OPERATIONAL RISK
AND
FINANCIAL INSTITUTIONS

OPERATIONAL RISK
AND
FINANCIAL INSTITUTIONS

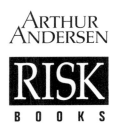

Published by Risk Books, a specialist division of Risk Publications.

Haymarket House
28–29 Haymarket
London SW1Y 4RX
Tel: +44 (0)171 484 9700
Fax: +44 (0)171 930 2238
E-mail: books@risk.co.uk
Home Page: http: //www.riskpublications.com

© Financial Engineering Ltd 1998

ISBN 1 899332 04 9 (case bound)

British Library Cataloguing in Publication Data
A catalogue record for this book is available from the British Library

Risk Books Commissioning Editor: Robert Jameson
Desk Editor: Ben Mullane
Copy Editor: David Michael
Typesetter: Laserscript Ltd

Printed and bound in Great Britain by Bookcraft (Bath) Ltd, Somerset.
Covers printed by Bookcraft.

A note from the sponsors

This book is correct to the best of our knowledge and belief at the time of going to press. It is, however, written as a general guide, so it is recommended that specific professional advice is sought before any action is taken.

CONTENTS

DEVELOPMENTS IN ANALYSING AND QUANTIFYING OPERATIONAL RISK

Preface

What defines a financial institution? Once the answer was simple: financial institutions offered credit and deposit facilities. More recently, as financial services diversified, thinkers in the industry suggested instead that financial institutions are institutions that manage *financial risks*. By this they generally meant credit risk and market risks such as interest rate or equity risk.

This ignores the untidy tangle of risks that lies between the offer of any service and its safe completion. This tangle is made up of all sorts of dangers that at first sight seem either unlikely or even unimportant – physical catastrophes, employee dishonesty or incompetence, inadequacies of systems and processes, regulatory risk, and various kinds of misunderstandings and miscommunications. Yet, in certain circumstances or combinations, even apparently unimportant risks can escalate and cause huge financial losses. The trigger might take the form of a spring-loaded derivative position. Often it is simply the *time* it takes to discover or act upon an otherwise trivial error – the end result being massive collateral damage to a bank's or institution's reputation.

Operational risks have leapt into the headlines over the last few years – the collapse of Barings Bank in 1995, the total destruction by fire of the Crédit Lyonnais trading room in Paris in 1996, the losses incurred by Morgan Grenfell Asset Management in the Peter Young affair also in 1996, and the unenforceability of contracts in the Russian markets in 1998. While the frequency of operational risk breakdowns are testament to their pervasive and powerful character, the unique nature of each breakdown complicates the task of addressing this class of risks. This is one reason why operational risk continues to prove the industry's blind spot, catching not only institutions with weak or lax controls, but also those renowned for their acuity.

Forensic reports reveal *one* common thread: working with and around the named perpetrators of operational losses were other professionals who failed to notice amber lights, put right obvious organisational problems, or grab responsibility for ringing the alarm. Where alarms were rung, senior managers often did not hear them. If they heard, they did not act. As the selection of cases described in Chapter 9 makes clear, few incidents truly come out of the blue. Aside from certain physical catastrophes, operational losses spring out of unfortunate *chains of events*, where different control points fail in sequence.

One reason for lapses and collapses in operational risk management is that, as an area embedded in the day-to-day detail of running a business, it has little appeal for managers. Preventing accidents that should never happen has been seen as protective, passive, tedious: the dull part of line management, a downside chore best shifted elsewhere. Also, it can be difficult to justify investments in risk avoidance. By definition, what the statisticians call "tail-end risks" can be ignored with impunity *most* of the time. As can the risk of housefire.

Things have begun to change. Provoked by sensational accounts of traders misbehaving and of physical disasters, as well as by sober detailed reports of more obscure catastrophes, institutions are waking up to the need for an imaginative programme of vigilance and preventative measures by senior management. Some rules of thumb are becoming known. Watch out for lapses during periods of expansion and market volatility (typically, problems surface during the subsequent bear market), for managers allowed to side-step best-practice organisational rules, for star performers (where there is reward, there is risk), for managers who don't take holidays or rotate, for over-reliance on black-box models and systems, for untested fail-safes, and for the one-sided exchange of an institution's reputation for a trader's bonus.

Yet the *science* of operational risk management for financial institutions lags far behind its equivalent in the manufacturing industries. Chief executives reaching for tools to identify, assess and manage operational risks have found themselves grasping thin air.

This book tries to show how some leading institutions, researchers and advisors are filling that gap. From the first chapter, where we offer a practically oriented discussion of how to start an operational risk programme, through to some intense discussion of quantification issues later in the book, we aim to convince the reader that there are now quite powerful approaches, methodologies, quantification tools and risk financing instruments available.

At this stage, many questions still have no answer. Others (especially the simplest, what is operational risk?) have too *many* answers for comfort. In ten years' time, there will be a textbook on the subject that is more complete and consistent. For the moment, we are happy to offer some thoughtful approaches to the last great frontier area of the financial risk management industry.

Arthur Andersen
December 1998

LIST OF PANELS

OPERATIONAL RISK: KEY THEMES AND EXAMPLES

Throughout this book special panels introduce key themes and offer illustrative examples:

CONTRIBUTORS

Gregory D. Cameron is the director of operational risk in the global risk management department of Fidelity Investments. He joined Fidelity in 1996 as an original member of a corporate team chartered to partner with Fidelity's diverse business units to establish a "best-in-class" risk management infrastructure. While at Fidelity, Greg has successfully instituted automated tracking of operational and credit losses, led the annual risk self-assessment survey and helped introduce Web-based products to collect and report risk information. Prior to joining Fidelity, he was a senior audit manager on General Electric's corporate audit staff. During his six years with GE, Greg participated in the introduction of the Six Sigma Quality Program, established risk management processes and performed internal control reviews. Most notably, while with GE he played a key role in the investigation of the $350 million trading debacle on Kidder Peabody's government bond desk. Greg earned his BA from St Lawrence University and is soon to become a Chartered Financial Analyst (CFA).

Michel Crouhy is senior vice president of global analytics, the market risk management division at the Canadian Imperial Bank of Commerce (CIBC). His responsibilities include the approval of all pricing models used in trading and for P&L calculation, the development of risk measurement methodologies, as well as the implementation of VAR models for market risk and credit risk, the implementation of the financial rates database for the bank, and the production of statistical and econometric studies related to risk management and model calibration. Prior to his current position at CIBC, Michel was a professor of finance at the HEC School of Management in Paris, where he was also director of the MS HEC in international finance. He has been a visiting professor at the Wharton School, University of Pennsylvania, and at UCLA. Michel holds a PhD from the Wharton School and is a graduate from Ecole Nationale des Ponts et Chaussées, France. He has published extensively in academic journals in the areas of banking, options and financial markets and is also associate editor of the *Journal of Derivatives*, the *Journal of Banking and Finance*, the *Journal of Risk*, and *Financial Engineering and the Japanese Markets*. Michel is a board member of the European Institute for Advanced Studies in Management (EIASM), Brussels. He has also served as a consultant to major financial institutions in Europe and in the areas of quantitative portfolio management, risk management, valuation and hedging of derivative products, forecasting volatility term structure and correlations.

Jonathan M. Davies is the executive director of North American operations risk at Warburg Dillon Read. He is responsible for incorporating the North American operations control environment into Warburg Dillon Read's operations risk measurement and risk management process and the development of an operations risk model. Jonathan has seven years experience at Warburg Dillon Read in many functions across operations, financial control and business unit control. Prior to his current role he was the global business unit controller for the interest rate derivatives business, managed from London. For two years, Jonathan was vice president for operational business development at Bankers Trust in London, and prior to that spent six years with Ernst & Young in London, where he qualified as an ACA in the financial services division before moving into management consultancy. He graduated from the University of Warwick with a BSc in molecular science.

Thomas C. Donahoe is a director at Metropolitan Life, and has been head of the derivatives unit since 1993. His responsibilities include the analysis and oversight of derivatives hedging strategies and co-ordinating the legal and regulatory issues for MetLife's General Account and affiliates occasioned by derivatives usage. Prior to MetLife, Tom was a vice president with Manufacturers Hanover Trust Company in the treasury unit. He was also a director with Scotiabank and Foreign Commerce Bank, trading and marketing futures and OTC derivatives, and worked in the enforcement division of the CFTC. Tom received his JD from Pace University and has an MBA from Fordham University, an MA from Catholic University, and a BSFS International Finance from Georgetown University. He is a member of the New York and Massachusetts Bars and has earned a Financial Risk Manager (FRM) designation. Tom is a frequent speaker on operational risk topics.

Matthew Fairless works in the office of the secretariat of the Global 2000 Coordinating Group, a private sector grouping of banks, securities firms and insurance companies, which includes over 200 firms. It aims to identify and provide resources for areas where co-ordinated initiatives will facilitate efforts by the financial community to improve the readiness of global financial institutions for the year 2000 date change. The group currently focuses its work in a number of areas, including firm readiness, country readiness and contingency planning. Matthew has participated in several UK financial sector working groups addressing testing, contingency planning, and disclosure. He previously spent two years as year 2000 programme manager for UBS, responsible for activities in Europe including applications, infrastructure and facilities.

Mark Fenton-O'Creevy is lecturer in management at the Open University Business School and visiting research fellow at the London Business School. He has an MBA and PhD in organisational behaviour from London Business School. Mark's research interests include the effects of cognitive biases on decision making and performance, barriers to strategic change in organisations and the relationship between employee relations systems and firm performance. He also acts as a consultant to a wide range of private and public sector organisations.

Dan Galai is the Abe Gray professor of finance and business administration at the School of Business Administration, Hebrew University, Jerusalem. He was a visiting professor of finance at INSEAD, and has also taught at the UCLA and the University of Chicago. Dr Galai holds a PhD from the University of Chicago and undergraduate and graduate degrees from the Hebrew University. He has served as a consultant for the Chicago Board of Options Exchange and the American Stock Exchange as well as for major banks. Dr Galai has published numerous journal articles on options, financial assets, and corporate finance, and was a winner of the first annual Pomeranze Prize for excellence in options research presented by the CBOE. He is a principal in IMGA PCM, which is engaged in portfolio management and corporate finance.

Douglas Hoffman is a managing director at Bankers Trust Company. He is head of the operational risk and insurance management unit within the corporate portfolio management group. His group's responsibilities include operational and event risk assessment and management, business vulnerability analysis and continuity planning, risk finance and insurance management. Douglas' group has been instrumental in the development of a proprietary operational Raroc methodology. Prior to joining Bankers Trust, he has been a principal and manager at a major international risk management and actuarial consulting firm, where he specialised in both risk management and insurance strategy consulting for financial service clients. In addition, Douglas served a range of other corporate, governmental, and non-profit firms. He is a frequent speaker and author of articles on operational and event risk management, insurance strategy, and financial services topics, and was founding editor of *BankRisk: The Bank Risk Management Quarterly*. Douglas served as founding chairman of the New York Clearing House Association (NYCHA) committee on business continuity planning, and is a past co-chair of the NYCHA risk and insurance committee. He holds BBA and MBA degrees with concentrations in risk management and insurance from the University of Georgia and is an associate in risk management (ARM) and a chartered property casualty underwriter (CPCU).

Paul Holmes joined Arthur Andersen as a director working in operational risk management with financial institutions. He has previously been global head of settlements at ING Barings, where his role included chairing the operational risk committee. Paul has worked in investment banking operations for the last 11 years. Before joining ING Barings he had worked at CS First Boston, Bankers Trust and Price Waterhouse. He has an industrial economics degree from Nottingham University and is a chartered accountant.

Norvald Instefjord is a lecturer in financial economics at the economics department of Birkbeck College. He joined the department four years ago after completing his PhD in finance at London Business School. Norvald's thesis was on security design and financial innovation, and he has written several academic papers in this area. His research interests include illiquid markets, capital structure choice, market microstructure, the takeover market, and managerial compensation. Recently, Norvald has been working with William Perraudin and Patricia Jackson on several projects including bank regulation, securities fraud, and credit derivatives.

Patricia Jackson is head of the regulatory policy division at the Bank of England, which advises on the financial stability implications of different approaches to prudential regulation and the lending of last resort and crisis management funds. She is a member of the Basle supervisors' committee, and in recent years has published research into the performance of VAR models and regulatory incentives. Patricia joined the Bank as an economist and originally worked on the euromarkets and forecasting interest rates before moving to monetary policy. From 1983, she worked on the issues arising from the Big Bang and carried out research into the effects of stamp duty on equity market turnover and risk-based capital for securities firms. From 1988 to 1990, Patricia was a deputy director of the securities and investments board and led the negotiations on a market risk standard. She then joined banking supervision and was responsible for the implementation of CAD. Patricia has an MSc in economics from Birkbeck College, London.

Stephen Kingsley graduated from the University of Bristol in 1973 and joined Arthur Andersen in that year. He qualified as a Chartered Accountant in 1976 and became a partner in 1986. Stephen currently acts as financial markets industry director for the EMEIA region of the firm and is responsible for developing the firm's business strategy in this market. More recently, he has led the build-up of the firm's financial risk management service line throughout the region. Throughout his career, Stephen has specialised in serving clients involved in the wholesale banking and securities markets, and in developing exchanges to meet participant demand. His work over recent years with financial institutions has focused on acting as engagement partner on projects designed to generate solutions in the area of risk management and control, of which a major element is the assessment and design of management information.

James Lam is president of Enterprise Risk Solutions, a risk management consulting, technology, and brokerage company. Prior to founding Enterprise Risk Solutions, he was chief risk officer at Fidelity Investments between 1995 and 1998. James' previous experience includes positions as chief risk officer at GE Capital Government Services, senior consultant at First Manhattan Consulting Group and vice president of strategic risk management at Glendale Federal Bank. In recognition of his contributions to the field of financial risk management, the Global Association of Risk Professionals (GARP) named him *Financial Risk Manager of the Year 1997*. James has authored or co-authored over 30 books and articles on a wide range of financial management and risk

management topics. He graduated summa cum laude with a BBA in finance and computers from Baruch College and currently serves as a founding member of Baruch's Business Advisory Council. James also has an MBA from UCLA Graduate School of Business.

Mark Laycock is group operational risk co-ordinator for the Deutsche Bank Group, which he joined in 1996. In this role he is working with businesses and their support functions to devise mechanisms for estimating risk, enhancing transparency and allocating capital as part of the Raroc process. Since receiving his MBA from Manchester Business School, Mark has worked for a number of financial institutions, where his roles have included trading a variety of capital market products and devising market risk methodologies. Immediately prior to Deutsche Bank, he worked in banking supervision for the Bank of England, where he was involved in the implementation of the capital adequacy directive, and establishing the traded markets team. Mark has published articles on euro-dollar futures, capital adequacy and marketing in the eurobond market.

Sonia Libaert currently works in operations for Warburg Dillon Read, where she joined as a graduate trainee in 1997. Since completing her training and working in ETD, she has moved into the operations risk measurement project. Sonia's roles include the development, construction and implementation of the projects' Web page, loss data collation and systems development, and the internal and external promotion of operations risk. She holds a BA in English literature and language from the University of Manchester.

Jason Love is a euro operations risk analyst at Warburg Dillion Read. The main function of his role is to minimise the impact of the introduction of the euro on operations risk in the organisation. Prior to this role he gained cross-product stream experience in operations control working on various projects to improve the control environment within Warburg Dillon Read. Jason is a chartered accountant, having spent three years with Deloitte and Touche (S.A.), where he performed his articles. He has a bachelors and honours degree in commerce, which he completed in 1994.

Robert M. Mark is an executive vice president at the Canadian Imperial Bank of Commerce (CIBC). His responsibilities at CIBC encompass corporate treasury and risk management functions, which have global responsibility to cover all market, trading related credit and operating risks for the wholesale and retail banks as well as for its subsidiaries. Robert's responsibilities also include managing the risk MIS, analytics, capital attribution and risk advisory units. He works in partnership with CIBC managers and ensures that all risks are accurately measured, controlled and managed, approves credits, and serves on the senior credit committee of the bank. Robert was also appointed to the board of the CIBC mortgage corporation. Prior to CIBC, he was the partner in charge of the financial risk management consulting practice at Coopers & Lybrand, managing director in the Asia, Europe, and capital markets group at Chemical Bank, and senior officer at Marine Midland Bank/Hong Kong Shanghai Bank Group. Robert earned his PhD from New York University, with a dissertation on

options pricing. He has an advanced professional certificate in accounting from NYU's Stern Graduate School of Business, where he has also been appointed an adjunct professor, and chairperson of the national asset/liability management association.

Nigel Nicholson is a professor of organisational behaviour and deputy dean (research) at London Business School. His major current research interests are on personality and leadership, risk and decision making among traders in the City, and applications of evolutionary psychology to work and organisational life. Nigel has published numerous books and articles on these topics, and a range of other areas, including careers and organisational change. He has held visiting appointments at several universities and been presented an award from the Academy of Management for his contribution to theory. Nigel also acts as a consultant to a variety of private and public sector organisations.

David O'Brien is an associate director in the operations risk function within Warburg Dillon Read. He joined SBC Warburg in 1996 and performed a variety of operations control functions before becoming involved in operations risk in August 1997. David is currently assisting with the implementation of a global operations risk recording process. He began his career in the financial services industry at James Capel & Co in 1989, where he worked on the development of counterparty risk requirement and client money calculation processes, before moving on to product control and then becoming a systems accountant for the finance function.

Michael K. Ong is head of enterprise risk management for ABN AMRO Bank. He is responsible for the management information and decision support function for the executive committee on enterprise-wide market, operational, credit, and liquidity risk, as well as Raroc and ROE models. Before joining ABN AMRO, Michael was head of corporate research unit at First Chicago NBD Corp, where he was chair of the global risk management research council and head of the market risk analysis unit. Prior to First Chicago NBD, he was responsible for quantitative research at Chicago Research and Trading Group (now NationsBanc-CRT) and has served as an assistant professor of mathematics at Bowdoin College. Michael is also an adjunct professor at the Stuart School of Business of the Illinois Institute of Technology. He received a BS degree in physics, cum laude, from the University of the Philippines, and his MA in physics, MS and PhD in applied mathematics from the State University of New York at Stonybrook. Michael is a member of the editorial board on the *Journal of Financial Regulation and Compliance,* and the *Journal of Risk*

William Perraudin is professor of finance at Birkbeck College, London, a fellow of the CEPR, and special advisor to the Bank of England. He holds degrees from Oxford, LSE and Harvard and has worked as an economist in the City and for the International Monetary Fund. Before coming to Birkbeck, William taught at Cambridge University and consulted extensively for private and public sector institutions. His research interests include contingent claims pricing, financial regulation, and risk management.

Yiannos Pierides is assistant professor of finance at the University of Cyprus, where he is responsible for teaching investments and option pricing. He has a BA in economics from the University of Cambridge, and earned his MBA and PhD in finance from the Sloan School of Management at MIT. Yiannos' research interests include derivatives pricing, portfolio management and corporate finance. His research has been published in the *Journal of Portfolio Management*, *Journal of Economic Dynamics and Control* and the *Handbook of Fixed Income Options*.

Chris Rachlin is head of group operational risk at The Royal Bank of Scotland plc (RBS). He is responsible for developing and implementing policies, processes and tools to ensure the RBS group identify and manage their operational risk effectively. Prior to joining RBS in 1997, Chris spent nine years at Coopers & Lybrand's risk management services group, where he advised international banks and regulators on aspects of operational risk and internal control. He was also responsible for producing the British Banker's Association and Coopers & Lybrand survey on operational risk management in banks.

André Rolland joined Arthur Andersen as a partner in 1997 to head the French financial risk management consulting practice. Over the last 20 years, he has gained extensive international experience at management level with JP Morgan, Credit du Nord, Thomson, and Banque Indosuez. André also lectures on capital markets and risk management at several graduate and professional institutions.

Tim Shepheard-Walwyn is a managing director in the corporate risk management department at UBS AG in Zurich. He began his career at the Bank of England, where he worked on international economics, monetary policy and banking supervision. Tim joined the Swiss Bank Corporation in 1987, where he held a number of positions in internal control and operations management, including a period as chief operating officer in Hong Kong. In 1996 he moved to SBC's head office to assist in the development of their approach to group-wide risk measurement and reporting. Following the merger with UBS he has been responsible for regulatory relations and risk awareness. He is the co-editor of *The Practice of Risk Management*, which provides a practical guide to the implementation of group-wide risk management and is chairman of the Global 2000 Coordinating Group.

Peter Slater is head of global operations risk at Warburg Dillon Read (WDR), responsible for various risk-orientated operations functions and operations risk policy development implementation and monitoring. Prior to WDR, he spent seven years at Midland Montagu, where he managed a range of operational units supporting the groups' wholesale businesses, including the group treasury and capital markets unit. Peter has also worked for Price Waterhouse in Hong Kong and Deloitte Haskins and Sells. He is a qualified accountant and read business studies at Sheffield University.

Emma Soane is research officer at London Business School, where she is conducting research into the individual and contextual influences on the market behaviour of finance professionals. Her research interests include the psychological aspects of individual and organisational decision making, risk taking, and risk management. Emma gained an MSc in occupational psychology from the University of Sheffield and is continuing to study at the university as a part time PhD student researching individual risk propensity.

Andrew Tinney is the lead partner responsible for providing services to investment banks at Arthur Andersen. He joined in 1986 and has responsibility for the global financial markets training programme. Andrew has developed, and lectures at, numerous in-house courses on the operation of UK and overseas equity and derivatives markets. He has considerable experience in dealing with UK and international financial institutions which are active in cash and derivatives markets, providing business integration (process reengineering, change enablement and programme management), technology and regulatory consulting. Andrew has undertaken a number of strategic assignments for trading exchanges and market participants, including the London Stock Exchange and Oslo Börs. In 1992 he led a major 18-month research project involving over 500 financial institutions, identifying key trends in banking and capital markets through to the year 2000. The findings were published in "Banking and Capital Markets – a strategic forecast" in conjunction with the Economist Intelligence Unit in 1993. In 1994 Andrew led the set up of Scottish Widows Bank, breaking new ground with the "Assurabanc" concept. He has worked with a number of blue chip global investment banks in re-engineering end-to-end processes including finance, settlements and treasury. Andrew was also the global controller for a major investment banking business.

Paul Willman is professor of organisational behaviour at London Business School. He has held positions at Imperial College, Cranfield University, and Oxford University. He is the author of several books and numerous academic articles on various aspects of organisational behaviour and a leader of the regulation initiative at London Business School.

Stavros A. Zenios is professor of management science at the University of Cyprus and senior fellow at the Wharton School, University of Pennsylvania, where he was an associate professor of decision sciences, and principal investigator with the HERMES laboratory for financial modelling. He has also held academic appointments at MIT, the universities of Bergamo and Milano, and the University of Haifa. Stavros' research focuses on large-scale optimisation, and on the use of parallel computers for the solution for large-scale problems arising in operations research applications. He is also involved in the development of management science models in finance, and especially for portfolio management. Stavros developed models for organisations such as the World Bank, Union Bank of Switzerland and Metropolitan Life. He has co-authored more than a hundred refereed articles and edited eight books, and is associate editor for several journals, including *Journal of Economic Dynamics and Control*, *SIAM Journal on Optimisation*, and the *ORSA Journal on Computing and Naval Research Logistics*. Stavros holds a BSc in mathematics and electrical engineering, and received his PhD from Princeton University in 1986.

STARTING POINTS AND INDUSTRY TRENDS

1

Operational Risk and Financial Institutions: Getting Started

Stephen Kingsley, André Rolland, Andrew Tinney and Paul Holmes
Arthur Andersen

Risk management has historically focused on market and credit risk. However, recent dramatic failures have shown that senior managers in financial institutions need to pay equal, if not greater, attention to operational risks if they are to safeguard against potential catastrophes – and if they are to continue to be able to work in the industry themselves.

It is increasingly apparent that the value-at-risk, risk scenario analysis and risk-adjusted performance measures on which senior managers now rely in much of the financial industry, are potentially misleading if they ignore operational risk. Operational risk measurement and management is not straightforward and as yet there is no established market practice to follow. One can, nonetheless, develop an approach using accepted risk management principles.

Whatever the area of risk, best practice risk management has three components:
❑ a workable system for identifying, capturing and measuring risks;
❑ a system for evaluating whether to accept, reject or take steps to reduce risks; and
❑ a system for ongoing validation of the control environment.

Table 1 lists the elements that unite these components, making them workable and practical. These elements also form the themes of the present chapter, which aims to help operational risk managers "get started" and provides some principles for the reader to consider.

Techniques for measuring operational risk need to be tailored to particular businesses, and to help readers see how this can be done we offer in the final section of the chapter a series of illustrations related to an overseas equity derivatives business.

Table 1. The elements of workable and practical risk management

1. An agreed conceptual framework that provides:
❑ a definition of operational risk;
❑ identification of the key components of operational risk;
❑ the role and responsibilities of the function;
❑ its organisational fit within risk management and the firm as a whole;
❑ its approach to measurement;
❑ its approach to reporting results; and
❑ its operating principles.
2. A systems and data architecture that provides timely, comprehensive and consistent information for decision taking and risk evaluation.
3. The resources, ie management and people.
4. The necessary tools, eg techniques for measurement.

Conceptual framework

DEFINITION OF OPERATIONAL RISK
As Figure 1 overleaf illustrates, the risk universe is typically categorised into several different kinds of risk.

❑ Market risk – risk of loss due to adverse movements in the mark-to-market value of the company's assets and liabilities.
❑ Credit risk – risk of loss through exposure to counterparty default.
❑ Strategic risk – risk of employing a strategy that fails to secure the optimum returns available from the capital employed.
❑ Business risk – risk of unfavourable fiscal, economic, competitive, legal, tax or regulatory changes in the markets.
❑ Operational risk – risk of loss caused by failures in operational processes or the systems that support them, including those adversely affecting reputation, legal enforcement of contracts and claims.

Readers of the other chapters in this book will notice that there is some debate regarding

1. Categories of risk

Core operational capability

Risks to core operational capability include the risk of premises, people or systems becoming unavailable due to:

❑ damage resulting from fire, bombs, technical or natural disasters;

❑ loss of utilities such as power, water, or transportation;

❑ employee disputes such as strikes or loss of key operational personnel; and

❑ inadequacy or loss of systems capabilities due, for example, to computer viruses or the "millennium timebomb".

These risks may seem obvious, but they can have unforeseen implications. One of the emerging areas of interest in operational risk management is how to assess and manage the cost of supporting longer term transactions. After all, for businesses that require the retention of key personnel and systems to manage exposures and administration, staff retention and continuity represent a considerable exposure in terms of their possible impact on future earnings.

People

People are arguably a company's most important resource. However, historically they have been overlooked when evaluating operational risk, as it is so difficult to measure and model the risks of:

❑ human error;

❑ lack of integrity and honesty;

❑ lack of segregation and risk of collaboration;

❑ lack of customer focus and professionalism;

❑ lack of teamwork and respect for the individual;

❑ reliance on key individuals;

❑ insufficient skills, training, management or supervision; and

❑ lack of a culture of control.

People risks continue to be the major contributory factor in many dramatic failures. For this reason, despite the difficulties of measuring them, they must be targeted in any programme that aims to improve risk management.

Client relationships

A financial institution largely derives its value from its reputation and its ability to place financial products with its client base. Here the key risks include:

❑ *Association.* There has been considerable financial cost and damage to the reputation of organisations publicly linked to undesirable clients such as money launderers, or notorious

whether to distinguish between strategic, business and operational risk, or treat them as one. Whichever definition is adopted, all risks must be captured somewhere, and in this chapter these three risk sources are treated as one and are covered by the term "operational risk".

What kinds of losses can operational risks give rise to? There are really three main categories:

❑ direct financial losses;

❑ indirect losses due to impairment of the firm's reputation and/or client relationships, or knock-on effects on other functions; and

❑ potential earnings foregone as a result of a lack of operational capability to transact business.

Historically, operational risk management has focused on direct financial consequences. However, recent events suggest that this greatly understates the risks and that possible damage to reputation and client relationships, and the hidden losses in terms of foregone opportunities, need to be emphasised.

KEY COMPONENTS OF OPERATIONAL RISK

The key components of operational risk involve:

❑ core operational capability;

❑ people;

❑ client relationships;

❑ transactional systems;

❑ safe custody;

❑ reconciliation and accounting

❑ change and new activities; and

❑ expense volatility.

individuals such as the British publisher Robert Maxwell, or those who have benefited from victims of events such as the Holocaust.

❏ *Client suitability.* There have been well-publicised lawsuits and regulatory and/or tax repercussions following the sale of allegedly unsuitable over-the-counter (OTC) derivative and pensions products and the use of unsuitable sales practices.

❏ *Client asset valuations.* False valuations and market risk assessments have been used to mislead or conceal losses as shown recently in various OTC derivative disputes.

❏ *Competitiveness.* Many customers and fund managers now allocate their business on performance criteria that include an assessment of the selling institution's operational risk management capability. These clients need to be *sure* that a financial institution is pursuing best practice in operational risk management, in just the same way that they have traditionally demanded reassurance about creditworthiness.

Transactional systems

Historically, assessments of the operational risk inherent in making any transaction have focused on settlement risk. Increasingly, however, they are understood to include:

❏ Data capture and processing. Financial institutions rely on prompt, accurate and efficient data capture and processing. Data quality also underpins all risk information. The level of investment in increasing the sophistication of risk management technique needs to be balanced against expenditure on improving underlying data quality.

❏ Confirmation and contractual documentation. Confirmations and pre-matching processes have become more automated – helping to reduce operational risk where master agreements exist covering a number of vanilla derivative products. However, more exotic products, including some OTC derivatives, require negotiated documentation that can take days, if not weeks, to finalise. Many senior line managers are not aware of the possible costs that could arise from unsigned or disputed documentation aggregated either by trade or by counterparty.

❏ Settlement operational risk. Operational risk information related to settlements has benefited from considerable innovation. In particular, new ways have been developed to translate voluminous data into meaningful management information and to control transactions in progress (and "fails" in the process) in a more proactive

manner. Yet the stakes are still high: losses caused by errors in the settlements process may reduce but the risk will not disappear, particularly for transactions in less-developed markets.

Safe custody

The providers of safe-custody services to the rest of the financial industry face major leveraged operational risks. The market in safe-custody services is consolidating because only a few organisations have the systems and capabilities to manage the risks of providing such services at a competitive cost. Risk is leveraged, in that custodial fees make up only a small proportion of the value of the assets that are under management. Once operational risk is included in risk-adjusted return on capital (Raroc), more firms may decide to withdraw from the market.

Reconciliation and accounting

The transactions in progress in any major financial institution commonly run to billions of pounds, so any exceptions and differences – ie trades that fall outside the normal parameters and processes for some reason – can be significant. The reconciliation of settlement transaction data with funding and accounting results is a key process in protecting a financial institution against undisclosed positions or undisclosed losses.

Change and new activities

In recent years, the financial industry has been marked by the high number and value of acquisitions and mergers. Whenever an institution is in the process of change or is developing new activities, it runs much higher operational risks than does a stable or existing business. A comprehensive and proactive operational risk function must be able to address: mergers, acquisitions and disposals, environment changes (such as the introduction of the euro and new tax laws and regulations), the implementation of new systems and re-engineering of processes, the launch of new products or entry into new markets, and the acquisition of new staff, clients, counterparties or suppliers.

Expense volatility

Income volatility analysis has historically focused on the components of revenue volatility and margins, typically ignoring the potential exposure to volatility in the cost base. Key risks include:

❑ Expenditure on technology. There is both the risk of spending more than the businesses can afford or not enough to remain competitive. A proactive function will factor costs associated with the "millennium timebomb" and the introduction of the euro into Raroc before, say, determining capital allocations or deciding whether to embark on or leave a particular business venture. ❑ Bonuses and variable compensation. Many firms find a significant proportion of so-called "variable compensation" is required to remain in business and this needs to be included and controlled as such.

ROLE AND RESPONSIBILITIES OF
OPERATIONAL RISK MANAGEMENT
The role or objectives of an operational risk management function are given in Table 2. Let us examine each of these in more detail. Readers might also like to consider them in relation to the illustrative examples we offer at the end of this chapter.

Avoiding potentially catastrophic losses
The primary role of an operational risk function is to support senior and line management in better understanding and managing their operational risks – particularly those risks with potentially catastrophic consequences. Partly this can be achieved by underlining the key sources of risk – eg the "commandments" in Panel 1. The operational risk function also provides senior managers with objective information from an independent source. It also has the power to take evasive action to mitigate undesirable levels of risk if line managers fail to take the necessary action.

Anticipating risk more effectively
An effective operational risk function enables the organisation to better anticipate critical operational risks and to adapt strategy and control processes to minimise these risks. It therefore considers both the risks associated with current business and the higher risks that would arise from change, new activities or an altering business environment. Anticipating risk is also likely to involve identifying scenarios within key business areas that either experience or commonsense suggest are likely to correlate with rising operational risks. For example, is a particular business area experiencing volatile markets, losing disproportionate numbers of staff, affected by a shifting legal or regulatory environment or implementing new mission critical systems?

Table 2. Objectives of an operational risk management function

❑ To avoid potential catastrophic losses.
❑ To generate a broader understanding of operational risk issues at all levels of the firm that touch on key areas of risk.
❑ To enable the organisation to anticipate risks more effectively.
❑ To provide objective measurements of performance.
❑ To change behaviour in order to reduce operational risk and to enhance the "culture of control" within the organisation.
❑ To provide objective information so that services offered by the organisation take account of operational risks.
❑ To provide support in ensuring that adequate due diligence is shown when carrying out mergers and acquisitions.

Objective performance measurement
Operational risk has historically been incorporated into risk performance measures by intuition, with different hurdle rates (ie minimum rates of return) being set according to management's perception of inherent risk. By incorporating value-at-operational-risk into their methodology, risk managers establish an objective basis for performance assessment and capital allocation.

Once an accepted methodology is in place, managers can better identify the issues and components they need to address in order to reduce operational risk and improve their returns.

Changing behaviour and enhancing the culture of control
Operational risk awareness and the techniques used to manage operational risk need to be approximately communicated and incorporated into performance measures. For example, responsibility for implementing approaches to operational risk and its ongoing management can be incorporated into compensation reviews, helping to motivate staff to change behaviour in order to reduce operational risk. Operational risk profiling, control assessment, risk measurement, and reporting contribute to improving control awareness and to understanding the culture of control. Personnel are also more motivated when their successes in reducing operational risk are measured and acknowledged by senior managers.

Streamlining services
The financial services industry offers an increasing number of products and it is common for these to cross-subsidise each other. Some

PANEL 1

THE 10 COMMANDMENTS

1. **Understand your profits**

   Large profits that you do not understand are more dangerous than large losses you do understand.

2. **Focus on distance**

   Operational risk increases with distance from head office.

3. **Honour the Sabbath**

   People who never take holidays or who always stay late are not necessarily paragons of corporate virtue: "lifestyle" choices may be used to mask business realities.

4. **Prepare to pay**

   There is no such thing as cheap risk management or segregation of duties.

5. **Invest with authority**

   The CEO is not the risk control function, but a risk control function without the CEO's backing will not prosper.

6. **Reconcile with diligence**

   Reconciliation problems usually presage losses: a debit balance in a suspense account is usually not an asset.

7. **Track the cash**

   Accounting entries can be manipulated; cash disbursements cannot. Cash is the fundamental control.

8. **Respect business quality**

   Volume is no substitute for value.

9. **Ensure it adds up**

   Accounting losses reflect business realities.

10. **Watch your systems**

    Computer systems are an open door into the heart of your business, and their integrity and security is not as complete as you think.

businesses offer complex services in order to attract or retain clients. In effect these businesses are trading increased operational risk in return for revenues. For example, brokerage clients are given free custody or derivative customers are given free daily position valuations. The potential operational risk from such activities may be substantial and needs to be separately priced and included in Raroc measures. Provisioning against operational risk encourages businesses to address these risks to allow writebacks on provisioning.

Helping to ensure due diligence in mergers and acquisitions

We mentioned in the previous section that mergers and acquisitions generate operational risks. The operational risk function should play a key role in due diligence reviews by advising senior managers on how the target company will change the overall operational risk profile of the group. It should also advise them of the target company's risk-adjusted capital and performance measures and report on management's capability for managing the target's operational risks should acquisition proceed.

ORGANISATIONAL FIT

Operational risk management must have independence, objectivity, and the capability and authority to operate effectively. This implies that it should be placed within the risk management function rather than within individual businesses. Risk management is responsible for supporting senior and line management in managing risk and for taking action to eliminate undesirable levels of risk where line management fails to take the necessary action.

A typical corporate governance model for operational risk is presented in Panel 2 overleaf. Individual responsibilities must be carefully defined to avoid ambiguity and to manage all risks properly.

APPROACH TO MEASUREMENT

High-level overviews

There are a number of methodologies evolving for measuring operational risk. These cover a spectrum from simplistic overviews to much more detailed calculations. The high-level overviews provide an operational risk capital number but, as we will see below, at present it is typically a number of little substance. Such methodologies are generally being replaced by the more detailed scientific calculations we describe later.

❑ *Expense-based model* An early view of operational risk was that all operational failures ultimately resulted in increased expenses. This often stemmed from an initial belief that operational risk was a back-office problem and the

OPERATIONAL RISK AND MANAGERIAL ACCOUNTABILITY

Senior managers hold ultimate collective responsibility for all aspects of risk management and control, including operational risk.

Regional managers are responsible for applying supervisory control over the businesses and activities in their location, and for managing their region's systems, facilities and people risks in particular.

Business and support function managers hold primary responsibility for ensuring effective operational risk management and control within their businesses, particularly in respect of transactional risks.

Risk functions (such as risk management, compliance, product control, security, human resources) are responsible for employing detective controls to assist line management in better controlling their risks and to safeguard the organisation should business managers fail to act.

Internal audit is responsible for reporting to the highest levels of management on the adequacy and effectiveness of controls. Some organisations have sought to assign operational risk measurement and reporting to internal audit. However this is not recommended as it is inconsistent with the treatment of market and credit risk and might compromise internal audit's need for complete independence and objectivity.

Committees are also typically used to oversee corporate governance and manage more significant risks. Below, we look at how these risk committees might relate to one another:

❑ the assets and liabilities committee (ALCO) monitors risk-adjusted capital and returns, together with funding by business, and controls capital allocations;

❑ the operational risk committee monitors and approves methodology, activity and key decisions;

❑ the new products/new markets committee approves new business;

❑ the information technology committee monitors the implementation of new systems and approves systems changes and spending on these; and

❑ the credit committee approves new clients and counterparties.

---

cost was mainly cost over-runs on system and overheads plus settlement errors.

Once expense data have been normalised for structural changes (ie changes to the structure of the firm that would otherwise distort the figures) a figure for the volatility of expenses can be derived (say 15%). This can be applied to budgeted expenditure to express operational risk as a number. It is a simple calculation and the data are readily available.

However, the result is counter-intuitive. Increased expenditure on improving the control environment, for example by upgrading controls or investing in systems to increase automation and security, actually results in increasing the operational risk capital charge. The calculation also:

❑ ignores the many operational risks that result in non-expense items such as reduced revenues, increased funding, or damage to the franchise;

❑ gives the user no insight into particular risks, exposures, or controls;

❑ does not motivate improved behaviour or the culture of control; and

❑ does not capture risks of change such as the "millennium timebomb" or the risk associated with new business ventures.

Following significant front-office operational losses such as those due to mis-selling derivatives investment products and pensions as well as losses due to the mis-pricing unlisted investments, the expense-based calculation seems unlikely to be used for long.

❑ *Income volatility* A common definition of operational risk is that it covers all risks that are not market or credit risks. This implies that if one could take historical income volatility and strip out the known market and credit risk elements, the remainder would be attributable to operational risks.

Again, a key advantage of this simple approach is that the historical data necessary to do this are likely to be readily available. This approach is an improvement over the expense-based method as it captures both revenue and cost effects, but:

❑ Historical data may not be a good guide to the future as they ignore structural changes such as new extremes in market volatility, new business ventures, the "millennium timebomb", or the introduction of the euro.

❑ The calculation does not capture opportunity costs or damage to the firm's reputation or franchise.

❑ Catastrophic or long-tail risks are likely to be largely ignored because they are unlikely to be included in historical data and the methodology does not readily enable data from external sources to be used.

❑ The result provides little insight into the particular risks, exposures and controls that need to be addressed and does little to motivate behavioural change to reduce actual losses or improve the control culture.

Thus, although the methodology is a significant advance over the expense-based model, it will not by itself be sufficient.

❑ *Capital asset pricing model* The capital asset pricing model (CAPM) assumes that all market information is included in the share price. Thus operational risk can be valued by looking at the effect of disclosed operational failures on the market capitalisation of the companies concerned. One can then use these observations to derive a value-at-operational-risk for a typical company in the same sector.

The great benefit of this approach is that it focuses on high-value risks and provides a value that incorporates all the effects of earnings risk, foregone opportunities, and damage to the reputation and franchise value of the firm.

However the method is partially flawed in that catastrophic risks often lead to bankruptcy rather than a diminution in value. Further, the level of risk is not affected by the particular controls and business risk characteristics of the firm concerned, and thus this approach will not motivate improved risk behaviour or control. It also does not help anticipate risks. The method is therefore unlikely to be used on its own but the exposures that it measures will be used in a more detailed calculation methodology.

More detailed calculation methodologies
There are two fundamental approaches to more detailed calculations of operational risk: top-down predictive mathematical modelling and bottom-up risk profiling.

Top-down predictive mathematical modelling
The top-down approach aims to measure the absolute and relative operational risks of businesses. It typically uses actuarial techniques such as Garch modelling of low-value,

high-incidence rate losses and change activities based upon the organisation's own loss experience, and chaos theory modelling of high-value, low-incidence rate losses and of risks in new activities based upon reported loss experience in the market. Using a predefined confidence level, a value-at-operational-risk can be derived and incorporated within risk and performance measures.

It should be emphasised that very few firms presently use such advanced techniques for measurement. So far, most firms have focused their efforts on improving the quality of information that they can use to manage down operational risks, whatever their size, rather than in enhancing the measurement methodology.

A limited number of firms already have functions specifically dedicated to high-value, low-incidence rate losses. These functions, sometimes known as "long-tail" risk teams, have established methodologies for evaluating exposures and the likelihoods of such rare events.

The top-down approach provides for a swift implementation of an operational risk measurement process and can quickly result in revised capital allocations and improved management information. However, few firms, if any, presently have the internal data that the model needs to hand. In the case of tail risk (very infrequent but catastrophic events), almost by definition, firms are highly unlikely to possess internal data.

Alternatively, if measurement is largely based on external data, the following concerns arise:

❑ External data may be unreliable or inappropriate as each firm's business and controls differ from those of every other firm. As most firms would choose not to make their operational failings public, the data are likely to understate the risks.

❑ External data tend to give rise to a relatively static model, as it considers the exposures and failings of the industry rather than the individual firm. Naturally, in reality, the operational risks of the individual firm are likely to be more volatile than the industry as a whole.

❑ Like other top-down models, the results do not tell senior management about the company's own failings or particular control issues.

❑ As the calculation is based on external data and does not incorporate an assessment of internal control, the process does not motivate business managers to change their behaviour or improve controls.

❏ The level of assumptions and the inability of management to have an effect on the model result may lead business managers to reject the validity or usefulness of the approach.

The top-down approach therefore represents a good start and best first estimate of the exposures but financial institutions will want to supplement it with operational risk profiling to capture improved accuracy and to help motivate individual line managers to reduce risk.

Bottom-up operational risk profiling

The bottom-up approach employs a detailed analysis of individual business processes, the controls in place and the identification and quantification of individual risks.

Using, say, a decision tree, the value at operational risk can be derived as a function of:

Value of potential losses
× chance of risk events occurring
× chance of controls not preventing loss
= value-at-operational-risk

The values and probabilities can be derived from management reports either directly or by using a score mechanism.

Operational risk profiling takes a significant amount of time to implement and requires particular care over how potential losses and probabilities are determined. It does, however, provide:
❏ ongoing assessment and upgrading of controls;
❏ improved information for management;
❏ greater awareness of, and insight into, the causes of operational losses;
❏ motivation to change methods and behaviour to reduce operational risk and improve control and returns from existing capital allocations; and
❏ a method of calculation that is transparent, and often secures better buy-in and acceptance of the result.

The illustrative examples that comprise the final section of this chapter show how operational risk profiling may be implemented in practice.

REPORTING RESULTS
When reporting operational risk measures, and especially when aggregating the results from different approaches to measuring operational risk, it is clearly important to understand what the amounts represent and imply.

Operational risk, like market and credit risk, cannot adequately be captured by a single figure; there is a range of potential outcomes with differing probabilities. Counter-intuitively, but in common with market risk, some operational risk events can result in a profit, not a loss (for example, if a firm contracts to sell when the client instructed to buy and the market then falls before the firm corrects the position, the trade error will generate a profit). The majority of outcomes can, however, be expected to be negative.

Risk reporting
When reporting various kinds of financial risk, institutions typically:
❏ evaluate the boundary of exposure to loss for a given confidence level known as the value-at-risk (VAR);
❏ analyse specific long-tail risks outside this confidence level; and
❏ analyse exposure to specific movements in market parameters, for example, to a parallel yield-curve shift of a single basis point.

The above calculations are based both on pre-set confidence levels and on assumptions concerning *duration* (the time expected to be required to liquidate any position), which can vary from, say, 10 days (in a market risk model) to a year (for credit risk). Volatile markets tend to throw a harsh spotlight on liquidity differences.

Similar assumptions need to be made when measuring operational risks and special care should be taken when aggregating results derived using different methodologies or from different areas of risk. It may be difficult to overcome many theoretical differences and difficulties in a completely satisfactory way – identifying correlation effects is particularly challenging – but the imprecision of the operational risk measure means that, with care, such differences are unlikely to be material.

Expected loss
Reporting Raroc requires the value of the expected loss rather than the boundaries or distribution of the potential loss. For example, suppose we take two businesses and make the following assumptions:
❏ each business employs $100 million of capital for infrastructure capital and to cover capital for market and credit risks;
❏ Business 1 generates a return before operational losses of $15 million, and Business 2 generates $20 million;
❏ Business 1 is in a low operational risk market and expected operational loss is $4 million

whereas Business 2 operates in a higher operational risk market and expected loss is $8 million;

❏ management seeks a minimum risk-adjusted return of 10%.

The operational risk component can be included either as an adjustment to returns or as an annuity on capital. In other words either

$$\text{Raroc} = \frac{\text{Budgeted returns} - \text{expected operational losses, or}}{\text{Allocated capital}}$$

or

$$\text{Raroc} = \frac{\text{Returns}}{\text{Capital plus annuity of expected operational losses}}$$

The results of both methods are presented in Table 3. It can be seen that, whichever method is used, Business 2 seems to be the most attractive proposition. The most suitable method will depend on individual needs but the first method is the most readily comprehensible.

OPERATING PRINCIPLES

If the operational risk management function is to be effective, it needs to act within agreed operating principles, which should be aligned with the operating principles of the rest of the risk management function. These would include the following areas.

Definition of data requirements

Operational risk management is responsible for defining and communicating its data requirements to the businesses and support functions.

Responsibility for data capture and integrity

The businesses and support functions are responsible for ensuring the completeness and integrity of data reported to risk management. Risk management, meanwhile, is responsible for exercising the secondary independent detective and diagnostic controls over data integrity.

Reporting of operational risk

Operational risk information would typically be reported weekly in summary form and in greater detail on a monthly basis. The format of the reports should be aligned with existing risk management information. An attribution methodology will be required for allocating a specific proportion of risk to different businesses, where those risks are shared.

Scheduling of formal operational risk committee meetings

This will depend on the type of firm but, depending on the rate of market change and the need for pro-active action, it is likely that meetings will be at least monthly. Ad hoc meetings may also be necessary in times of market turbulence.

Members of the operational risk committee

A board member should be assigned responsibility for the operational risk function. The membership of the committee will mirror that of the market and credit risk committees and include the most senior levels of management. It will probably be chaired by the chief executive officer, and administered by risk management.

Empowerment

The powers of the operational risk function should be documented and known throughout the organisation. The operational risk function should also have the capacity to exercise those powers, particularly their power to reduce unauthorised levels of risk where line management has failed to do so.

Systems and data architecture

ARCHITECTURE WITHIN THE UNDERLYING SYSTEMS

Systems need to be configured so that, for each of the identified operational risks:

❏ the potential for loss on current and proposed business is valued;

❏ the attributes determining the likelihood of loss are identified;

❏ the attributes determining the likelihood of controls failing to prevent loss are identified; and

❏ the actual historical experience of such loss is identified.

Table 3. Comparison of Raroc calculation methods

	Business 1	Business 2
Returns excluding operational risk	15%	20%
Raroc returns adjusted for operational risk	$\frac{15-4}{100} = 11\%$	$\frac{20-8}{100} = 12\%$
Raroc capital adjusted for operational risk	$\frac{15}{100+40} = 10.7\%$	$\frac{20}{100+80} = 11.1\%$

To be able to provide the systems specification, the business and risk management should first agree the potential operational risks for which data are sought, the attributes determining the likelihood of loss, and the attributes determining the likelihood of controls failing to prevent loss.

Due to the scale of the task involved, senior managers need to determine the risks that they regard as having greatest significance. These should be modelled first. Risk management should translate this into a common top-down risk-focused approach and incorporate it into their strategy both by modifying existing systems and by ensuring that the requirements are specified into future systems.

DATABASES TO HOLD INFORMATION

Many underlying systems will probably run using batch processing and the data will not be accessible in real-time. Indeed, access to most systems needs to be scheduled so that it meshes efficiently with the requirements of the information technology function. Accordingly, current data should be fed from the underlying systems into databases after the end of day's batch run, and the risk system should access its data from the databases rather than the underlying systems. Should one of the underlying systems crash or not run feed data, the risk system can revert to the most recent data held. Table 4 outlines the information that databases will need to hold.

A RISK SYSTEM THAT EXTRACTS DATA,
APPLIES MODELS, AND REPORTS

In common with other risk systems this will include:

❑ interface with the above databases containing information and approved models;

❑ an audit trail so that the calculations are transparent;

❑ access to the system to enable appropriate individuals to add explanations and comparative information as this is required; and

❑ reporting modules to present and communicate data.

In designing the risk systems architecture it is necessary to consider ease of formatting data for management reporting, the most appropriate scheduling for downloading to databases, the effect of data being drawn at different times, and the mechanism for identifying where the data held are not current. Panel 3 looks at some

---

Table 4. Database contents

Databases will need to be able to hold the following information:

1. Current data to enable any further analysis that management may need in order properly to understand reported exposures, and the actions necessary to reduce or eliminate them. This means that that the underlying data must be held at the transactional level, rather than being aggregated before being fed into the database. It should be possible to view this information by age, value, product and location. To be most effective the data also needs to be available on a view-only basis to the businesses and support functions concerned. Typically, a financial data warehouse would meet these requirements.

2. Historical data to enable modelling based on past experience and to allow line management to investigate and fully understand the causes of earlier losses and how to reduce them in future. Past exposures also highlight trends in performance. This modelling process is discussed in more depth in Chapter 8 of the present volume.

3. Data on future or proposed transactions and changes to transactions. For high-risk areas, a report of proposed transactions can be most useful to senior managers. Looking at transactions "in the pipeline", as it were, is essential if senior managers are to take action – including deciding whether or not to accept the associated operational risk.

4. An approved models database holding the models to be used to convert the data on exposures into reportable risk amounts.

5. A database of external data observations. The nature of this database depends on the measurement methodology used and should be updated with external data as specified by risk management.

---

common problems in building useful databases for operational risk.

Resourcing

MANPOWER

The role of the operational risk function is to add a secondary level of control rather than to control risks directly. Accordingly there should already be a number of people within the business lines directly involved in managing operational risk. The manpower requirement for the operational risk function should be relatively limited.

SKILL SET

There is a clear need for quantitative and analytical skills in the operational risk management function, together with an appreciation of the other sections of risk management with which the operational risk function will integrate, aligning methodologies and reports.

Operational risk personnel also need a thorough understanding of the organisation's businesses and their processes, the drivers of risk – particularly reputation and client relationship

KEY PROBLEMS IN BUILDING USEFUL DATABASES

A lack of data is often the greatest obstacle risk managers face when trying to measure operational risk. Here are some common problems:

❑ *Valued exposure data* Existing management information deals with many operational characteristics such as volumes and ageing of transactions but it rarely values the potential for loss. To overcome this, transaction values or mark-to-market values may have to be used as a proxy for potential loss.

❑ *Franchise value losses* The effect of a failure on the value of the organisation's reputation and its client relationships may be the greatest risk but it is unlikely to be valued. A value derived from current profitability will be required for modelling.

❑ *Opportunity costs* Operational failures that reduce capability result in an opportunity loss rather than a realised loss. Opportunity costs are typically not valued or reported and, if included, they may well need to be calculated and shown separately.

❑ *Business environment and strategy losses* Care needs to be taken to ensure that operational losses are not mixed or confused with strategic or business losses for which the accounting differs.

❑ *Market data* The reputational or franchise effects of operational failures are such that financial institutions will often not report them and thus any published market data are understated and need to be adjusted.

❑ *Low-incidence, high-value events* Catastrophic losses are naturally extremely rare events, and available data are limited, so the results of calculations intended to cover this kind of operational loss should be treated with caution. Market conditions in the later part of 1998 highlighted how volatile risks can be in terms of timing and effect. Empirical modelling tends only to capture median events – possible but extreme events tend not to be captured.

❑ *Human behaviour and people risks* It is hard, if not impossible, to measure the potential for dishonest behaviour or obtain data on risks posed by other people but as these are frequently the root cause of operational failures they must be included on a best-effort basis.

❑ *Data on controls* Failures typically result from breakdowns in a number of controls rather than in just one, and thus the probability of controls not being effective is more complex than simply looking at individual risks and individual controls.

risk – and the processes of control. Increasingly they need to understand personnel risks, and here some behavioural science and psychological analyses discussed in Chapter 10 may be helpful.

Historically operational risk personnel have been recruited from the back offices. Increasingly, however, the necessary skill set is more likely to be found in the front office.

MANAGEMENT
Analysis of the collapse of Barings Bank revealed that operational risks and failings had been identified long before the collapse but that the company had failed to properly escalate and address the problems.

An effective operational risk function requires:

❑ appropriate management and staff supervision to ensure that risks and exposures are properly analysed and escalated to the correct level;
❑ access to, and support, of the highest levels of management;
❑ buy-in from business and support

management to the process and acceptance of their responsibility to react;
❑ management awareness of the sources of revenues and the causes of losses; and
❑ an action-tracking mechanism to ensure necessary action is taken.

Techniques for measurement – illustrative example of how to risk profile an individual business
BACKGROUND ASSUMPTIONS
In this section we use the example of a Russian equity derivative trading business to illustrate how an individual business can be risk profiled. While we have added some background detail to bring the example to life, we should stress that what follows is a purely hypothetical exercise and that the numbers used in the accompanying tables do not reflect market realities. In addition, the following assumptions are made:

❑ There is only one business line. This consists of Russian equity-structured products such as pass-through notes and options based upon

Table 5. Financial data for the Russian equity-trading business example

Annual revenues	$100 million
Direct costs:	
London/NY	$20 million
Moscow	$10 million
Bonus pool costs:	
London/ NY	$15 million
Moscow	$5 million
Annual budgeted profit before tax	$50 million
Client data:	
Number of client accounts	250
Value of client positions in safe custody	$250 million
Gross delta equivalent value of portfolios on which valuations are quoted	$750 million
Funding data:	
Funding facility	$100 million

Table 6. Risks, data sources and illustrative expected loss

Risk	Data source	Illustrative expected operational loss estimate ($ million)
1. Client relationship		
Suitability	External	0.7
Association	External	0.2
Valuations	External	0.5
2. Transactional		
Data capture and processing	Internal	0.1
Confirmations	Internal	0.2
Payment/delivery	Internal	0.1
3. Safe custody		
Loss of securities	Internal	0.2
Corporate actions	Internal	0.1
4. Reconciliations and accounting		
Cashflow differences	Internal	0.1
Nostro/depot breaks	Internal	0.1
Accounting breaks	Internal	0.2
Systems capability	Internal	0.4
Valuations	Internal	0.1
5. Core operational capability		
Physical damage	External	0.2
Fraudulent access	External	0.2
Year 2000 problems, introduction of the euro	Internal	0.4
Tax recovery	External	0.2
Licence retention	External	0.1
6. People		
Dishonesty and human error	External	0.5
Retention	Internal	0.1
7. Change activities	Internal	0.1
8. Expense volatility	Internal	0.2
	Total	$5 million

underlying traded Russian shares. The products are delta hedged using positions in the underlying shares. The shares are sourced through the bank's local Moscow office.

❑ It is a client-driven business and the traders have the mandate only to hedge exposures arising from client trades in the structured products.

❑ Products are sold through a special purpose vehicle owned by the bank and within the UK tax group.

❑ The client base consists predominantly of US institutions.

We also assume that the team assessing the operational risk has the rudimentary data outlined in Table 5 available to it. Finally, we assume that $10 million of current year's revenues depends on the launch of new products.

We noted earlier that measuring operational risk is not an exact science. The team looking at this Russian equity business would need to continually challenge the credibility of results and to retain transparency within both the calculation methodology and the final result.

ROUND-TABLE DISCUSSION
A good first start for the team would be to initiate a round-table discussion between the business support heads, internal auditors and the legal department. They would need to set out:
❑ the key operational risks involving exposures greater than $1 million;
❑ annualised expected operational loss; and
❑ the probable range of potential outcomes and their respective probabilities.

Annualised expected operational losses can be hard to conceptualise for comparatively rare events. However, looking at the market as a whole and then calibrating the result to the particular trading desk concerned can facilitate this. Thus, in this example, if one wanted to estimate expected loss from a claim arising from an unsuitable product being sold to a client one could estimate the likely annual value of claims in the market as a whole for this type of product and then apply the firm's market share to that value.

Another approach is to agree the premium that the business would be willing to pay to insure itself against potential operational risks. Actual operational risk insurance is more problematic to implement, but the methodology for determining how much it would be *worth* paying is applicable to this case.

Table 6 shows what the results from such a round-table analysis might look like. (Like the other figures in this section, these amounts are illustrative only and have not been mathematically derived.) In this illustration we assume that the round-table group decides that the expected operational loss is $5 million. This in itself is a useful rule of thumb, however, the group decides to try to refine its estimates using the more detailed risk profiling to which we will now turn.

OPERATIONAL RISK PROFILING THE RUSSIAN EQUITY BUSINESS

As noted earlier operational risk profiling is based on the following calculation:

$$\begin{aligned} &\text{Value of potential losses} \\ &\times \text{ chance of risk events occurring} \\ &\times \text{ chance of controls not preventing loss} \\ &= \text{value-at-operational-risk} \end{aligned}$$

For each of the risks established by the round-table we therefore require data valuing exposures to key operational risks and data on probability of a risk materialising and internal controls failing to prevent that loss. The probability is derived from a tree encompassing the factors determining whether the risk event will occur and whether internal controls will prove effective or whether a loss will materialise. As many factors may be involved, a score table may provide an expedient and transparent methodology for deriving the probability.

A score table works as follows. For each of the factors determining likelihood a score is ascribed either subjectively or using data. There may be, say, five factors where four are given a score out of 10 and the one key factor is given a score out of 50. The scores are then totalled and translated into a probability using a table that might look like Table 7.

To calculate the expected annualised loss, all probabilities need to be converted into *expected risk events per annum* and the data modelled to give the *average value of each loss event*.

One of the hardest tasks is to determine the exposure data on which to impose the assigned probability. The overriding goal is to ensure that the final result, the expected loss estimate, is realistic.

In the following section of risk profiles, "risk value" describes the *expected annual loss* from the operational risks concerned. Again, the probabilities, scores and exposures are

Table 7. A score table

Score	Probability assigned (%)
0–25	0.1
25–50	0.5
50–75	2.5
75–100	10.0

Table 8. Profile estimates compared to initial estimate

Risk	Operational risk expected annualised loss ($ million)	
	Initial estimate	Profile estimate
1. Client relationship		
Suitability	0.7	0.17
Association	0.2	0.30
Valuations	0.5	0.30
2. Transactional		
Data capture and processing	0.1	0.07
Confirmations	0.2	0.24
Payment/delivery	0.1	0.12
3. Safe custody		
Loss of securities	0.2	0.22
Corporate actions	0.1	0.07
4. Reconciliations and accounting		
Cashflow differences	0.1	0.15
Nostro/depot breaks	0.1	0.24
Accounting breaks	0.2	0.27
Systems capability	0.4	0.45
Valuations	0.1	0.16
5. Core operational capability		
Physical damage	0.2	0.17
Fraudulent access	0.2	0.26
Year 2000 risks, introduction of the euro	0.4	0.25
Tax recovery	0.2	0.22
Licence retention	0.1	0.12
6. People		
Dishonesty and human error	0.5	0.35
Retention	0.1	0.04
7. Change activities	0.1	0.12
8. Expense volatility	0.2	0.2
Total	$5 million	$4.49 million

illustrative rather than derived. Whereas Table 8 sums up the risk profiling exercise by showing how these more detailed profile estimates compare to the initial round-table discussion, the subsequent tables show how each of the profile estimates was arrived at in rather more detail.

The risk profiles
CLIENT RELATIONSHIP EXPOSURE
Client suitability

Risk	Russian equities are inherently a high-risk investment for the client and are categorised as non-marketable securities for regulatory purposes. The key client suitability risks could result in the following claims: ❑ The bank is assisting the investor in avoiding regulations designed to limit investment to marketable (suitable) securities. ❑ The client is not fully aware of the risks of Russian equities or the salesman has misrepresented those risks. ❑ The person committing to the trade on behalf of the client was not authorised to do so and the bank should have known that he was not. Even if there is no litigation a significant loss on the trade could prejudice other business with the client.
Exposure measure	The potential for loss to the client from the transactions – ie its VAR and any losses to date.
Key controls	Enforcement of "know-your-client" procedures and requirements concerning documented support (indemnity) to verify that clients may purchase such securities. All clients should be sent, and be required to acknowledge receipt of, a specific statement of risk concerning Russian equities and derivatives. Stratified client signatory requirements so that transactions with VARs above predetermined levels need increasing levels of seniority both within the firm and within the client company to authorise them.
Probability of loss measure	Value-at-risk of open client trades stratified by client type – ie market professionals (low risk) investment funds (moderate risk) and private clients (high risk). Also use reports with mark-to-market (MTM) on deals with pending disputes/litigation and deals with risk statements not issued and returned. Any external and internal data on incidence of client suitability lawsuits, plus any data on Russian equity lawsuits in particular.

Illustration

	VAR $M	Probability %	Risk value $ million
VAR on open trades:			
Market professional	20	0.02	0.0
Investment funds	30	0.05	0.02
Private clients	25	0.2	0.05
MTM on open trades:			
In dispute/ litigation	10	0.5	0.05
No risk statement	50	0.1	0.05
			Total $0.17 million

Initial estimate from modelling market-observed loss data $0.2 million

Association

Risk	The ownership of the local Russian brokers cannot be determined with the same certainty as with Western counterparts. There is a higher inherent risk that they or the securities that they trade may be linked to individuals or organisations or activities with which the bank would not wish to be associated.
Exposure measure	The main impact would be on the firm's reputation, and the bank's own research function can best estimate how the share value of the firm would change if such an event occurred and was published.
Key controls	New counterparties should be subject to detailed background checks and approval by both local and regional credit committees. "Pending trade" and other suspense accounts should be purged daily and controls should be established to prevent trades settling from dummy client accounts.
Probability of loss measure	Value of aged transactions (older than one day) in pending, dummy client or other suspense account. Internal rating on effectiveness of new counterparties checking procedures and approvals.

Illustration

Research calculates the average reputational loss at being $1 million per event.

	Exposure value $ million	Probability Measure	Score out of 10	Probability	Risk value $ million
Aged transactions in suspense accounts	1	500 trades	6	0.2 events	0.2
Other accounts	1	250 client accounts	4	0.1 event	0.1
					Total $0.3 million
				Initial estimate from modelling market observed loss data $0.2 million	

Valuation sent to clients

Background	Asset management clients generally need daily valuations of their position to determine the net asset values of their funds and to calculate conversion rates for new money and redemptions. Other clients need the information for their own management reporting or satisfying their auditors. Banks typically provide clients with daily valuations.
Risk	Erroneous valuations can lead to litigation to recover redemptions or to pay investors if they were misled. False valuations may have been used either by salesmen where they sought to conceal from the client that the product they sold has lost money or by the client in collaboration with the salesman seeking to conceal the loss from his superior or investors.
Exposure measure	The value of transactions for which valuations are provided to the client is stratified between market professionals, asset managers and private clients.
Key controls	Valuations must only be issued from the back office and only with disclaimers and in a format approved by legal advisers. All valuations must be signed off by the relevant trader and the price quoted for valuation must be one at which the trader is willing to trade should the client wish to unwind.
Probability of loss measure	Combination of internal data and the much-publicised external data on relevant lawsuits. An internal score could be used to assess the likelihood of the above issuance controls not being in place.

Illustration

	Exposure value $ million	Score out of 10	Probability %	Risk value $ million
Valuations sent to clients/ market professional	500	2	0.01	0.05
asset management	200	2	0.1	0.2
private client	50	2	0.1	0.05
				Total $0.3 million
				Initial assessment $0.5 million

TRANSACTIONAL EXPOSURE
Data capture and processing

Risk	There is a risk of errors in data capture and processing, resulting in the firm hedging or funding illusory positions. There is a risk that unexplained front-to-back-office differences are due to unauthorised activity or trading errors that have not been accounted for.
Exposure measure	Unexplained front-to-back-office position or funding breaks that are balance sheet debits.
Key controls	Direct dealer input and straight-through processing, and automation. Daily sign off and explanation of front-to-back position and funding position reconciliations.
Probability of loss measure	Ageing. These are daily reconciliations and the longer the unexplained difference has persisted the more likely a loss will crystallise.

Illustration

	Exposure value $ million	Probability %	Risk value $ million
Unexplained front-to-back office position differences:			
❑ less than 5 days old	200	0.01	0.02
❑ 5–30 days old	5	1	0.05
❑ over 30 days	0	8	–
			Total $0.07 million
			Initial assessment $0.1 million

Confirmations

Background	Only limited transaction details are confirmed over the telephone when a deal is struck, and the deal might not be taped due to local laws. A more detailed written confirmation is issued and signed in due course. There is typically a master agreement under which individual agreements are issued and can, for example, be netted. The International Swaps and Derivatives Association (ISDA) has standardised this process.
Risk	Key risks from deals pending signed documentation are: ❑ the client subsequently denies knowledge of the trade or disputes trade details that affect its value and risk characteristics; ❑ the confirmation includes an error to the bank's detriment and becomes binding once issued and signed; ❑ the counterparty defaults and lack of contractual documentation prevents or delays recovery.
Exposure measure	Mark-to-market value of transactions where documentation has not yet been signed. This is stratified by the client and aged from transaction date.
Key controls	Sales should be restricted until the client has signed a master agreement. The key economic terms in the confirmation should be signed off by both front and back office prior to issuance. Confirmations should be issued using standard templates agreed by legal advisers. Legal advisers should approve any changes that are subsequently negotiated. Confirmations should be issued and collected according to strict schedules with limits (by salesmen and by counterparty) on the mark-to-market value of transactions with unsigned documentation. Key economic terms should be agreed separately on large exposures.
Probability of loss measure	Probabilities stratified to give higher rates for older transactions and for non-market professionals. Rates themselves are derived from the business's own experience. Any actual dispute is taken as a credit or market risk and provisioned for separately.

Illustration

	Exposure value $ million	Probability %	Risk value $ million
Market counterparties:			
❑ less than 5 days	100	0.05	0.05
❑ greater than 5 days	20	0.2	0.04
Non-market professionals:			
❑ less than 5 days	50	0.1	0.05
❑ greater than 5 days	20	0.5	0.1
			Total $0.24 million
			Initial assessment $0.2 million

Payment/delivery

Background	The central depository is only used for settling certain shares. Others are settled by the Registrar by free delivery/free payment. The registrars are not all in Moscow and there are logistical problems between time of free delivery to the Registrar and time the personnel return with the documentation to the office. It may be necessary for the settlement clerk to telephone that delivery has taken place. In many emerging markets, it may not be possible to confirm the counterparty's settlement instructions to published sources.
Risk	The settlement clerk is: ❏ misled or deceived at the Registrar's office; ❏ forced to lie at gun-point; ❏ impersonated; and ❏ defrauding in collaboration with the counterparty. The settlement details are incorrect due to negligence or falsification either internally, by the counterparty or by another.
Exposure measure	Value of transactions in process.
Key controls	Counterparty standard settlement instructions should be reconfirmed either to published sources or directly with the counterparty back-office. All counterparties should be issued with own standard settlement instructions. Payment should only made when the settlement clerk returns to the office with a signed purchase-and-sale agreement/custody statement.
Probability of loss measure	Historic experience by counterparty, with higher rates for counterparties with less trading history and those without a recognised Western parent.

Illustration

	Exposure value $ million	Probability %	Risk value $ million
Pending settlements:			
❏ local counterparts	10	0.1	0.01
❏ western counterparts	20	0.05	0.01
Failed trades:			
❏ local counterparts	3	2	0.06
❏ western counterparts	2	1	0.04
			Total $0.12 million
			Initial assessment $0.1 million

SAFE CUSTODY
Loss of securities

Risk	For shares not held with a central depository the custodial risks are high. Custodians pass on the risks to the beneficial owner. These risks include: ❏ the risk that the Registrar deletes the ownership record in error, fraudulently, or to prevent foreign ownership; ❏ the risk that the Registrar acts on a fraudulent instruction and fails to make good; ❏ the risk that the Registrar's records are lost or fraudulently adjusted.
Exposure measure	The value of securities in custody, stratified by Registrar or sub-custodian.
Key controls	Use of central depositories wherever possible. Use of approved sub-custodians. Staff rotation and regular interaction with Registrars. Specifically, holdings should be re-confirmed at least monthly.
Probability of loss measure	External published data on market losses experienced.

Illustration

	Exposure value $ million	Probability %	Risk value $ million
Securities held directly at Registrar	50	0.2	0.10
Securities held by approved custodian	200	0.06	0.12
			Total $0.22 million
			Initial assessment $0.2 million

Corporate actions

Risk	The firm could fail to act upon, or receive the benefit of, a corporate action due to either lack of knowledge of the corporate action or other internal operational failure.
Exposure measure	Percentage of assets in custody based upon prevailing dividend yields.
Key controls	Use of external corporate action advisory services to supplement other resources.
Probability of loss measure	Data drawn from own experience or externally if internal data are too limited.

Illustration

	Custody value $ million	Exposure value $ million	Probability %	Risk value $ million
Securities held directly with Registrar	50	2	1	0.02
Securities held by approved custodian	200	10	0.5	0.05
				Total $0.07 million
				Initial assessment $0.1 million

RECONCILIATIONS AND ACCOUNTING
Cashflow differences

Risk	The diary of cashflows is a key tool for the management of both funding and valuing positions. The cashflow diary for determining cash requirement by nostro is also essential for efficient funding. Breaks between the front-office system, settlement system and accounting system sometimes reflect incorrect funding and valuations or failure to secure all entitlements. If the cashflow diary is incorrect, nostro funding will be incorrect and trades may fail or nostros may be over-funded (resulting in foregone interest).
Exposure measure	Unexplained debit balances, stratified by age.
Key controls	Straight-through processing together with a daily reconciliation and explanation/clearance of differences.
Probability of loss measure	Subjective probabilities skewed for ageing of items and distinguished between potential profit and loss versus potential funding exposure. A database of losses can be built up by reason code to facilitate a more precise probability of loss and to assist in managing their clearance.

Illustration

	Exposure value $ million	Probability %	Risk value $ million
Cashflow breaks:			
❑ less than 5 days	50	0.1	0.05
❑ 5–30 days	5	1	0.05
❑ over 30 days	1	5	0.05
			Total $0.15 million
			Initial assessment $0.1 million

Nostro/depot breaks

Background	The reconciliation of the bank's record of its cash and stock balances with the statement of balance/holding provided by its counterparty is a key control. Systems now enable any differences thrown up by the reconciliation process to be explained in terms of unmatched transactions aggregating to the out-of-balance position. Differences need to be segregated between timing differences (ie the firm's own records are more up-to-date than the latest counterparty statements), failures made by the counterparty, and failures made by the bank.
Risk	The firm's record of cash and stock positions is overstated due to misappropriation, processing error or other failure resulting in a loss to the bank. The nostro break may reflect a failed settlement, where the bank's exposure is to the possible mark-to-market cost of unwinding the trade rather than to the full contract value. The break may leave nostros overdrawn or over-funded, leading to additional funding expenses or opportunity costs. Failure to receive a timely statement may indicate operational problems at the counterparty, or a deliberate suppression of information in an attempt to conceal a fraud.
Exposure measure	Unexplained breaks should be recorded together with the length of time they have been left unreconciled (ie they should be "aged"), and debits should be segregated from credits. Systems should be able to separate out those that have arisen because no current statement is obtainable.
Key controls	Independent daily preparation and reporting of nostro reconciliations and breaks. Timely explanation of breaks and supervision and reviews of reconciliation preparation; explanation of items and clearance.
Probability of loss measure	Probabilities are skewed to increase with the age of unexplained debit. Over time, individual probabilities of loss can be allocated to each reason for a break. This necessitates allocating a code to each reason for a break and more sophisticated data-gathering, but it increases the precision and usefulness of the risk measurement.

Illustration

Nostro depot breaks	Exposure value $ million	Probability %	Risk value $ million
Explained timing differences:			
❏ less than 5 days	150	0.0	0.0
❏ 5–30 days	50	0.1	0.05
❏ over 30 days	10	0.2	0.02
Unexplained debits:			
❏ less than 5 days	200	0.01	0.02
❏ 5–30 days	20	0.5	0.10
❏ over 30 days	1	5	0.05
			Total $0.24 million
			Initial assessment $0.1 million

Accounting breaks

Background	Systems that offered all the functions a bank might want to use would quickly become unwieldy and inefficient, so it is common for banks to use separate but interconnected systems in the front office, in settlements and in the finance section. The data held within these systems are systematically reconciled for consistency.
Risk	Differences between the general ledger and either the front office or the settlement system's records may represent unreported losses, unauthorised activity or other irregularities.
Exposure measure	The main measure is unreconciled or unexplained aged debits. However unreconciled credits can also represent failures or unauthorised activity and should be captured and reported.
Key controls	Periodic independent reconciliations between systems and investigation and explanation of differences under suitable authorisation and supervision.
Probability of loss measure	The potential financial risks can be modelled from past experience. The potential risk that the breaks represent unauthorised activity or irregularities is likely to be judgmental but can be derived using a score system and probabilities based, say, on audit ratings.

Illustration

Accounting debit breaks	Exposure value $ million	Probability %	Risk value $ million
Front-office versus finance:			
❑ less than 5 days	50	0.1	0.05
❑ 5–30 days	10	0.5	0.05
❑ over 30 days	1	5	0.05
Settlements versus finance:			
❑ less than 5 days	2	1	0.02
❑ 5– 30 days	20	0.5	0.1
❑ over 30 days	0	10	
			Total $0.27 million
			Initial assessment $0.2 million

Systems capability

Background	Straight-through processing, automation and strong technology controls are key components of reducing operational risk. Systems functionality is tailored around existing products and newer and more complex products are either "worked around" on the main systems or managed off-line on spreadsheets.
Risk	System deficiencies can prevent timely processing and can create significant inefficiencies as well as increasing the risk of error, or of manipulation, such as the creation of illusory profits (as experienced by Kidder Peabody).
Exposure measure	Composite of average daily transaction value processed and value of client and firm positions.
Key controls	New product approval process/technology committee to limit business on non-core systems to that which the manual workarounds and spreadsheets can reasonably control.
Probability of loss measure	Score-based probability derived from: ❑ Proportion of manual interfaces and manual journals. ❑ Time taken to produce daily profit and loss data. ❑ Value of positions accounted for on spreadsheets.

Illustration

Systems capability	Exposure value $ million	Risk rating out of 10	Probability %	Risk value $ million
OTC options	40	9	0.5	0.20
Pass through notes	100	6	0.1	0.10
Russian equity trades	100	5	0.05	0.10
Funding trades	50	2	0.1	0.05
				Total $0.45 million
				Initial assessment $0.4 million

Valuations

Background	Not all positions can be readily valued from an externally quoted price and thus traders' marks are needed to both price cash equity positions and volatility assumptions underlying the options values.
Risk	Positions are mispriced, potentially leading to incorrect hedging and therefore unrecognised market exposure, an overstatement of profits, incorrect statement of accounting and regulatory capital, and overpayment of bonuses. It can also lead to incorrect strategic decisions such as continuance of loss-making activities or inappropriate allocation of capital and resources.
Exposure measure	Gross position values.
Key controls	Independent daily revaluation of positions and diagnostic pricing controls.
Probability of loss measure	Pricing difference history potentially skewed with a score mechanism to reflect complexity of the product, liquidity of the market, tenure of the traders and of the controllers, etc.

Illustration

Systems capability	Exposure value $ million	Risk rating out of 10	Probability %	Risk value $ million
OTC options	10	9	0.5	0.05
Pass through notes	20	6	0.4	0.08
Russian equity trades	5	5	0.4	0.02
Funding trades	5	2	0.2	0.01
				Total $0.16 million
				Initial assessment $0.1 million

CORE OPERATIONAL CAPABILITY
Physical damage

Background	Physical damage can materialise from a variety of causes from terrorist bombings and fires to malicious damage by employees. Evaluating the operational risks helps focus business resumption plans and is necessary to optimise insurance cover.
Risk	The risk is that the firm will not be able to conduct new transactions or manage its risk positions due to its premises or the technology within them being unavailable. There is also the risk of loss in value of such fixed assets and there is additional loss to the extent that the cost of the disruption is not covered by insurance.
Exposure measure	Value of fixed assets adjusted for insurance cover. The VAR of the business's positions may be a reasonable proxy for potential market exposures with the durations adjusted to reflect the time delay expected to recalculate positions and to be able to resume hedging activity. Lost revenues may be taken as both average daily client-driven revenues for the expected downtime period plus an additional cost for disruption to the client relationship.
Key controls	All businesses should have documented and tested disaster recovery and business resumption plans that detail the procedures to be employed in the event of business disruption. Insurance may be obtained. If not, the risks should be evaluated and the likely costs self-funded.
Probability of loss measure	Natural disasters are published and the probability of such risk events can be obtained by calculating modes from such public data and supplementing them with a component for potential internal threats, and data on the business's own system failures. The probabilities should reflect insurance cover. The probabilities of controls not being effective can be rated according to how current the plans are and when they were last tested.

Illustration

Core operational capability	Exposure value $ million	Risk rating out of 10	Probability %	Risk value $ million
Fixed assets	10	2	1	0.1
Business disruption:				
❑ OTC options	10	9	0.5	0.05
❑ Pass through notes	5	6	0.2	0.01
❑ Russian equity trades	5	5	0.2	0.01
❑ Funding trades	1	2	0.2	0.0
				Total $0.17 million
				Initial assessment $0.2 million

Fraudulent access

Risk	Risk of financial loss due to persons being able to misappropriate funds or cause other damage via unauthorised access to the firm's premises or systems. Risk that viruses enter the firm's systems, prevent orderly operations and contaminate information.
Exposure measure	Firm and client assets up to the limit of funding lines. Downtime while viruses are removed and data recreated.
Key controls	Physical access controls, systems with secured access and password controls, enforced segregation of duties and supervision, and detective controls. Specific technology controls around access to, and interfaces with, external systems to prevent viruses.
Probability of loss measure	The bank should be able to have a good database of internal fraud losses and be able to access external data either from regulators or fraud prevention specialists. Similarly for data on viruses. The incidence rate will need to reflect the higher-than-average fraud risk of operating in a country such as Russia.

Illustration

Core operational capability	Exposure value $ million	Risk rating out of 10	Probability %	Risk value $ million
Fixed assets	10	8	0.5	0.1
Payment systems	100	7	0.1	0.1
Custody and settlement systems and processes	100	3	0.05	0.05
Viruses	2	3	0.5	0.01
				Total $0.26 million
				Initial assessment $0.2 million

The "millennium timebomb" and the euro

Risk	The risk that the firm's systems, including its interfaces with counterparts, suppliers and exchanges, are either unavailable or unable to operate due to either "the millennium timebomb" or the introduction of the euro.

Exposure measure	The cost of downtime should euro capability or the "millennium timebomb" not be addressed by January 1, 1999 and January 1, 2000.
	    The value of business lost should business activities need to be restricted due to unavailability of systems.
	    The cost of fines or penalties from counterparties, suppliers, clients or exchanges.

Key controls	Systematic eradication of the "millennium timebomb" problem.
Probability of loss measure	This is likely to be calculated by detailed bottom-up plans by system with probabilities and alternative plans in the event of failure being defined.

Illustration

	Exposure value $ million	Risk rating out of 10	Probability %	Risk value $ million
Euro	1	1	0.1	0.0
"Millennium timebomb"	50	7	0.5	0.25
				Total $0.25 million
				Initial assessment $0.4 million

Tax recovery

Background	In pricing the structures, the traders will have made assumptions in respect of Russian and UK income and capital gains taxation that may or may not be passed through to the client (according to the deal structure). There is no tax treaty between Russia and the UK and, as in many emerging markets, Russian tax law is sometimes ambiguous and uncertain.
Risk	There is a risk that tax costs exceed expectations and that the amounts built into pricing, or a negligent act, could leave the firm exposed to a tax loss that it cannot pass through to the client.
Exposure measure	Timing of tax receivable balance and discounted value of future tax recoveries included within the valuation.
Key controls	Ideally such tax risks are passed through to the client. Otherwise key controls are to obtain independent advice on key tax risks and to keep tax balances current.
Probability of loss measure	The internal or external tax adviser used in the transactions should be able to make the initial assessment, which can be supplemented by measures based on the ageing of current tax receivables.

Illustration

Taxation	Exposure value $ million	Risk rating out of 10	Probability %	Risk value $ million
Receivable balance:				
❑ Current year	4	4	1	0.04
❑ Previous year	2	7	4	0.08
❑ Greater than 2 years	1	10	10	0.10
				Total $0.22 million
				Initial assessment $0.2 million

Licence retention

Background	Capability to access the Russian market and transact hedge trades and funding at efficient prices may depend on retaining a licence that permits the company to trade in the US and the Russian market.
Risk	Risk of loss of sales or trading capability or efficiency as a result of losing US or Russian operating licence. Retention of the licence to be able to sell the product to US clients is likely to be of greater value and concern.
Exposure measure	The potential exposure is greater than just for this business line, as a failure by this business line may lead to all businesses being precluded from operating in these markets.
Key controls	Compliance with relevant regulatory laws and requirements.
Probability of loss measure	Withdrawal of licences are published and thus an initial estimate could be obtained from public data. This could then be tailored by factors determined by the legal and compliance function.

Illustration

Licence retention	Exposure value $ million	Risk rating out of 10	Probability %	Risk value $ million
Russian licence	2	4	1	0.02
US licence	200	2	0.05	0.1
				Total $0.12 million
				Initial assessment $0.1 million

PEOPLE
Dishonesty

Risk	Risk of loss either of the business's own assets or of clients' funds under the firm's fiduciary responsibility arising from the dishonest activities of one or more employees. Such losses risk the firm's reputation as being a secure custodian. Losses recovered by insurance can be expected to be paid for in higher future premiums. Risk of loss of the business's own assets and of those of clients due to human error of employees.
Exposure measure	The level of access to clients' funds and to the business's own funds and the borrowing facilities given to the business and its support functions.
Key controls	Segregation of duties, authorisation and supervisory controls to limit the opportunity for dishonesty. Use of references and credit checks to try to avoid hiring dishonest employees. Alignment of reward mechanisms to risk appetite to avoid unduly motivating dishonest behaviour. Automation and supervision control human error risk.
Probability of loss measure	An initial probability estimate may be available from internal and external data. The probability should then be skewed by, say, internal audit rating to tailor it to the company and promote improvement.

Illustration

People risk	Exposure value $ million	Risk rating out of 10	Probability %	Risk value $ million
Front-office personnel:				
❏ Local	50	4	0.2	0.1
❏ Overseas	100	2	0.1	0.1
Back-office personnel:				
❏ Local	20	5	0.5	0.1
❏ Overseas	100	1	0.05	0.05
				Total $0.35 million
				Initial assessment $0.5 million

Reliance on key individuals

Background	The firm's value is in part reflected by the value ascribed to its employees. For some businesses or activities successful operation may depend on the retention of key individuals who hold the necessary knowledge, capabilities or contacts. In most cases their unexpected loss will cause a temporary problem while they are replaced.
Risk	The firm is not able to continue ordinary activities following the unexpected loss of a few key individuals.
Exposure measure	This would have to be calculated in detail but, as an initial estimate, a proportion of VAR and, say, one month's revenues could be taken.
Key controls	A structured approach to job rotation, skill sharing and succession planning. Flexible outsourcing arrangements and automation reduce exposure to loss of particular back-office personnel.
Probability of loss measure	The probability could be scored through an assessment of: ❑ tenure with the firm; ❑ percentage of employees with identified potential successors; and ❑ degree of cross-training and job rotation.

Illustration

People retention risk	Exposure value $ million	Risk rating out of 10	Probability %	Risk value $ million
Front-office personnel:				
❑ Local	2	4	1	0.02
❑ Overseas	5	2	0.2	0.01
Back-office personnel:				
❑ Local	1	5	1	0.01
❑ Overseas	0	1	0.1	0
				Total $0.04 million
				Initial assessment $0.1 million

CHANGE ACTIVITIES

Risk	Risk of loss through uncontrolled change activity. Three particular change activities are identified as higher risks for this business: Introduction of new products that the firm does not have the expertise to manage or process. Risks of error are higher in the early stages of a product launch where the firm is learning by experience. There is also the potential to miss business opportunities due to an overly bureaucratic change management process. Introduction of new clients may facilitate addition of unsuitable clients or may create opportunities for insertion of fraudulent settlement instructions into the systems. New system developments could prevent orderly processing or may enable employees to compromise system controls.
Exposure measure	Investment cost of new activities plus the reputational damage arising from the failure of a new activity. Profit at risk if budgeted new opportunities are not captured.
Key controls	A change management process that ensures that changes are implemented only with after testing and with suitable controls.
Probability of loss measure	An initial assessment can probably be made from the firm's historic experience in change management. For new product risk this can be refined to the limits of risk set for the business in its start-up phase.

Illustration

Change activities	Exposure value $ million	Risk rating out of 10	Probability %	Risk value $ million
New products	10	5	1	0.1
New clients	5	4	0.2	0.01
New systems	5	2	0.2	0.01
				Total $0.12 million
				Initial assessment $0.1 million

EXPENSE VOLATILITY

Background	The particular risk for this business is that the products are priced with an assumed cost of support for dynamic hedging and administration during the product term. Costs may exceed expectations for many reasons but a key consideration should be evaluating the support costs if there were no new business to allocate fixed costs to, ie if the business were only supporting the orderly run-off of transactions.
Risk	The risk that the costs of supporting the business are higher than anticipated. 　The risk that entering such business is committing to future costs that would not be covered by revenues from existing transactions.
Exposure measure	Factor of operating cost base and average duration to expiration of outstanding transactions.
Key controls	Disciplined cost budget challenge process. 　Reserving (pricing) policies for transactions of longer maturities and in markets with little liquidity in which to unwind.
Probability of loss measure	Score based on volatility of costs.

Illustration

Expense volatility	Exposure value $ million	Risk rating out of 10	Probability %	Risk value $ million
Current year's costs	30	5	0.3	0.1
Future costs committed to in current transactions	5	7	0.2	0.1
				Total $0.2 million
				Initial assessment $0.1 million

2

New Trends in Operational Risk Measurement and Management

Douglas G. Hoffman
Bankers Trust

The business environment for financial institutions has changed dramatically in recent years. Technological advances, the information revolution, open global markets, advances in financial products, and now the advent of electronic commerce have all driven this change. The resulting business complexity, and the need to manage the risks associated with it, have given rise to a new field called operational risk management.

The urgency of this need has been underscored numerous times in recent years by headlines filled with loss events ranging from rogue trading to system failures, accounting improprieties, fraud, improper sales practices, landmark legal judgements and settlements, terrorist acts, sabotage, attacks on systems, and regulatory violations, to name only a few.

Operational risk has assumed a prominent position on the agenda of senior management at major financial institutions partly because of these losses, but also because of a convergence among several other key trends in risk management. In this chapter, we focus on these trends, as well as on changes in the underlying risk factors that might exacerbate the situation even further. Some of the trends – both causal and resultant – in this newest area of risk management include:

❑ enterprise-wide risk management and operational risk recognition;
❑ macro- and micro-operational risk factor trends;
❑ operational risk definition trends;
❑ risk management organisational challenges;
❑ data and operational risk models: concept, construction and challenges;
❑ new risk information measures and applications for improved decision making;
❑ expanded risk finance applications; and

❑ linkages between risk-based capital methods and risk finance.

This chapter also reviews some of the work of Bankers Trust, a pioneer in operational risk measurement and management, including early research into operational risk-based capital and the implementation of operational risk management generally.

Operational risk definitions, trends and driving forces

DEFINITIONS
No discussion of operational risk would be complete without some comment about definitions. So many professionals have approached the subject from different perspectives that finding common ground at the outset is essential. For instance, the subject has been approached by operations and processing managers, corporate risk managers, insurance risk managers, market and credit risk managers, auditors, and consultants. Each has brought a different perspective.

Regardless of one's perspective, there is a trend today toward recognition that the universe of operational risk includes, but is broader than, operations or processing risk (ie *operations* risk). It transcends all business lines, and spans front-, middle- and back-office business operations. It is broader than the realm of conventionally insured risks, and it is broader than studies of control failures.

The current operational risk management strategy at Bankers Trust began in 1992 with a serious and complex study of operational risk that asked a very simple question: what risks were *not* being addressed by market and credit risk management models and functions? Answering the question led us to identify risks associated with key resources of the firm, such as its relationships, people/human capital,

NEW TRENDS IN

OPERATIONAL

RISK

MEASUREMENT

AND

MANAGEMENT

technology/processing, physical assets and other external sources.

We looked at multiple-dimension loss scenarios involving each, including their direct impact and cost, their indirect business disruption and interruption, and legal considerations. By doing so, we found that we could get closer to the underlying source, circumstances and causative factors for each loss event. For instance, by focusing on "people risk" one may be more inclined to analyse the human behaviours that might cause negative outcomes, whether they be corporate, cultural, peer pressure, simple carelessness and inadequate control, or dishonest tendencies. In contrast, conventional approaches to defining risks, whether borrowed from the auditing, regulatory, or insurance communities, tend to focus on the outcome or symptom (eg the problem may be seen as a compliance, reporting or legal risk) rather than the underlying behaviour.

Although the latter terms might be useful for classification purposes and in re-engineering control functions, they have limited value in analysing causation. After all, the objective should be to facilitate and promote effective risk-managed behaviour, not just to measure the degree of compliance with controls. Whatever categories one chooses for analysing operational risk, they should have a solid foundation for practical risk management.

If all this does not present enough of a challenge, regulators have been anxious to see *reputation risk* – possible damage to a bank's credibility and standing – considered alongside operational risks. Reputation risk is a key consideration and a factor in many operational events, particularly for banks, and especially where human behaviour is concerned. However, it is probably the most difficult area to quantify.

EXPONENTIAL GROWTH OF OPERATIONAL
RISK: DRIVING FORCES/RISK FACTORS
What is it about operational risk that has altered the risk landscape in recent years? In describing its growth, the word "exponential" may not be too strong.

First, financial products and transactions, and technology are all more complex than ever before. Second, technological advances in the 1980s and early 1990s have given rise to financial engineering, affording firms the ability to dissect and analyse multiple dimensions of financial risks, applying hedges where advantageous. This evolution has been key in transforming corporate risk profiles and enabling reduction of the financial (ie market and credit) risk profiles for corporations and financial service firms alike. At the same time, however, this evolution has given rise to an entirely new phenomenon.

It has enabled greater transaction *complexity* and created the need for more robust data management structures, given that many of these financial structures cross many markets and product types. The underlying technology has also facilitated greater transaction *velocity*. In turn, however, this has led to an even greater reliance on essential systems – both central and distributed on desktops – along with greater reliance on key people who understand them. It has become more challenging to control and monitor these systems, and most banks are less and less capable of operating manually should the technology itself fail. And so the cycle continues. Further advances contribute to the expansion of operational risk. The latest wave – the advent of electronic commerce – has ushered in yet another phase of change in the business and risk landscape, along with risk issues of confidentiality, identity, compromise and repudiation.

Several other major factors have already been contributing to the growth of areas of operational risk. They include the continued global trend toward litigation as a dominant method for settling disputes, an increased frequency of large-scale natural disasters in recent years, constant change and evolution in the regulatory landscape, and problematical issues in operational risk transfer (the ability of insurance and other risk transfer products to align effectively to operational risk classes).

METAMORPHOSIS OF OPERATIONAL RISK
AND MANAGEMENT THINKING
Operational risk has been a challenge for financial service firms for years, but because, historically, disasters arising from operational risk occur relatively infrequently, its full impact in terms of the losses it causes has not been recognised until recently. One-off events, while causing both major embarrassment and/or the collapse of organisations, were considered to be extremely rare and so were thought of as "aberrations".

At the same time, other types of operational risks seemed to be characterised by frequent relatively small and predictable events such as processing errors, reconciliation

31

NEW TRENDS IN
OPERATIONAL
RISK
MEASUREMENT
AND
MANAGEMENT

breaks, or system glitches, accompanied by the one-in-five-or-ten-year large system failure and loss, defalcation or customer dispute.

This changed in recent years, when a whole series of life-threatening or fatal operational loss events at a number of different financial firms caused reorganisation, management shake-ups, a re-focusing on control environments and a new focus on operational risk. Even more noteworthy was that these events occurred at high-profile and respected firms in the US and Europe, underscoring the danger of ignoring this area.

This series of loss events, in the evolving risk landscape, changed management's perceptions and priorities forever. Coupled with the advent of increased management and directorship accountability, and reinforced by legal actions against officers and directors, a chain reaction had been set in motion. Suddenly there is a new recognition of the importance of identifying, understanding, measuring and finding more creative approaches to managing operational risks given their complexity and potentially devastating impact on firms.

One noteworthy development is the September, 1998 release of a White Paper on operational risk management by the Bank for International Settlements (BIS) Basle Committee on Banking Supervision. It states that "managing operational risk is becoming an important feature of sound risk management practice in modern financial markets" and "encourages banks to share with their supervisors the development of new techniques to identify, measure, manage and control operational risk."

Perhaps one irony with operational risks is that today some may not only drive the need for operational risk management but may also give rise to macro-economic events, which in turn create a need for even greater focus on operational risk management. Take, for example, the risks posed by the introduction of European monetary union and the euro, and also the "year 2000" or "Y2K" computer systems risk. In the short term, economic activity created by the need to adjust systems and prepare for these risks may provide a spark to the global economy. In the time remaining up to and including the trigger dates, however, we might not only see system failures but we can fully expect postponement of new system investment. Along with both may come a rash of legal allegations relating to conversion problems and systems failures with respect to system under-investment

that further contribute to business and economic downturn. In the wake of economic stress, a lower tolerance for risk may result, together with an even greater need to manage downside operational risk.

In summary, management, bank boards, and regulators have all begun asking the question "what else besides credit and market losses can put our firm at substantial risk?" How do we define, measure and manage operational risks? Can we hedge them? How can we think more holistically about risk on an enterprise-wide basis so that we are not blind-sided in the future?

Operational risk management in practice

This section will focus on the kind of demands made by senior managers, organisational considerations, the evolution of operational risk management at Bankers Trust, and operational risk modelling considerations.

DEMANDS FROM SENIOR MANAGERS

In the wake of headline losses and business and technology changes, many chief executives and senior managers have concluded that they must:

❏ understand more fully the extent of the impact of operational risk (risk identification and risk capital measurement);

❏ obtain management information about operational risk, its sources and causative factors;

❏ determine capital adequacy for operational risk just as they have done for market, credit and liquidity risks;

❏ effect risk mitigation through clearly assigned ownership of, and responsibility for, risk management;

❏ provide incentives for risk management through performance measures such as risk capital attribution and links to incentive compensation;

❏ make better-informed decisions about hedging or risk financing (risk reserves, insurance and other financing techniques); and

❏ combine the net impact of operational risk with credit and market risk potential for a firm-wide view of risk, and aggregated risk capital adequacy.

ORGANISING FOR OPERATIONAL RISK MANAGEMENT

Most risk managers live by the principle that responsibility for risk management should reside

NEW TRENDS IN

OPERATIONAL

RISK

MEASUREMENT

AND

MANAGEMENT

with those in the best position to manage it. This generally dictates that line management "owns" the risk and is held accountable for its management. But, in practice, risk management is a partnership between corporate and line management. Corporate management is usually in the best position to capture a broad perspective of the firm's risk exposure, including the larger scale impact of operational interdependency and concentration risks, and to capitalise on economies of scale in hedging the risk. In contrast, line management should be responsible for day-to-day operational risk, both of the "expected" and "unexpected" kind. Thus, a corporate risk management function can add significant value by sharing, and offering an analysis of, the bigger picture with the line managers who must manage the individual risks on a daily basis.

The contribution of risk management functions can be categorised in two ways. One involves providing a business-wide or firm-wide *process and framework* to ensure consistency in approach. At both line-management and corporate levels, this role generally involves policy setting, developing risk management standards, monitoring, portfolio management (of data or of hedges, etc), and measuring firm-wide operational risk capital.

The second is a *transactional role*, which is most critical at the line management level but should include centralised risk management as well. The latter might include active involvement/consultation in deal review because of specialised knowledge at the corporate level. (eg of risk management techniques such as contract engineering, or of insurance and risk finance management).

Together, centralised operational risk management's involvement in the two dimensions – process and transactional – lessen the danger that a centralised function might either find itself too detached from the firm's business flow or miss the big picture (eg unlikely but severe forms of loss that threaten the existence of the firm).

CASE EXAMPLE – OPERATIONAL RISK MANAGEMENT EVOLUTION AT BANKERS TRUST

As noted, as part of our strategy at Bankers Trust, we began looking at operational risk management as part of an early attempt at enterprise-wide risk management – filling out a spectrum of risk measurement. We had already

developed models for market and credit risk, and now the question was "what's missing?" Thus, in 1990, we began capturing risks outside of our usual risk measurement criteria (ie beyond the 99% confidence level), and calling them "long-tail event risks". (This kind of very severe, unexpected risk can devastate a firm, and is increasingly referred to in the industry as "tail risk".) We also began capturing risks of a non-market and credit variety. The trick was not only to identify them but, at a later stage, to measure them.

Our first pass involved a simple form of scenario analysis at the corporate level. We asked key managers about the loss scenarios that were most likely to "keep them awake at night". Admittedly many of these losses involved credit and market risks, but often there was also an operational risk dimension (eg large-scale failure of key systems, overarching regulatory change, class legal actions, loss of key people).

The exercise involved a systematic investigation in terms of risk identification, assessment of probabilities, past frequencies and severities, or identification of past losses and, most important of all, of effective risk mitigation measures. We also looked at whether the necessary risk finance/insurance was in place, or even available.

We continued this early attempt at tracing large-scale firm-wide long-tail event risks, as we were calling them, over several years. In 1992 we set out to identify a methodology that might align with our market and credit risk functions. Our objectives were simple enough. They spanned:

❑ risk measurement, in supporting capital adequacy and attribution;

❑ risk mitigation, in support of strategic decision-making (decisions to invest, disinvest or divest) and to provide support for the risk control environment; and

❑ risk finance, in providing tools to support decision-making relative to risk finance designs and insurance/reinsurance purchases.

This time we initiated our scenario analysis approach by business. After several detailed reviews, however, we realised that, whereas the analysis served as an informative exercise from a loss potential perspective, its results were too subjective to be useful for consistent risk-based capital measurement or attribution purposes, particularly where strategy decisions were involved.

33

NEW TRENDS IN
OPERATIONAL
RISK
MEASUREMENT
AND
MANAGEMENT

PANEL 1

TWIST IN THE TAIL

Operational tail risk is perhaps the dimension of operational risk most often misunderstood, and therefore also overlooked, by management. Simply stated, it is the representation of events that, while extremely improbable, are also extremely severe in terms of loss should they occur.

When plotted as an aggregate loss probability distribution, by definition the vast majority of outcomes fall in the "body" of the distribution. If managers do not look beyond this part of the distribution and venture into the more detailed statistical measures of operational risk, they are assessing risk only at expected levels – often defined as the distribution that covers 67% of possible outcomes or one standard deviation.

It is not until one examines extreme probabilities that cover 95% or 99% of possible outcomes (ie two and three standard deviations) that one is considering tail risk.

Let's consider an example involving computer systems risk. With many systems, one might expect routine outages of relatively minor duration, say from one or two minutes to an hour, over the course of a year. In the case of non-critical systems, this might be acceptable.

When considering a more critical system, such as money transfer, market data feeds systems for trading operations, or customer service systems for funds management operations, the tolerance of "downtime" is much lower. Failures of even five minutes might be unacceptable and, by definition, less expected as well. In fact, the expected outages might fall in the range of seconds, if tolerable at all.

So, for various kinds of systems, one can identify types of events that would naturally fall in the expected range of a probability distribution, as well as those that are less acceptable and, hopefully, less probable. They may be less probable because they are inherently unlikely or because they have been engineered out of the system.

Where does this take us? For a start, risk managers can begin to build subjective scenarios of loss events and to map these against subjectively estimated probabilities of the risk event occurring, and thereby create a subjective loss distribution. Or they might decide to examine the empirical data on loss events. At Bankers Trust, we have done both. That is, early in our programme we found that we needed to build subjective scenarios. With time, we invested in the extensive collection and collation of empirical data not only to reflect our own experience but to track that of other firms as well. The data help to confirm our expectations of loss scenarios and their likely outcomes.

But, you may ask, "what about tail-risk scenarios that have never been experienced or logged before, but can be imagined?" For these cases, such as large-scale outages involving critical systems, we would still want to have an option of mapping the assumed probability of the loss event into our collection of empirical event frequencies and loss severity for technology disasters. We call these our "synthetical data points" and we believe that a sprinkling of these in combination with empirical data provides a far more robust database than one would have in using solely empirical data, or solely hypothetical scenarios.

The real message here, however, is that managers *must* consider the "long tail" risk. This can be done in singular fashion either by analysing the experience of other unfortunate firms that have suffered large losses in areas that you have not, or by dreaming up some of your own worst case nightmares.

The confidence of the result can be boosted, of course, by analysing numerous events and then producing simulation results from Monte Carlo or other models. At Bankers Trust, we have used our database of both our own and others' experience, supplemented by some hypothetical scenarios and our analytical methods, to produce results up to a 99% confidence level.

With the data and analyses in hand, a risk manager is in a far better position to discuss the control investment options available to re-engineer an outcome. Through investment in control measures, a firm might reduce further the probability of an unlikely event happening (although the change might be academic), or it might minimise the possible size of the outcome should the event occur (far more important).

Operational risk analysis and modelling

RISK INFORMATION IS THE KEY TO
EFFECTIVE BUSINESS OPERATIONAL RISK
MANAGEMENT

Operational risk information is becoming critically important for both business line management and at corporate levels in many financial firms. In fact, it is clear that, looking ahead, the most successful risk managers will be adept at *collection, analysis and presentation of relevant risk information, balanced with effective hands-on risk-mitigation measures*. Data management and focused risk systems will be crucial.

In this section, we will explore the background to risk/performance measures, types and

NEW TRENDS IN
OPERATIONAL
RISK
MEASUREMENT
AND
MANAGEMENT

conceptual bases for operational risk models, the unique complexities of operational risk modelling, and new frontiers of operational risk analysis.

DATA CHALLENGES

At the outset, one must recognise that there are unique challenges in managing operational risk data. First, and most obvious, its availability in useable formats is a significant problem. With the exception of relatively small loss events, most of which represent processing risk (errors, outages, and system glitches for example), data about larger and "unexpected" losses are not readily available. This is either because such events have not occurred, because they have only occurred very infrequently, or because they have not been documented and data have not been collected.

Second, most organisations that *have* attempted to measure their own operational risk have done so in a vacuum, and thus are only working with their own firm's (hopefully) limited experiences of operational losses. This yields an incomplete picture – the sample is too small for meaningful statistical analysis.

Third, although loss events can be dissected, post-mortems conducted, and lessons identified, the exercise often merely results in observations concerning the circumstances that were in place prior to, and at the time of, the loss. The relationship between cause and effect has all-too-often not been proven statistically. Neither has the relationship between the loss and the control variables – such as the relative effectiveness of security access controls or the importance of the separation of duties – been proven statistically. Thus in both areas there is room for data collection and correlation analysis.

RISK/PERFORMANCE MEASURES

To give managers a full and complete view of the firm-wide risk at their firms, operational risk must be represented in terms that are comparable with market and credit risk. Thus, before beginning any modelling exercise it is crucial to consider how the results can be aligned with those from other risk disciplines – otherwise the operational risk number will be left hanging in a "modelling vacuum". Thus one would be well advised to begin by finding a common language that aligns with the language used in credit and market risk measurement.

For some firms, particularly corporations, this might involve a financial measure such as

economic value added (EVA). For financial firms, daily price volatility (DPV), value-at-risk (VAR), or risk-adjusted return on capital (Raroc) might seem obvious places to start. But when it comes to operational risk, DPV and VAR are less relevant as day-to-day variations of operational risk are invariably difficult to measure.

At Bankers Trust, operational Raroc has been our primary risk measure for many years. We completely overhauled operational Raroc during 1992–5 and introduced these upgraded models during the first quarter of 1996. One of our objectives was to confirm the capital adequacy of the firm, given the inclusion of operational risk. Thus, we reintroduced our risk measurement model in a significantly upgraded analytical format. Other objectives were to support our risk-control environment and to support strategic decision making. To meet this second set of objectives, we needed an incentive-based system. The concept of operational Raroc seemed perfectly aligned with this need. Under our system, operational risk capital is attributed to business units according to measures of their operational risk profiles derived from our model. This raises the performance hurdle for business and engineering operational risk management, and puts it squarely on the agendas of the individual business managers.

TYPES AND CONCEPTUAL FOUNDATIONS OF MODELS

There are a number of possible conceptual foundations for operational risk modelling, of course. For instance, one could make a case for any combination of the following:

❑ *Factor-derived models.* These apply loss and/or causal factors to build a bottom-up prediction of loss expectancies.

❑ *Economic pricing models.* These base forecasts on economic models. One such operational risk model uses the capital asset pricing model (CAPM) to suggest a relative distribution of pricing of operational risk among the other price determinants for capital.

❑ *Scenario analysis/subjective loss estimate models.* These are used to capture diverse opinions, concerns and experience/expertise of key managers, and represent them in matrix and graphic form.

❑ *Statistical/actuarial/(data-based) loss potential models.* These use actual loss data to construct representations of loss frequencies and severity in the form of statistical probability distributions. Simulation techniques are then used to combine the distributions in modelling possible loss scenarios for the future.

From a modelling standpoint, as already noted, an obvious difference between operational risk and credit or market risk is the availability of data. For more liquid markets, price data for market risk measurement are plentiful. For credit risk, although default and other data may not be nearly as plentiful, they have been more so in recent years. In contrast, operational data, predictors and models are still in their relative infancy.

Another challenge in operational risk modelling, discussed in detail in Panel 1, is the need to measure and represent "tail risk" in such a way that business managers are convinced of its importance.

Returning to our list of demands from senior managers, let's explore the various models with each demand in mind.

❑ *Factor-derived models* might be derived from various risk factors or risk indicators that serve to characterise a risk profile. For instance, the combination of error rates, failed reconciliations, employee training expenditure, turnover, and investment in both new and existing (maintenance) systems might project an interesting, albeit partial, picture of the operational risk profile of a business. If the trends are observed over time, the picture can be even more informative and when mapped along with changes in the underlying business, such as transaction volume or values, the analysis provides even greater meaning – see Figure 1. In themselves, these trends at best only project the *evolution* of a risk profile. Is it evolving toward higher or lower risk? While they might be trended forward through regression analysis, they will only produce a relative future value of the individual or aggregated factors – not necessarily a loss outcome in any absolute terms. Thus, these models might be considered to be partially representative of *cause* or causation only, not *effect*, in contrast to a loss scenario or actuarial model. It is only when these factor or causation profiles are combined with representations of outcome that they reach their full potential, as we discuss below.

❑ *Economic pricing models*. Some firms have chosen to measure operational risk through an economic derivation. At least one such firm has applied the CAPM to its financial data and, by this means, has derived an economic formula for operational risk. It used CAPM's systematic risk component as a start toward dissecting compo-

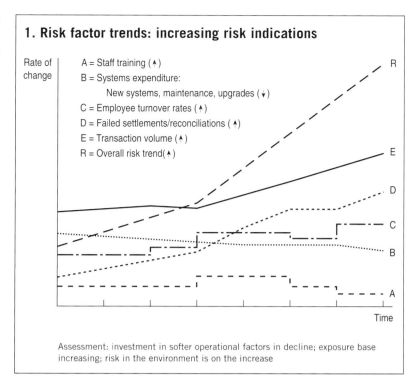

1. Risk factor trends: increasing risk indications

Rate of change

A = Staff training (↑)
B = Systems expenditure:
     New systems, maintenance, upgrades (↓)
C = Employee turnover rates (↑)
D = Failed settlements/reconciliations (↑)
E = Transaction volume (↑)
R = Overall risk trend(↑)

Time

Assessment: investment in softer operational factors in decline; exposure base increasing; risk in the environment is on the increase

nents that contribute to the firm's risk profile. Reportedly, they then found the approach useful in dimensioning a figure for the aggregate operational risk to the firm's capital. Without other information, the approach would only be useful in considering aggregate capital adequacy. In itself it would lack information value about specific operational risks. For instance, what loss scenarios are likely to produce the worst possible aggregated outcome for a one-year horizon? What scenarios would represent more moderate outcomes? For this underlying information, one must look further, to other models and analyses.

❑ *Loss-scenario models* can be useful in many ways and have been applied for years. Figures 2 and 3 illustrate the beginning and end of a very simple loss-scenario model. Figure 2 illustrates part of a risk assessment matrix. Individual loss scenarios such as this one and others are then represented in terms of their probability and severity, and can be summarised in a single exhibit. The exhibits sometimes take the form of a "risk map" such as the one shown in Figure 3. These combined exhibits are useful in representing the qualitative nature of operational risk. They are similar to the first risk-assessment exercise we applied at Bankers Trust for operational risk modelling. By definition, these models are more descriptive than quantitative, but they are useful in beginning to represent both the qualitative and quantitative dimensions of scenarios

36

NEW TRENDS IN
OPERATIONAL
RISK
MEASUREMENT
AND
MANAGEMENT

2. Risk assessment matrix

Risk/scenarios: system distribution	Description	Loss potential
Outage	Short-term service interruptions of critical systems: 1–3 hours	US$50,000–100,000 range
Failure	Moderate to long-term disruption; three hours to several days; risk of errors during period/manual processing, if possible.	US$5 million–US40 million range

3. Aggregated risk map

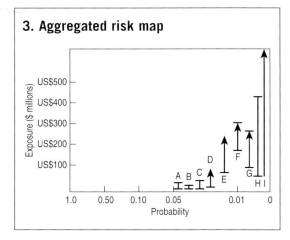

for which extensive data are lacking. They can also represent a wide variety of loss situations, including potential operational risk losses that are still emerging, such as electronic commerce-related risks or risks involving intellectual capital. Another advantage is that they can capture the precise details of the loss scenarios envisaged by the managers surveyed. However, their subjectivity can be their weakness, particularly when there is a need to convince one's audience of a possible outcome.

❏ *Statistical/actuarial models* can also be applied. Actuarial methods, of course, have been used by insurers and insurance risk managers for years in projecting the potential outcomes of singular risk classes (such as general liability, workers' compensation, medical malpractice costs). We cannot do justice to them in the space available here. Very simply stated, they are derived from loss and exposure data. By constructing representative distributions of loss frequencies and loss severity data, the actuary has a basis for further analyses, for example by combining the two in a Monte Carlo simulation.

❏ *Combination models.* In most cases, a combination of model types yields the best results. This was our conclusion at Bankers Trust, and it formed the basis of the phase of upgraded model development and implementation that we embarked on in the first quarter of 1996, in which we applied each of these approaches.

THE UNIQUE COMPLEXITIES OF OPERATIONAL RISK

One of the analytical challenges in dealing with operational risk is the difficulty of modelling complex, multi-factor risks. It is also important to recognise the need to model *interdependencies* between businesses. For instance, there is a risk of loss whenever one business "hands over" a transaction to another part of the company, especially if there are gaps in the responsibilities of professionals during the hand-off. Any model of risk should attempt to represent these interdependencies by first identifying business lines within the firm that rely on one another (those that rely on the business in question or on which it depends), then consider the downside risk of a failed hand-off.

Another area of complexity is *integration* risk, that is, the risk of gaps in responsibility that result from acquisition, restructuring or reorganisation. Here, too, one can start by illustrating transaction flow.

Third, there is *concentration* risk. All the risk process models can be rendered useless if they do not consider the possibility of a single event disrupting the firm's entire operation (a "long-tail" event). Thus, any firm-wide representation of operational risk must look at singular concentrations such as the risk to a home office location, to a primary trading floor, to a processing centre, or data centres.

Clearly all three areas described above present unique challenges to those modelling operational risks.

ANALYTICAL TRENDS – NEW FRONTIERS

Some tools are already available to deal more effectively with complex operational risks. For instance, stress testing (combining the long-tail risk scenario analysis with acturial loss potential models) can and should be applied to all models as a reality check. And there is some evidence that additional new tools might be developing to deal more effectively with complex operational risks. These might include the application of social psychology on trading floors, for instance,

37

NEW TRENDS IN
OPERATIONAL
RISK
MEASUREMENT
AND
MANAGEMENT

BUILDING AN OPERATIONAL LOSS DATABASE

At Bankers Trust, we began building an operational loss database in 1993. We have found it invaluable in:

❏ supporting analysis and projections;

❏ selecting individual large losses for use in stress testing our models;

❏ conducting loss cause analysis by selecting loss patterns; and

❏ supporting risk finance and insurance decision making.

Our database consists of two sections: our own ("internal") losses and losses of other firms ("external" losses). Each has its own advantages and disadvantages (see Table), but when taken together, the subsections complement one another. For firms building databases of external events, the sources include Internet searches, research services (eg Lexus/Nexus), companies' own regulatory filings, newspapers/magazines, insurance company publications/insurance industry publications, and government-sponsored studies.

Table. Internal versus external data: comparison of advantages/disadvantages

Database section	Advantages	Disadvantages
Internal losses	❏ Serves as the best direct reflection of a firm's own loss experience and potential	❏ A firm's own experience would normally be light on "tail risk" losses, thus making it difficult to use alone in forecasting future events
	❏ Ease and economy of data collection	❏ Taken in isolation, internal losses are too inward focused
External losses	❏ Natural bias of loss information in the public domain is toward large, newsworthy events generally underrepresented in internal databases (ie "tail losses")	❏ Losses may not be directly relevant to any one firm; user must select relevant losses from the overall population
	❏ A firm can learn much by studying and avoiding the mistakes of others, not to mention dodging the economic loss	❏ Data collection and management challenges
Combination	❏ When combined, internal and external loss data can provide an insightful overall picture of loss potential	❏ Data management challenges

some aspects of which are discussed in Chapter 10 of this book, and the use of non-traditional mathematical thinking and modelling along the lines of complexity theory. W. Michael Waldrop referred to this in his book *Complexity* in 1993 and it may well simply be a matter of time before the non-traditional thinking that he highlights makes its way into corporate risk management and control functions.

Case example: the evolution of operational risk models at Bankers Trust

At Bankers Trust the choice of measurement tools was an easy one. Risk-adjusted return on capital has been applied at Bankers Trust since the 1970s. As its characteristics – a one-year time horizon and a 99% confidence level – are far more relevant to operational risk's more gradual

evolutionary tendencies than many other risk measures, it served as an appropriate basis for our updated models.

Our next challenge was to find an analogue for market price volatility. After some deliberation, we concluded that actual operational loss experience would fit the bill. Observing the occurrence and volatility of actual losses at all firms in the global marketplace painted a valuable picture. The variance of losses from small routine errors, re-works and claims to larger-scale failures, re-designs, and legal costs provided operational risk's own unique picture of volatility.

BANKERS TRUST'S OPERATIONAL LOSS DATABASE

In 1993, we began construction of the industry's first operational loss database (see Panel 2). Initially, we began by capturing and studying

NEW TRENDS IN
OPERATIONAL
RISK
MEASUREMENT
AND
MANAGEMENT

the characteristics of any loss event that did not have its basis in a market or credit loss (any loss event that was not caused by a market move or the inability of a party to meet its obligations). Our early analysis resulted in the observations that:

❑ because of the relatively sparse nature of operational loss data relative to market risks, for instance, we should hold our numbers of risk classes to a minimum;

❑ also because of sparse data at Bankers Trust alone (thankfully), we would use industry data to supplement our own; and

❑ we should class the losses by type distinction (ie by resource/asset or causation), which will be meaningful for future analysis.

With these considerations in mind, Bankers Trust business operational risk classes developed an identity of their own. A definition of operational risk evolved that centred on control failures, errors, business disruptions, or external events related to:

❑ relationships (such as customer-, regulatory-, shareholder-related relationships);

❑ people/human capital (employee errors; injury to or loss of key people, intellectual property and employment-related liability, for example);

❑ physical assets (such as loss of physical business location, property; loss of customer assets);

❑ technology resources (for example systems failure, programming errors, hacking; loss of hardware or applications); and

❑ other external/regulatory issues (for example, external fraud risk, regulatory change risk – see Table 1).

The exercise helped us to develop our own considered definition of operational risk and learn much about the causes and costs of loss. We concluded that loss to, or involving, the firm's key resources, as outlined above, was most relevant from a risk management standpoint. Again, contrast this with conventional audit or insurance risk classes that are more control-oriented or symptomatic in nature ("segregation of duties risk" or "disaster recovery risk", on the one hand, or compliance or "legal liability risk" on the other, for example).

Our operational risk classes also allowed us to focus on the direct loss exposures (ie risk of loss of key technology, for instance), or indirect consequences (such as legal liability or business disruption involving technology). They also served as one of the bases of our operational risk models.

Table 1. Operational risk/exposure class definitions

Primary operational risk/exposure classes are:

Relationship risks

Non-proprietary losses caused to a firm and generated through the relationship or contact that a firm has with its clients, shareholders, third parties or regulators (eg accommodations/reimbursements to clients, settlements or penalties paid etc).

People/human capital risks

The risk of loss caused intentionally or unintentionally by an employee (ie an employee error, employee misdeed etc.) or involving employees, such as in the area of employment disputes, intellectual capital etc.

Technology and processing risks

The risk of loss caused by a piracy, theft, failure, breakdown or other disruption in technology, data or information; also includes technology that fails to meet the intended business needs.

Physical risks

The risk of loss through damage of bank-owned properties or loss to physical property or assets for which the firm is responsible.

Other external risks

The risk of loss caused by the actions of external parties, such as in the perpetration of fraud on the bank, or in the case of regulators, the promulgation of change that would alter the firm's ability to continue operating in certain markets.

All five exposure classes include several dimensions of risk, including direct economic loss, the economic impact of indirect loss or business disruption, and/or legal liability.

LEVELS OF MODELLING AT BANKERS TRUST

Operational risk models at Bankers Trust have been, and remain, evolutionary in nature. Bankers Trust developed its first-generation estimation as early as 1979. As noted, re-evaluation of that estimation began in 1992. In 1996, we introduced our first phase (phase I) of the current generation of models that have served to measure and attribute operational risk capital to Bankers Trust business lines. They can be characterised as two key processes applied in advancing operational risk management in the firm, and we have applied them actively since that time.

❑ *Risk measurement process.* Using the loss data gathered, in combination with selective *loss scenario* modelling, we apply an *actuarial* model and Monte Carlo simulation to develop loss potential by our five risk classes and in terms of the firm as a whole.

❑ *Capital attribution process.* Using a broad array of risk factors (currently approximately 60), we attribute the firm-wide risk capital, using a *factor-derived* model to each of the firm's

39

NEW TRENDS IN
OPERATIONAL
RISK
MEASUREMENT
AND
MANAGEMENT

business lines and profit centres. We also attribute capital charges for one-off outstanding risk and control issues that deserve special attention as add-ons.

We recognise that the entire area of operational risk management holds opportunities for further development, but the combination of our model processes have demonstrated the value of a top-down portfolio approach toward firm-wide risk and class-wide risk measurement at various levels of confidence (ie expected loss and outward to a 99% confidence level). We have the benefit of a well-populated and information-packed loss distribution, combined with a representation of long-tail risk. When our attribution process is applied, we have the added benefit of a bottom-up factor-based model and representation of risk predictors that can also be quantified, traced and trended.

In our current Phase II, we have been engaged in additional work on new factor models and incentive credits using data specific to individual business lines in order to supplement our firm-wide models.

All of these dimensions are captured in our proprietary Operational Risk Control Analysis (ORCA) data warehouse, analysis and communication interface application, for use in data compilation, sorting and analysis.

The need for operational risk MIS

In addition to modelling operational risk, there is a clear need for improvement in the quality of information about operational risk available to senior management. Using management information systems like lights on a control panel, much value can be gained in the decision-making process by simply reporting on areas including, but not limited by, the following:

❑ losses and loss-cause analyses;

❑ linking analyses to outstanding control issue tracking; or to

❑ specific risk variables/indicators (such as a compilation of extensive processing technology or other risk class data);

❑ risk class/concentration-of-risk representations;

❑ identification of candidates for incentives and accountability;

❑ risk factor comparative and trend analyses;

❑ risk finance and insurance coverage alignments (eg the cost of risk analyses); and

❑ effect on the balance sheet and the profit and loss statement.

Trends in operational risk hedging and risk finance

In market risk management, the prospect of hedging risk is often engineered directly into a trading decision. Often, the consideration is not so much *whether* to hedge risk but rather how *much* of it can be hedged away. As a back-to-back hedge or a portfolio hedge can often be applied with minimal basis risk, the trader or risk manager understandably and naturally often talks only in terms of net exposure (unless of course the hedge fails or has a significant chance of failure).

In operational risk the dynamics are completely different. Operational risk is embedded throughout a business and cannot easily be stripped out. Its consequences cannot be escaped simply because of the existence of a hedge – even one that performs precisely as intended. In the case of technology systems or processing risk, either the firm suffers an outage or it does not. It does not much matter whether the event is *insured*. And often it does not even matter whether the processing operations can be *outsourced*. Either the firm's own trading or settlement operations are disrupted or they are not.

Of course, it may be possible to hedge away the immediate economic impact, either through insurance or outsourcing, but the firm still lives with the disruption and any reputational impact that might come with it.

This is not to imply that the hedging of operational risk is unimportant. The firm has an interest in offsetting the economic effects of a loss, and might well be derelict in its duties in the eyes of stakeholders if it does not explore such options. But it does suggest that the important question of risk financing resides a few steps later in the risk management process than it does in the case of market risk. Generally, one explores the possibilities offered by risk financing only after the risk has been identified, analysed, and reasonable risk control measures have been engineered and applied.

CAN ANY OF THESE RISKS BE REASONABLY HEDGED OR FINANCED?
Simply stated, one can hedge the economic effects of operational risk either through contractual risk transfer or through risk finance and insurance techniques. A firm's application of contractual risk transfer is often quite unique to each individual business deal, trade or process, so we will not dwell on it here. (In fact entire books are available on the practice of contractual

NEW TRENDS IN
OPERATIONAL
RISK
MEASUREMENT
AND
MANAGEMENT

risk management and key considerations.) Suffice it to say that it should not be overlooked as an option.

In contrast, and despite the fact that numerous texts are also available on risk finance and insurance, we will venture into this subject *from the perspective of operational risk management* because few have approached the subject from this direction to date.

RISK FINANCE AND INSURANCE: OBJECTIVES
Most financial firms arrange for risk finance and insurance programmes for two main reasons, even though they might not identify them explicitly:
❑ to protect their earnings;
❑ to protect their balance sheet;
❑ or perhaps, both.

Non-financial corporate firms might also arrange for risk finance and insurance to protect cashflow or liquidity, but that often is not a prime objective for financial entities (at least not from an operational risk management perspective).

Ironically, these key objectives also find themselves at the nexus of contention between insurers and insureds. That is, because few insurance claims are settled without some degree of tension (with the possible exception of life insurance claims), very few of them are also actually settled (decided) and paid within the same quarterly accounting period as that in which the underlying loss was booked. Thus, from an accounting perspective, earnings for the period have *not* been protected.

Also because of this timing phenomenon, the balance sheet is often not protected. Here the problem is complicated by the fact that many large financial firms cannot purchase limits of coverage large enough to protect their balance sheets. The winds of change may be beginning to blow, however, as capital market solutions have been explored to bring increased limit capacity to the traditional insurance markets.

MARKET TRENDS IN RISK FINANCE: WHILE
THE INSURANCE MARKET HAS FIDDLED . . .
The growth of operational risk, and its relationship to the insurance industry, conjures up images of Nero fiddling as Rome burns. Far be it for me to predict obsolescence of sectors of the industry, but it seems likely that there will be casualties along the way as insurance companies fail to keep up with the needs of their target market.

Why these predictions of gloom and doom for conventional players? The suggestion is based not only on the nexus of contention described above, but also on the mismatch that exists between the needs of financial firms and the breadth of coverage offered by most of the insurance firms that are in the business of serving them. Some evidence for this is provided by the industry's own statistics. For instance, one of the industry's organisations, the Surety Association of America, has for many years published the aggregated underwriting results of its member firms in the area of commercial crime insurance and financial institution bonds (or bankers' blanket bonds). The results showed that in the areas underwritten (employee dishonesty and related crime coverage areas), the firms' aggregated results have for years paid out 20–65% of the premiums collected for these coverages in the form of claim settlements, leaving the balance to cover expenses and profit, not to mention the investment income earned on the cashflow. For any extreme exceptions to these results one has to look back to the mid-1980s when, for a few short years, aggregate loss payments actually exceeded premiums.

The confident insurance executive would call these figures for recent years a great result – very profitable indeed. There are flaws in that logic. Independently, in our studies of operational risk at Bankers Trust, and analyses of the value of insurance as a hedge, we noted countless examples of crime- and fraud-related losses suffered by financial firms that would *not* have resulted in claims covered by conventional bond coverage, or any other conventionally written coverage for that matter. Thus one must question whether these insurers are being responsive to market needs. When we map all the other types of operational risk, such as technology failures, disruption, data security failures, electronic commerce risks, employee errors, to name only a few, against the entire array of conventionally available insurance coverage, the gaps are even more obvious.

It is difficult to settle on a precise rate of performance, but on several different surveys of the broad range of our database of industry losses, we found that (in the aggregate) insurers' conventional off-the-shelf coverages respond to only about 10–30% of the losses when both type and size are considered. Even to achieve the higher end of that range one must assume that payments would be made in cases where the loss scenarios contained one or more parts that might be problematical from a claim perspective (for example, they might run afoul of policy terms, conditions or exclusions). This high-end assumption seems optimistic, indeed.

What is the point of all this? Lest there be any confusion, it is not to attack the insurance industry but merely to point out that if one thinks that operational risk can simply be insured away, one is sadly mistaken. Insurance has its place but, to use a phrase from statistical risk management, the basis risks are enormous.

Some strategic application of risk finance tools can certainly increase the odds of a more palatable result for the financial firm. That is, a selective use of funded self-insurance, captive insurance companies, finite or funded deals, when woven into a risk finance programme instead of – or as a supplement to – conventional insurance, might just do the trick.

APPLYING NEW DEFINITIONS TO RISK
FINANCE
As a first step toward a better result one must break out of the conventions of the insurance industry and the insurance-like risk classes that drive many risk finance and insurance programmes. Insurance conventions force a risk manager to think in classes such as blanket bonds, with their narrow definitions of crime risk, rather than starting more broadly with all the possible sources of people/human capital and external fraud risk. It is the same with technology and processing risk, and so on.

At Bankers Trust, our operational risk-based capital methodology provided a conceptual escape. That is, we forced ourselves to work with our broad definition of operational risk: the loss potential from control failures, errors, or external events involving people, relationships, technology and processing, physical assets and other external factors – not insurance risk classes.

TRENDS IN RISK FINANCE STRATEGY:
TRANSLATING STRATEGY TO
IMPLEMENTATION
The broad view that comes with analysis of all of the operational risks that might impair a firm's capital position risk, coupled with the reality of the basic risk finance objectives noted above, will probably force change. Even at a more basic level, a financial firm's own analysis that compares risk finance cost measures of recoveries against *both* expenditures and underlying loss over time will most certainly bring *demands*

for change. Already some insurance underwriters at Lloyd's of London, in Europe and the US, are beginning to entertain more holistic and coordinated insurance approaches for operational risk classes, rather than for traditional insurance classes.

A more comprehensive risk finance strategy for a financial firm might involve "earnings protection" or loss accounting smoothing at relatively low levels of risk, attempts to improve the timing or alignment of accounting treatment for losses and recoveries, and targeted large-loss coverage as a start toward "balance sheet protection".

This strategy might suggest using an integrated programme of risk finance including:
❑ self-funding of losses and captive insurance vehicles for relatively low level risk types, where data suggest this is an efficient form of protection;
❑ conventional insurance and reinsurance only where the firm needs to be covered against medium levels of risk.

Then, breaking completely out of the insurance paradigm, one might explore a blend of catastrophe insurance and capital markets "coverages" for the balance sheet protection tranche.

Some of the keys to risk finance evolution must certainly involve separating action from market talk, obtaining substantial commitments of capacity through key relationships, and confirmation of the desired accounting and tax treatment as appropriate. All the while one must revisit the objectives of the individual firm with regard to risk finance (ie is the emphasis on earnings or balance sheets protection?).

Conclusion: the view forward – where do we go from here?
Clearly, the approach that an individual firm will take with regard to operational risk will depend on the style of its management and the firm's overall culture. Whether it places all of its emphasis on more granular audit-based control systems, or blends these with risk measurement and incentive systems at a higher firm-wide level, and/or introduces softer, perhaps less measurable risk factors, depends partly on the effect the programme is expected to have on human behaviour.

In any event, we can certainly expect that the increased complexity of business operations will dictate a greater emphasis on, and investment in, data collection and analytics, with a view toward more heroic attempts at building operational risk

NEW TRENDS IN
OPERATIONAL
RISK
MEASUREMENT
AND
MANAGEMENT

models for measurement, analysis and incentives toward management of these risks. Senior managers are seeking better definition of operational risk – and better risk management information systems. Thus, risk information will be key. Performance measurement tools will also be essential in creating incentives/disincentives for effective risk management behaviour.

On the regulatory front, the 1998 BIS paper was a first indication of where we are headed. Because of the stakes involved, it is simply a matter of time before operational risk measurement and management are much more closely scrutinised. At that point in time, improved measurement and management of operational risks might become a requirement.

Organisationally, firms will have to invest in operational risk management groups and analytics. The challenge will be in coalescing teams of people schooled in the broad range of disciplines represented by the underlying operational risks.

Last, there are encouraging signs that the financial and insurance markets will continue to evolve toward providing more effective "hedges" for broader areas of operational risk than have been addressed by the insurance markets alone in the past.

The precise direction that risk managers responsible for operational risk modelling, measurement, management and risk finance will take in future months and years is unclear. What is clear, however, is that operational risk itself can be expected to grow in size and complexity given the anticipated evolution of business systems and the increased interdependency of organisations. If recent industry losses are any indication, the need for risk management will continue to evolve along with it. All of these trends make for interesting and challenging times ahead.

IMPLEMENTING NEW APPROACHES TO OPERATIONAL RISK

3

Key Steps in Building Consistent Operational Risk Measurement and Management

Michel Crouhy, Dan Galai and Robert Mark
Canadian Imperial Bank of Commerce; Hebrew University, Jerusalem; Canadian Imperial Bank of Commerce

Operational risk in financial institutions can be briefly defined as the risk that external events, or deficiencies in internal controls or information systems, will result in a loss – whether the loss is anticipated to some extent or entirely unexpected. Operational risks are often associated with human error, system failure, and inadequate procedures and controls. They reduce a bank's effectiveness in terms of its ability to compete and adapt to change, as well as management's ability to respond to unexpected circumstances.

Failure to identify an operational risk, or to defuse it in a timely manner, can translate into a huge loss. Most notoriously, the actions of a single trader at Barings Bank, who was able to take extremely risky positions in a market without authority or detection, led to losses ($1.5 billion) that brought about the liquidation of that bank.

The Bank of England report on Barings Bank revealed some lessons about operational risk. Firstly, management teams have the duty to understand *fully* the businesses they manage. Secondly, responsibility for each business activity has to be *clearly* established and communicated. Thirdly, relevant internal controls, including independent risk management, *must* be established for all business activities. Fourthly, top management and the audit committee must ensure that significant weaknesses are resolved *quickly*.

Looking to the future, banks are becoming aware that technology is a double-edged sword. The increasing complexity of instruments and information systems increase the potential for operational risk. Unfamiliarity with instruments may lead to their misuse, and raise the chances of mispricing and wrong hedging; errors in data feeds may also distort a bank's assessment of its risks. At the same time, advanced analytical techniques combined with sophisticated computer technology create new ways to add value to operational risk management.

In this chapter we look at how Canadian Imperial Bank of Commerce (CIBC) has attempted to meet these present and future challenges by constructing a framework for operational risk control. After explaining what we think of as a key underlying rule – the control functions of a bank need to be carefully integrated – we examine the typology of operational risk. We describe four key steps in implementing bank operational risk, and highlight some means of risk reduction. Finally, we look at how a bank can extract value from enhanced operational risk management by improving its capital attribution methodologies.

For reasons that we discuss towards the end of the chapter, it is important that the financial industry develops a consistent approach to operational risk. We believe that our approach is in line with the findings of a recent working group of the Basle Committee in autumn 1998 (Panel 1), as well as with the 20 best-practice recommendations on derivative risk management put forward in the seminal Group of Thirty (G30) report in 1993 (Panel 2).

Typology of operational risks

Operational failure risk and operational strategic risk, as illustrated in Figure 1, are the two main categories of operational risks. These categories can also be defined as "internal" and "external" operational risks.[1]

KEY STEPS IN
BUILDING
CONSISTENT
OPERATIONAL
RISK
MEASUREMENT
AND
MANAGEMENT

BASLE COMMITTEE ON BANKING SUPERVISION – SEPTEMBER 1998 PAPER

A working group of the Basle Committee on Banking Supervision recently interviewed 30 major banks from various member countries to discover their approaches to the management of operational risk. Several common themes that emerged during these discussions were published in a short paper dated September 1998. The paper pointed out while there is no agreed universal definition of operational risk, many banks have defined operational risk as any risk not categorised as market or credit risk. Here is a personal summary of selected other findings, while the full paper can be accessed on the web.[1]

Management oversight

Overall the interview process uncovered a strong and consistent emphasis on the importance of management oversight and business line accountability for operational risk. Those banks that are developing measurement systems for operational risk often are also attempting to build some form of incentive for sound operational risk management practice by business managers. The focus on operational risk management as a formal discipline has been recent but was seen by some banks as a means to heighten awareness of operational risk.

Risk measurement, monitoring and management information systems

Most banks that are considering measuring operational risk are at a very early stage, with only a few having formal measurement systems. The report indicated that measuring operational risk requires both estimating the probability of an operational loss event and the potential size of the loss.

Risk monitoring

Banks often have some form of monitoring system for operational risk without formal statistically defined operational risk measures. For example, many of the banks interviewed monitor operational performance measures such as volume, turnover, settlement fails, delays and errors. Several banks monitor operational losses directly, with an analysis of each occurrence and a description of the nature and cause of the loss provided to senior managers or the board of directors.

Control of operational risk

A variety of techniques are used to control or mitigate operational risk. Most banks noted in the interviews that internal controls are seen as the major tool for managing operational risk. Banks also cited insurance as an important mitigator for some forms of operational risk. Several banks have established a provision for operational losses similar to traditional loan loss reserves. Banks are also exploring the use of reinsurance (in some cases through captive subsidiaries) to cover operational losses.

View of possible role for supervisors

Most banks agreed that the process is not sufficiently developed for the bank supervisors to mandate guidelines specifying particular measurement methodologies or quantitative limits on risk.

The Basle Committee believes that publishing their summary of survey results will provide banks with an insight into the management of operational risk. Banks were encouraged to share with their supervisors new techniques for identifying, measuring, managing and controlling operational risk.

1 At Web Site: www.bis.org

Operational failure risk covers the risks that might arise from a breakdown of people, processes and technology. These risks originate *within* the firm and are directly under the control of the management.

Operational strategic risk is the risk associated with such items as political upheavals, shifting societal needs, changes in regulatory or government policy, tax regime changes and so on. Operational strategic risk originates *outside* the firm, since it stems mainly from external factors that are not under the bank's direct control. It affects the relationship with clients, government

agencies, regulatory agencies, suppliers, contractors, outside service providers, affiliations, competitors, etc.

This chapter focuses on operational failure risk, ie on the internal factors enumerated in Table 1 that can and should be controlled by management. However, one should observe that a failure to address a strategic risk issue can translate into an operational failure risk. For example, a change in the tax laws is a strategic risk. The failure to comply with the tax laws is an operational failure risk. Furthermore, from a business unit perspective it might

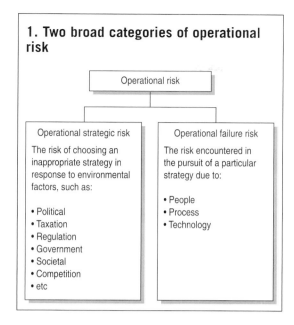

1. Two broad categories of operational risk

Operational risk

Operational strategic risk

The risk of choosing an inappropriate strategy in response to environmental factors, such as:

• Political
• Taxation
• Regulation
• Government
• Societal
• Competition
• etc

Operational failure risk

The risk encountered in the pursuit of a particular strategy due to:

• People
• Process
• Technology

be argued that external dependencies include support groups *within* the bank, such as information technology. In other words, the two types of operational risk are interrelated and tend to overlap.

The key to implementing bank-wide operational risk management

Operational risk is often managed on an ad hoc basis, and banks can suffer from a lack of coordination among functions such as risk management, internal audit, and business management. Most often, there are no common bank-wide policies, methodologies or infrastructure. As a result there is also often no consistent reporting on the extent of operational risk within the bank as a whole. Furthermore, bank-wide capital attribution models rarely incorporate meaningful measures of operational risk.

We believe that a partnership between a business and its infrastructure – internal audit and risk management – is the key to success. How can this partnership be constituted? In particular, what is the nature of the relationship between operational risk managers and the bank audit function?

Firstly, the necessary operational risk information has to travel from the operational environment (which includes infrastructure, corporate governance and business units) to the operational risk management function. In return, the operational risk management function must provide operational risk analyses and policies to all units on a timely basis – as well as generating firm-wide and regulatory risk reports, and working with the audit function.

Secondly, the various businesses in the bank implement the policy, manage the risks and generally run their business.

Thirdly, at regular intervals the internal audit function needs to ensure that the operational risk management process has integrity, and is indeed being implemented along with the appropriate controls. In other words, auditors analyse the degree to which businesses are in compliance with the designated operational risk management process. They also offer an independent assessment of the underlying design of the operational risk management process. This includes examining the process surrounding the building of operational risk measurement models, the adequacy and reliability of the operations risk management systems and compliance with external regulatory guidelines, etc. Audit thus provides an overall assurance on the adequacy of operational risk management.

A key audit objective is to evaluate the design and conceptual soundness of the operational risk value-at-risk (VAR) measure, including any methodologies associated with stress testing, and the reliability of the reporting framework. Audit should also evaluate the operational risks that affect all types of risk management information systems – whether they are used to assess market, credit or operational risk itself – such as the processes used for coding and implementation of the internal models. This includes examining controls concerning the capture of data about market positions, the accuracy and completeness of these data, as well as controls over the parameter estimation processes. Audit would typically also review the adequacy and effectiveness of the processes for monitoring risk, and the documentation relating to compliance with the qualitative/quantitative criteria outlined in any regulatory guidelines.

Regulatory guidelines typically also call for auditors to address the approval process for vetting risk pricing models and valuation systems used by front and back-office personnel (for reasons made clear in Panel 3), the validation of any significant change in the risk measurement process, and the scope of risks captured by the risk measurement model. Audit should verify the consistency, timeliness and reliability of data sources used to run internal models, including the independence of such data sources. A key role is to examine the accuracy and appropriateness of volatility and correlation assumptions as well as the accuracy of the valuation and risk transformation calculations. Finally, auditors should examine

KEY STEPS IN
BUILDING
CONSISTENT
OPERATIONAL
RISK
MEASUREMENT
AND
MANAGEMENT

PANEL 2

GROUP OF THIRTY RECOMMENDATIONS: DERIVATIVES AND OPERATIONAL RISK

In 1993, the Group of Thirty (G30) provided 20 best-practice risk management recommendations for dealers and end-users of derivatives. These have proved seminal for many banks structuring their derivatives risk management functions, and here we offer a personal selection of some key findings for operational risk managers in other types of institutions who may be less familiar with the report.

The G30 working group was composed of a diverse cross-section of end-users, dealers, academics, accountants, and lawyers involved in derivatives. Input also came from a detailed survey of industry practice among 80 dealers and 72 end-users worldwide, involving both questionnaires and in-depth interviews. In addition, the G30 provided four recommendations for legislators, regulators, and supervisors.

The G30 report noted that the credit, market and legal risks of derivatives capture most of the attention in public discussion. Nevertheless, the G30 emphasised that the successful implementation of systems, operations, and controls is equally important for the management of derivatives activities. The G30 stressed that the complexity and diversity of derivatives activities make the measurement and control of those risks more difficult. This difficulty increases the importance of sophisticated risk management systems and sound management and operating practices. These are vital to a firm's ability to execute, record, and monitor derivatives transactions, and to provide the information needed by management to manage the risks associated with these activities.

Likewise, the G30 report stressed the importance of hiring skilled professionals: Recommendation 16 states that one should *"ensure that derivatives activities are undertaken by professionals in sufficient number and with the appropriate experience, skill levels, and degrees of specialisation"*.

The G30 also stressed the importance of building best-practice systems. According to Recommendation 17, one should *"ensure that adequate systems for data capture, processing, settlement, and management reporting are in place so that derivatives transactions are conducted in an orderly and efficient manner in compliance with management policies"*. Furthermore, *"One should have risk management systems that measure the risks incurred in their derivatives activities based on their nature, size and complexity"*.

Recommendation 19 emphasised that accounting practices should highlight the risks being taken. For example, the G30 pointed out that one *"should account for derivatives transactions used to manage risks so as to achieve a consistency of income recognition treatment between those instruments and the risks being managed"*.

People

The survey of industry practices examined the involvement in the derivatives activity of people at all levels of the organisation. The survey indicated a need for further development of staff involved in back-office administration, accounts, and audit functions, etc. Respondents believed that a new breed of specialist, qualified operational staff, was required. The survey pointed out that dealers (large and small) and end-users face a common challenge of developing the right control culture for their derivatives activity.

The survey highlighted the importance of the ability of people to work in cross-functional teams. The survey pointed out that many issues require input from a number of disciplines (eg trading, legal, and accounting) and demand an integrated approach.

Systems

The survey confirmed the view that dealing in derivatives can demand integrated systems to ensure adequate information and operational control. The survey indicated that dealers were moving toward more integrated systems, between front- and back-office (across types of transactions).

The industry has made a huge investment in systems, and almost all large dealers are extensive users of advanced technology. Many derivative groups have their own research and technology teams that develop the mathematical algorithms and systems necessary to price new transactions and to monitor their derivatives portfolios. Many dealers consider their ability to manage the development of systems capabilities an important source of competitive strength.

For large dealers, there is a requirement that one develop systems that minimise manual intervention as well as enhance operating efficiency and reliability, the volume of activity, customisation of transactions, number of calculations to be performed, and overall complexity.

Systems that integrate the various tasks to be performed for derivatives are complex. Because of the rapid development of the business, even the most

49

KEY STEPS IN
BUILDING
CONSISTENT
OPERATIONAL
RISK
MEASUREMENT
AND
MANAGEMENT

sophisticated dealers and users often rely on a variety of systems, which may be difficult to integrate in a satisfactory manner. While this situation is inevitable in many organisations, it is not ideal and requires careful monitoring to ensure sufficient consistency to allow reconciliation of results and aggregation of risks where required.

The survey results indicated that the largest dealers, recognising the control risks that separate systems pose and the expense of substantial daily reconciliations, are making extensive investments to integrate back-office systems for derivatives with front-office systems for derivatives as well as other management information.

Operations

The role of the back-office is to perform a variety of functions in a timely fashion. This includes recording transactions, issuing and monitoring confirmations, ensuring legal documentation for transactions is completed, settling transactions, producing information for management and control purposes. This information includes reports of positions against trading and counterparty limits, reports on profitability, and reports on exceptions (requiring action to be taken such as outstanding confirmations, limit excesses, etc).

There has been significant evolution in the competence of staff and the adequacy of procedures and systems in the back office. Derivatives businesses, like other credit or securities businesses, give the back-office the principal function of recording, documenting, and confirming the actions of the dealers. The wide range of volume and complexity that exists among dealers and end-users has led to a range of acceptable solutions.

The long timescales between the trade date and the settlement date, which is a feature of some products, means that errors not detected by the confirmation process may not be discovered for some time.

While it is necessary to ensure that the systems are adequate for the organisation's volume and the complexity of derivatives activities, there can be no single prescriptive solution to the management challenges that derivatives pose to the back-office. This reflects the diversity in activity between different market participants.

Controls

Derivative activities, by their very nature, cross many boundaries of traditional financial activity. Therefore the control function must be necessarily broad, covering all aspects of activity. The primary element of control lies in the organisation itself. Allocation of responsibilities for derivatives activities, with segregation of authority where appropriate, should be reflected in job descriptions and organisation charts.

Authority to commit the institution to transactions is normally defined by level or position. It is the role of management to ensure that the conduct of activity is consistent with delegated authority. There is no substitute for internal controls; however, dealers and end-users should communicate information that clearly indicates which individuals within the organisation have the authority to make commitments. At the same time, all participants should fully recognise that the legal doctrine of "apparent authority" may govern the transactions to which individuals within their organisation commit.

Definition of authority within an organisation should also address issues of suitability of use of derivatives. End-users of derivatives transactions are usually institutional borrowers and investors and as such should possess the capability to understand and quantify risks inherent in their business. Institutional investors may also be buyers of structured securities exhibiting features of derivatives. While the exposures to derivatives will normally be similar to those on institutional balance sheets, it is possible that in some cases the complexity of such derivatives used might exceed the ability of an entity to understand fully the associated risks. The recommendations provide guidelines for management practice and give any firm considering the appropriate use of derivatives a useful framework for assessing suitability and developing policy consistent with its overall risk management and capital policies. Organisational controls can then be established to ensure activities are consistent with a firm's needs and objectives.

Audit

The G30 pointed out that internal audit plays an important role in the procedures and control framework by providing an independent, internal assessment of the effectiveness of this framework.

The principal challenge for management is to ensure that internal audit staff has sufficient expertise to carry out work in both the front- and back-offices. Able individuals with the appropriate financial and systems skills are required to carry out the specialist aspects of the work. Considerable investment in training is needed to ensure that staff understand the nature and characteristics of the instruments being transacted and the models that are used to price them.

Although not part of the formal control framework of the organisation, external auditors and regulatory examiners provide a check on procedures and controls. They also face the challenge of developing and maintaining the appropriate degree of expertise in this area.

KEY STEPS IN
BUILDING
CONSISTENT
OPERATIONAL
RISK
MEASUREMENT
AND
MANAGEMENT

the verification of the model's accuracy through an examination of the back-testing process.

To achieve all this the bank's risk management team will need to develop policy, design the operational risk measurement methodology and build the necessary infrastructure. The operational risk management group will then be able to monitor and analyse the risks, implement methodologies such as risk-adjusted return on capital (Raroc), and actively manage residual risk using tools such as insurance.

In our experience, eight key elements (Figure 2) are necessary to successfully implement such a bank-wide operational risk management framework. They involve setting policy, identifying risk and designing a common language, constructing business process maps, building a best-practice measurement methodology, providing exposure management, installing a timely reporting capability, performing risk analysis (inclusive of stress testing) and allocating economic capital. Let's look at these in more detail.

❑ *Develop well-defined operational risk policies* This includes articulating explicitly the desired standards for risk measurement. One also needs to establish clear guidelines for practices that may contribute to a reduction of operational risks. For example, the bank needs to establish policies on model vetting, off-hour trading, off-premises trading, legal document vetting, etc.

❑ *Establish a common language of risk identification* For example, people risk would include a failure to deploy skilled staff. Process risk would include execution errors. Technology risk would include system failures, etc.

❑ *Develop business process maps of each business* For example, one should map the business process associated with the bank's dealing with a broker so that it becomes transparent to management and auditors. One should create an "operational risk catalogue", as illustrated in Table 1, which categorises and defines the

Table 1. Types of operational failure risks

People risk	Incompetency
	Fraud
	Etc.
Process risk:	
A. Model risk *(See Panel 3)*	Model/methodology error
	Mark-to-model error
	Etc.
B. Transaction risk	Execution error
	Product complexity
	Booking error
	Settlement error
	Documentation/contract risk
	Etc.
C. Operational control risk	Exceeding limits
	Security risks
	Volume risk
	Etc.
Technology risk	System failure
	Programming error
	Information risk (See Panel 4)
	Telecommunication failure
	Etc.

various operational risks arising from each organisational unit. This includes analysing the products and services that each organisational unit offers, and the action one needs to take to manage operational risk. This catalogue should be a tool to help with operational risk identification and assessment. Again, the catalogue should be based on common definitions and language (lexicons such as those in Panel 4 can help here).

❑ *Develop a comprehensible set of operational risk metrics* Operational risk assessment is a complex process. It needs to be performed on a firm-wide basis at regular intervals using standard metrics. In the early days, as illustrated in Figure 3, business and infrastructure groups performed their own self-assessment of

2. Eight key elements to achieve best practice operational risk management

1. Policy
2. Risk identification
3. Business process
4. Measurement methodology
5. Exposure management
6. Reporting
7. Risk analysis
8. Economic capital

Best practice

3. The process of implementing operational risk management

Increased knowledge

Self assessment of each discipline

Assessment based on well designed objective operational metrics

Operations risk assigned economic capital

First class risk management

51

KEY STEPS IN
BUILDING
CONSISTENT
OPERATIONAL
RISK
MEASUREMENT
AND
MANAGEMENT

operational risk. Today, self-assessment has been discredited – the self-assessment of operational risk at Barings Bank contributed to the build up of market risk at that institution – and is no longer an acceptable approach. Sophisticated financial institutions are trying to develop objective measures of operational risk that build significantly more reliability into the quantification of operational risk.

To this end, operational risk assessment needs to include a review of the *likelihood* of a particular operational risk occurring, as well as the *severity* or magnitude of the impact that the operational risk will have on business objectives (see Panel 4 for a definition of the italicised terms). This is no easy task. It can be challenging to assess the probability of a computer failure, or of a programming bug in a valuation model, and to assign a potential loss to any such event. We will examine this challenge in more detail in the next section of this chapter.

❏ *Decide how one will manage operational risk exposure, and take appropriate action to hedge the risks* The bank should address the economic question of the cost–benefit of insuring a given risk for those operational risks that can be insured.

❏ *Decide on how one will report exposure* For example, a summary report for the Tokyo equity arbitrage business at CIBC is shown in Table 2.

❏ *Develop tools for risk analysis and procedures for when these tools should be deployed* For example, risk analysis is typically performed as part of a new product process, periodic business reviews, etc. Stress testing should be a standard part of the risk analysis process. The frequency of risk assessment should be a function of the degree to which operational risks are expected to change over time as businesses undertake new initiatives, or as business circumstances evolve. This frequency may be reviewed as operational risk measurement is rolled out across the bank. A bank should update its risk assessments more frequently (say semi-annually) following the initial assessment of operational risk within business units. Further, one should reassess whenever the operational risk profile changes significantly (eg implementation of a new system, entering a new service, etc).

❏ *Develop techniques to translate the calculation of operational risk into a required amount of economic capital* Tools and procedures should be developed to enable businesses to make decisions about operational risk based on risk/reward analyses, as we discuss in more detail later in the chapter.

Table 2. Operational risk reporting worksheet

The overall operational risk of the Tokyo Equity Arbitrate Trading desk is low

	Risk Profile
1. People risk	
❏ Incompetency	Low
❏ Fraud	Low
2. Process risk	
A. Model risk	
❏ Model/methodology error	Low
❏ Mark-to-market error	Low
B. Transaction risk:	
❏ Execution error	Low
❏ Product complexity	Low
❏ Booking error	Low
❏ Settlement error	Low
❏ Documentation/contract risk	Medium
C. Operational control risk	
❏ Exceeding limits	Low
❏ Security risk	Low
❏ Volume risk	Low/medium
3. Technology risk	
❏ System failure	Low
❏ Programming error	Low
❏ Information risk	Low
❏ Telecommunication failure	Low
Total operational failure risk measurement	**Low**
Strategic risk	
❏ Political risk	Low
❏ Taxation risk	Low
❏ Regulatory risk	Low/medium
Total strategic risk measurement	**Low**

A four-step measurement process for operational risk

Clear guiding principles for the operational risk measurement process should be set to ensure that it provides an appropriate measure of operational risk across all business units throughout the bank. Figure 4 illustrates these principles. By "objectivity" we mean that

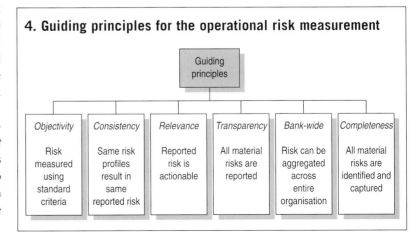

4. Guiding principles for the operational risk measurement

Objectivity	Consistency	Relevance	Transparency	Bank-wide	Completeness
Risk measured using standard criteria	Same risk profiles result in same reported risk	Reported risk is actionable	All material risks are reported	Risk can be aggregated across entire organisation	All material risks are identified and captured

KEY STEPS IN
BUILDING
CONSISTENT
OPERATIONAL
RISK
MEASUREMENT
AND
MANAGEMENT

PANEL 3

MODEL RISK

Model risk relates to the risks involved in the erroneous use of models to value and hedge securities. Model risk is typically defined as a component of operational risk. Model risk may seem to be insignificant for simple instruments (such as stocks and straight bonds) but can become a major operational risk for institutions that trade sophisticated OTC derivative products and execute complex arbitrage strategies.

The market price is (on average) the best indicator of an asset's value in liquid (and more or less efficient) securities markets. However, in the absence of such a price discovery mechanism, theoretical valuation models are required to "mark-to-model" the position. In these circumstances the trader and the risk manager are like the pilot and co-pilot of a plane which fly under Instrument Flight Rules (IFR), relying only on sophisticated instruments to land the aircraft. An error in the electronics on board can be fatal to the plane.

Pace of model development

The pace of model development has accelerated to support the rapid growth of financial innovations such as caps, floors, swaptions, spread options and other exotic derivatives. These innovations were made possible by developments in financial theory that allow one to efficiently capture the many facets of financial risks. At the same time, these models could never have been implemented on the trading floor had the

growth in computing power not accelerated so dramatically.

In March 1995, Alan Greenspan commented, "The technology that is available has increased substantially the potential for creating losses". Financial innovations, model development and computing power are engaged in a sort of leapfrog, whereby financial innovations call for more model development, which in turn requires more computing power, which in turn results in more complex models. The more sophisticated the instrument, the larger the profit margin – and the greater the incentive to innovate.

If the risk management function does not have the authority to approve (vet) new models, then this dynamic process can create significant operational risk. Models need to be used with caution. In many instances, too great a faith in models has led institutions to make unwitting bets on the key model parameters – such as volatilities or correlations – which are difficult to predict and often prove unstable over time.

The difficulty of controlling model risk is further aggravated by errors in implementing the theoretical models, and by inexplicable differences between market prices and theoretical values. For example, we still have no satisfactory explanation as to why investors in convertible bonds do not exercise their conversion option in a way which is consistent with the predictions of models.

operational risk should be measured using standard objective criteria. "Consistency" refers to ensuring that similar operational risk profiles in different business units result in similar reported operational risks. "Relevance" refers to the idea that risk should be reported in a way that makes it easier to take action to address the operational risk. "Transparency" refers to ensuring that all material operational risks are reported and assessed in a way that makes the risk transparent to senior managers. By "bank-wide" we mean that operational risk measures should be designed so that the results can be aggregated across the entire organisation. Finally, "completeness" refers to ensuring that *all* material operational risks are identified and captured.

As pointed out earlier, one can assess the amount of operational risk in terms of the likelihood of operational failure (net of mitigating controls) and the severity of potential financial

loss (given that a failure occurs). This suggests that one should measure operational risk using the four-step operational risk process illustrated in Figure 5. Below, we discuss each step in more detail.

INPUT (STEP 1)
The first step in the operational risk measurement process is to gather the information needed to perform a complete assessment of all significant operational risks. A key source of this information is often the finished products of other groups. For example, a unit that supports a business group often publishes reports or documents that may provide an excellent starting point for the operational risk assessment.

Relevant and useful reports (eg Figure 6), include audit reports, regulatory reports, etc. The degree to which one can rely on existing documents for control assessment varies.

Different types of model risk

Model risk, as illustrated in the figure, has a number of sources:

❏ the data input can be wrong;

❏ one may wrongly estimate a key parameter of the model;

❏ models may give rise to significant hedging risk;

❏ the model may be flawed or incorrect.

In fact, when they talk about model risk most people are referring to this last risk source. It is a particular worry when trading derivatives, as modern traders rely heavily on the use of mathematical models which involve complex equations and advanced mathematics. Flaws may be caused by mistakes in the setting of equations, or wrong assumptions may have been made about the underlying asset price process. For example, a model may be based on a flat and fixed term structure, while the actual term structure of interest rates is steep and unstable.

Various levels of model risks

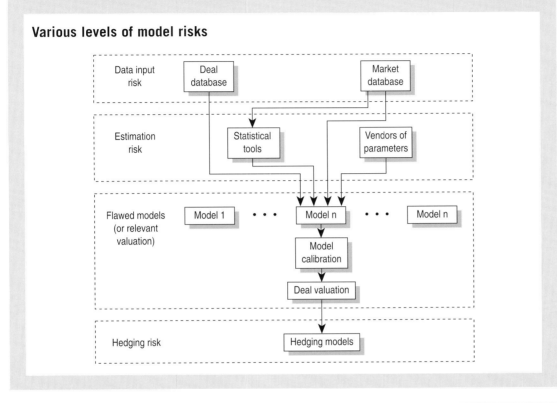

5. The operational risk measurement process

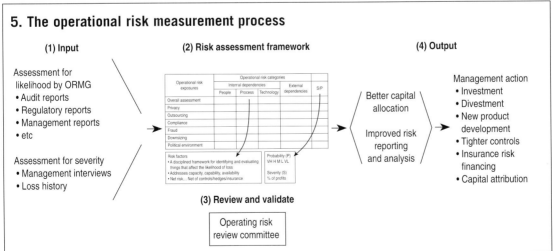

For example, if one is relying on audit documents as an indication of the degree of control, then one needs to ask if the audit assessment is current and sufficient. Have there been any significant changes made since the last audit assessment? Did the audit scope include the area of operational risk that is of concern to the present risk assessment?

KEY STEPS IN
BUILDING
CONSISTENT
OPERATIONAL
RISK
MEASUREMENT
AND
MANAGEMENT

6. Sources of information in the measurement process of operational risk: the input

Assessment for:

Likelihood of occurrence	Severity
• Audit reports	• Management interviews
• Regulatory reports	• Loss history
• External reports	
• Management reports	
• Expert opinion	
• BPR (business recovery plan)	
• EMU (European Monetary Union)	
• Business plans	
• Budgets	
• Operations plans	

As one works through the available information, gaps often become apparent. These gaps in information are filled through discussion with the relevant managers. Information from primary sources needs to be validated, and updated as necessary. Particular attention should be paid to any changes in the business or operating environment since the information was first produced.

Typically, there is not sufficient reliable historical data available to confidently project the likelihood or severity of operational losses. One often needs to rely on the expertise of business management, until reliable data is compiled, to offer an assessment of the severity of the operational failure for each of the key risks identified in Step 2. The centralised operational

risk management group (ORMG)[2] will need to validate any such self-assessment by a business unit in a disciplined way. Often this amounts to a "reasonableness" check that makes use of historical information on operational losses within the business and within the industry as a whole.

The time frame employed for all aspects of the assessment process is typically one year. The one-year time horizon is usually selected to align with the business planning cycle of the bank. Nevertheless, while some serious potential operational failures may not occur until after the one-year time horizon, they should be part of the current risk assessment. For example, one may have key employees under contract working on the year 2000 problem – the risk that systems will fail on January 1, 2000. These personnel may be employed under contracts that terminate more than 12 months into the future. However, while the risk event may only occur beyond the end of the current one-year review period, current activity directed at mitigating the risk of that future potential failure should be reviewed for the likelihood of failure as part of the *current* risk assessment.

RISK ASSESSMENT FRAMEWORK (STEP 2)

The "input" information gathered in Step 1 needs to be analysed and processed through the risk assessment framework sketched in Figure 7. The risk of unexpected operational failure, as well as the adequacy of management processes and controls to manage this risk, needs to be identified and assessed. This assessment leads to a measure of the net operational risk, in terms of likelihood and severity.

Risk categories

We mentioned earlier that operational risk can be broken down into four headline *risk categories* (representing the risk of unexpected loss) due to operational failures in people, process and technology deployed within the business – collectively the *internal dependencies* – and *external dependencies*.[3]

Internal dependencies should each be reviewed according to a common set of factors. Assume, for illustrative purposes, that we examine these internal dependencies according to three key components of capacity, capability and availability. For example, if we examine operational risk arising from the people risk category then one can ask:

❑ Does the business has enough people (capacity) to accomplish its business plan?

7. Second step in the measurement process of operational risk: risk assessment framework

Operational risk exposures	Operational risk categories				
	Internal dependencies			External dependencies	S/P
	People	Process	Technology		
Overall assessment					
Privacy					
Outsourcing					
Compliance					
Fraud					
Downsizing					
Political environment					

Risk factors
• A disciplined framework for identifying and evaluating things that affect the likelihood of loss
• Addresses capacity, capability, availability
• Net risk... Net of controls/hedges/insurance

Probability (P)
VH H M L VL

Severity (S)
% of profits

VH: very high, H: high, M: medium, L: low, VL: very low

❑ Do the people have the right skills (capability)?

❑ Are the people going to be there when needed (availability)?

External dependencies are also analysed in terms of the specific type of external interaction. For example, one would look at clients (external to the bank, or an internal function that is external to the business unit under analysis), government regulatory agencies, suppliers (internal or external), contractors, out-sourced service providers (external or internal), investments, affiliations and competitors, etc.

Net operational risk

Operational risks should be evaluated net of risk mitigants. For example, if one has insurance to cover a potential fraud then one needs to adjust the degree of fraud risk by the amount of insurance.

Connectivity and inter-dependencies

The headline risk categories cannot be viewed in isolation from one another. Figure 8 illustrates the idea that one needs to examine the degree of interconnected risk exposure across the headline operational risk categories, in order to understand the full impact of any risk. For example, assume that a business unit is introducing a new computer technology. The implementation of that new technology may generate a set of interconnected risks across people, process and technology. Have the people who are to work with the new technology been given sufficient training and support?

All this suggests that the overall risk is likely to be higher than that accounted for by each of the component risks considered individually. Similarly, the severity or financial impact assessment could be greater (or may be less) than the sum of the individual severity assessments.

Change, complexity, complacency

One should also examine the sources that drive the headline categories of operational risk. For example, one may view the drivers as falling broadly under the categories of: change, complexity, and complacency.

Change refers to such items as introducing new technology or new products, a merger or acquisition, or moving from internal supply to outsourcing, etc. *Complexity* refers to such items as complexity in products, process or technology. *Complacency* refers to ineffective management of the business, particularly in key operational risk areas such as fraud, unauthorised trading, privacy and confidentiality, payment and settlement, model use, etc. Figure 9 illustrates how these underlying sources of a risk connect to the headline operational risk categories.[4]

Net likelihood assessment

The likelihood that an operational failure may occur within the next year should be assessed (net of risk mitigants such as insurance) for each identified risk exposure and for each of the four headline risk categories (ie people, process and

KEY STEPS IN
BUILDING
CONSISTENT
OPERATIONAL
RISK
MEASUREMENT
AND
MANAGEMENT

8. Connectivity of operational risk exposure

Dependencies

Internal External

Operations risk due to:

People Process

Technology

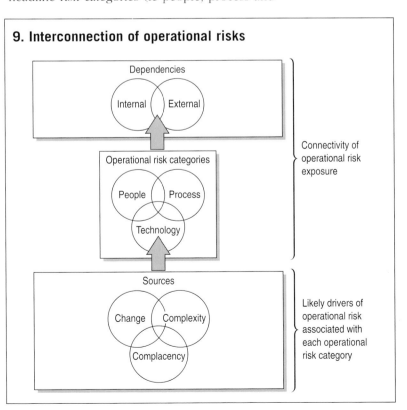

9. Interconnection of operational risks

Dependencies

Internal External

Operational risk categories

People Process

Technology

Sources

Change Complexity

Complacency

Connectivity of operational risk exposure

Likely drivers of operational risk associated with each operational risk category

KEY STEPS IN

BUILDING

CONSISTENT

OPERATIONAL

RISK

MEASUREMENT

AND

MANAGEMENT

LEXICON OF RISK

It is critical that operational risk management groups are clear when they communicate with line management (in one direction) and senior managers (in the other). It can help to publish internally a lexicon of key terms. Here are some examples:

❏ Expected loss refers to the loss an institution anticipates or expects in connection with a business or risk source. It is a function of the likelihood of failure and the likely loss severity given that a failure occurs.

❏ Failure refers to an interruption in business activities that is manifested in terms of a severe but (in the CIBC lexicon) non-catastrophic financial loss.

❏ Likelihood refers to the chance or possibility that an operational risk will result in an operational failure.

❏ Risk assessment refers to the measurement of operational risk that exists within a business unit.

Initially, risk assessments are likely to be conducted at a high level with lower, more detailed assessments planned for the future.

❏ Risk category refers to the main types of operational risk that occur in the bank. The four principal risk categories used by CIBC are people, process, technology and external dependencies.

❏ Risk exposure refers to the specific event or situation that produces operational risk. Although the amount of risk exposures may be unlimited, the risk manager's attention naturally focuses on the most relevant risk exposures for a given business unit. An example of a risk exposure is outsourcing.

❏ Severity refers to the dollar impact (ie financial loss) that results from an operational failure.

---

technology, and external dependencies). Since it is often unclear how to quantify these risks, this assessment can be expressed as a rating along a five-point likelihood continuum from very low (VL) to very high (VH) as set out in Table 3.

Severity assessment
Severity describes the potential loss to the bank given that an operational failure has occurred. Typically, this will be expressed as a range of dollars (eg $50 million to $100 million), as exact measurements will not usually be possible. Severity should be assessed for each identified risk exposure. As we mentioned above, in practice the operational risk management group is likely to rely on the expertise of business management to recommend appropriate severity amounts.

Combining likelihood and severity into an overall operational risk assessment
Operational risk measures are constrained in that there is not usually a defensible way to combine the individual likelihood of loss and severity assessments into an overall measure of operational risk within a business unit. To do so, the likelihood of loss would need to be expressed in numerical terms – eg a medium risk represents a 5–10% probability of occurrence. This cannot be accomplished without statistically significant historical data on operational losses.

Table 3. Five-point likelihood continuum

Likelihood that an operational failure will occur within the next year

VL	Very low (very unlikely to happen: less than 2%)
L	Low (unlikely: 2–5%)
M	Medium (may happen: 5–10%)
H	High (likely to happen: 10–20%)
VH	Very high (very likely: greater than 20%)

The fact is that for the moment the financial industry measures operational risk using a combination of both quantitative and qualitative points of view. To be sure, one should strive to take a quantitative approach based on statistical data. However, where the data are unavailable or unreliable – and this is the case for many risk sources at the moment – a qualitative approach can be used to generate a risk rating. Neither approach on its own tells the whole story: the quantitative approach is often too rigid, while the qualitative approach is often too vague. The hybrid approach requires a numerical assignment of the amount at risk based on both quantitative and qualitative data.

Ideally, one would also calculate the correlation between the various risk exposures and incorporate this into the overall measure of business or firm-wide risk. Given the difficulty of doing this, for the time being risk managers are more likely to simply aggregate individual severities assessed for each operational risk exposure.[5]

57

KEY STEPS IN
BUILDING
CONSISTENT
OPERATIONAL
RISK
MEASUREMENT
AND
MANAGEMENT

Table 4. Example of a risk assessment report for Business Unit A

| Operational risk scenarios | Likelihood of event (in 12 months) | | | | | |
| | Internal dependencies | | | External dependencies | Overall assessment | Severity $million |
	People	Process	Technology			
Outsourcing	L	VL	VL	M	M	50–100
Privacy	L	M	VL	L	L	50–100
Compliance	L	VL	VL	VL	L	35–70
Fraud	L	L	VL	VL	L	5–10
Downsizing	L	VL	VL	L	L	5–10
Political environment	VL	M	VL	VL	L	5–10
Overall assessment	L	M	VL	L	L	150–300

Sample risk assessment report

What does this approach lead to when put into practice? Assume we have examined Business Unit A and have determined that the sources of operational risk are related to:

❏ outsourcing;
❏ privacy;
❏ compliance;
❏ fraud;
❏ downsizing; and
❏ the political environment.

The sample report, as illustrated in Table 4, shows that the business has an overall "low" likelihood of operational loss within the next 12 months. Observe that an overall assessment has led to an overall exposure estimate of $150 to $300 million.

The summary report typically contains details of the factors considered in making a "likelihood" assessment for each operational risk exposure (broken down by people, process, technology and external dependencies) given an operational failure.

REVIEW AND VALIDATION (STEP 3)

What happens after such a report has been generated? First, the centralised operational risk management group (ORMG) reviews the assessment results with senior business unit management and key officers in order to finalise the proposed operational risk rating. Key officers include those with responsibility for the management and control of operational activities (such as internal audit, compliance, IT, human resources etc.). Second, ORMG typically presents its recommended rating to an operating risk rating review committee – a process similar that followed by credit rating agencies such as Standard & Poors. The risk committee comments

on the ratings prior to publication. ORMG may clarify or amend its original assessment based on feedback from the rating review committee, and agrees with the committee a final assessment.

OUTPUT (STEP 4)

The final assessment of operational risk, will be formally reported to business management, and the centralised Raroc group, and the partners in corporate governance (such as internal audit, compliance, etc.) As illustrated in Figure 10, the output of the assessment process has two main uses. Firstly, the assessment provides better operational risk information to management for use in improving risk management decisions. Secondly, the assessment improves the allocation of economic capital to better reflect the extent of operational risk being taken by a business unit, a topic we discuss in more detail below. Overall, operational risk assessment guides management action – for example, in deciding whether to purchase insurance to mitigate some of the risks.

The overall assessment of the likelihood of operational risk and severity of loss for a business unit can be plotted to provide relative information on operational risk exposures across the bank (or a segment of the bank) as shown in Figure 11. Of course, Figure 11 is a very simplified way of representing risk, however for many

10. Fourth step in the measurement process of operational risk: output

KEY STEPS IN

BUILDING

CONSISTENT

OPERATIONAL

RISK

MEASUREMENT

AND

MANAGEMENT

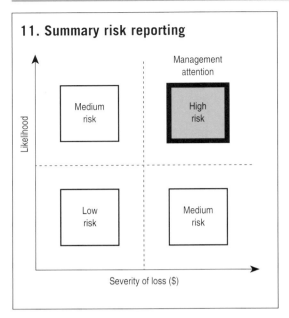

11. Summary risk reporting

Management attention

Likelihood

Medium risk

High risk

Low risk

Medium risk

Severity of loss ($)

operational risks presenting a full probability distribution is too complex to be justified – and may even be misleading given the lack of historical evidence. In Figure 11, one can see very clearly that if a business unit falls in the upper right-hand quadrant then the business unit has a high likelihood of operational risk and a high severity of loss (if failure occurs). These units would be the focus of management's attention.

A business unit may address its operational risks in several ways. Firstly, one can avoid the risk by withdrawing from a business activity. Secondly, one can transfer the risk to another party (eg say through insurance or outsourcing). Thirdly, one can accept and manage the risk, say, through effective management, monitoring and control. Fourthly, one can put appropriate fall-back plans in place in order to reduce the impact should an operational failure occur. For example, after management identifies the sources of operational risks in its organisation, it can ask several insurance companies to submit proposals for insuring those risks. Of course, not all operational risks are insurable, and in the case of those that are insurable the required premium may be prohibitive. The strategy and the eventual decision should be based on a cost–benefit analysis.

Capital attribution for operational risks

By attributing economic capital to operational risks we can make sure that businesses that take on more operational risk are assigned a greater allocation of capital and incur a transparent capital charge. The idea is that this, in turn, will

allow whole firms and individual businesses to use risk/reward analysis to improve their operational decisions.

In many banks, the methodology for translating operational risk into capital is developed by the Raroc group in partnership with the operational risk management group. One approach to allocating economic capital is really an extension of the risk measurement and ranking process we described above. For example:

❑ First assign a risk rating to each business based on the likelihood of an operational risk occurring, for example, on a scale of 1 for "very low" operational risk to 5 for "very high". This rating should be assigned to reflect the probability of a failure occurring, inclusive of mitigating factors introduced by management.

❑ Second, the degree of severity of the risk should be determined given the operational risk has occurred. Risk severity is estimated utilising a combination of internal loss history, losses at other banks and management judgement, etc.

❑ Third, a risk rating is assigned based on combining the likelihood and severity operational risk calculation. A review group ensures consistency and integrity of the operational risk rating process on a bank-wide basis, so that the result is a "relative" risk rating for each business that can then be used to attribute capital up to the desired "all-bank operational risk capital amount".

Note that for the purposes of capital allocation we need to take special account of the kind of worst-case scenarios of operational losses illustrated in Figure 12. To understand this diagram, remember that operational risks can be divided into those losses that are expected and those that are unexpected. Management, in the ordinary course of business, knows that certain operational activities will fail. There will be a "normal" amount of operational loss that the business is willing to absorb as a cost of doing business (such as error correction, fraud, etc.). These

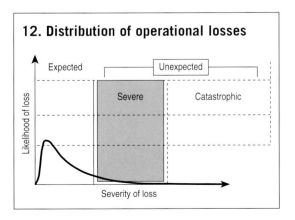

12. Distribution of operational losses

Expected

Unexpected

Likelihood of loss

Severe

Catastrophic

Severity of loss

KEY STEPS IN
BUILDING
CONSISTENT
OPERATIONAL
RISK
MEASUREMENT
AND
MANAGEMENT

Table 5. Distribution of operational losses

	Expected event (high probability, low losses)	Unexpected event (low probability, high losses)	
		Severe financial impact	Catastrophic financial impact
Covered by	Business plan	Operational risk capital	Insurable (risk transfer) or "risk financing"

failures are explicitly or implicitly budgeted for in the annual business plan and are covered by the pricing of the product or service. We assume that a business unit's management is already assessing and pricing expected failures.

By contrast, the focus of this chapter, as illustrated in Figure 12, is on *unexpected* failures, and the amount of economic capital which should be attributed to business units to absorb those losses. However, as the figure suggests, unexpected failures can themselves be further subdivided:

❏ *Severe but not catastrophic losses* Unexpected severe operational failures, as illustrated in Table 5, should be covered by an appropriate allocation of operational risk capital. These kinds of losses will tend to be covered by the measurement processes described in the sections above.

❏ *Catastrophic losses* These are the most extreme but also the rarest forms of operational risk events – the kind that might destroy the bank entirely. Value-at-risk (VAR) and Raroc models are not meant to capture catastrophic risk, since potential losses are calculated up to a certain confidence level and catastrophic risks are by their very nature extremely rare. Banks will attempt to find insurance coverage to hedge catastrophic risks since capital will not protect a bank from these risks.

Although VAR/Raroc models may not capture catastrophic loss, banks can use these approaches to assist their thought process about insurance. For example, it might be argued that one should retain the risk if the cost of capital to support the asset is less than the cost of insuring it. This sort of risk/reward approach can bring discipline to an insurance programme that has evolved over time into a rather ad hoc set of policies – often where one type of risk is insured while another is not, with very little underlying rationale.

Banks have now begun to develop databases of historical operational risk events in an effort to quantify unexpected risks of various sorts. They are hoping to use the databases to develop statistically defined "worst case" estimates that

may be applicable to a select subset of a bank's businesses – in the same way that many banks already use historical loss data to drive credit risk measurement.

It should be admitted that this is a new and evolving area of risk measurement. A bank's internal loss database will most likely be extremely small relative to the major losses in certain other banks. Hence, the database should also reflect the experience of others. Blending internal and external data requires a heavy dose of management judgement.

Some banks are moving to an integrated or concentric approach to the "financing" of operational risks. This financing can be achieved via a combination of external insurance programmes (eg with floors and caps), capital market tools and self-insurance. Where risks are self-insured, the risk should be allocated economic capital.

How will the increasing emphasis on operational risk and changes in the financial sector affect the overall capital attributions in banking institutions? In the very broadest terms, we would guess that the typical capital attributions in banks now stand at around 20% for operational risk, 10% for market risk and 70% for credit risk (Figure 13). We would expect that both operational risk and market exposures

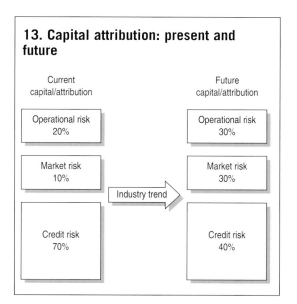

13. Capital attribution: present and future

PANEL 5

INFORMATION RISK

Many risk management systems are developed to perform unique functions, and in some cases the functions may overlap. A typical operational risk problem is the fragmentation of existing systems such that one cannot easily communicate across them (the "islands of automation" problem). Defining and measuring operational risk in an integrated fashion is the key to controlling it. One needs to find some way of integrating technology for the purposes of implementing an effective overall risk management system covering market, credit and operational risk.

This implies that financial institutions must develop a *risk management information system* infrastructure as a critical foundation to meet their risk management goals to avoid what might be termed "information risk". The risk management system should be designed to support the transportation and integration of risk information from a variety of technology platforms (legacy systems) as well as from multiple internal and external legacy systems. Information should be delivered error free to the risk management system – if necessary, from around the world.

Institutions are also likely to require a *risk warehouse*, cleansed of bad data and populated with relevant operational information. Specifically, the information should be reconciled or verified if possible to ensure that an accurate measure of operational risk is being reported. The risk warehouse should also store a time series of operational data in its financial database. The risk reports should be generated regularly by an analytic engine that has been designed within the risk management system. The analytic engine should be built with a flexible architecture that will be able to accommodate new risk measures in the future.

might evolve in the future to around 30% each – although of course much depends on the nature of the institution. The likely growth in the weighting of operational risk can be attributed to the growing risks associated with people, process, technology and external dependencies. For example, it seems inevitable that financial institutions will experience higher worker mobility, growing product sophistication, increases in business volume, rapid introduction of new technology and increased merger/acquisitions activity – all of which generate operational risk.

14. Integrated risk models

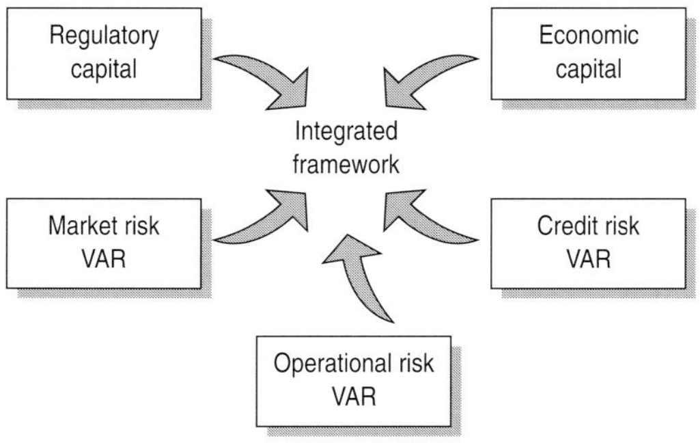

Integrated operational risk

At present, most financial institutions have one set of rules to measure market risk, a second set of rules to measure credit risk, and are just beginning to develop a third set of rules to measure operational risk. It seems likely that the leading banks will work to integrate these methodologies (Figure 14). For example they might attempt to integrate market risk VAR and credit risk VAR with a new operational risk VAR measure.

Developing an integrated risk measurement model will have important implications from both a risk transparency and a regulatory capital perspective. For example, if one simply added a market risk VAR plus an operational risk VAR plus a credit risk VAR to obtain a total VAR (rather than developing an integrated model) then one would overstate the amount of risk. The summing ignores the interaction or correlation between market risk, credit risk and operational risk.

The Bank for International Settlement (1988) rules for capital adequacy are generally recognised to be quite flawed. We would expect that in time regulators will allow banks to use their own internal models to calculate a credit risk VAR to replace the BIS (1988) rules, in the same way that the BIS 1998 Accord allowed banks to adopt an internal models approach for determining the minimum required regulatory capital for trading market risk.

The banking industry, rather than the regulators, sponsored the original market VAR methodology. (In particular, JP Morgan's release of its RiskMetrics product.) Industry has also sponsored the new wave of credit VAR

61

KEY STEPS IN
BUILDING
CONSISTENT
OPERATIONAL
RISK
MEASUREMENT
AND
MANAGEMENT

PANEL 6

TRAINING AND RISK EDUCATION

One major source of operational risk is people – the human factor. Undoubtedly, operational risk due to people can be mitigated through better educated and trained workers, especially in the case of critical activities. (With the rider that it is costly to select better people and train them more thoroughly, and this added cost should be evaluated against the benefit of reduced operational risk). Training in the sense of risk education is also crucial: first-class risk education is a key component of any optimal firm-wide risk management programme. Staff should be aware of why they may have to change the way they do things. Staff are more comfortable if they know new risk control procedures exist for a good business reason. Staff need to clearly understand more than basic limit monitoring techniques (ie

the lowest level of knowledge illustrated in the figure below). Managers need to be educated on the mathematics behind risk analysis. In other words, managers need to be educated on the means by which risk is measured.

Business units, infrastructure units, corporate governance units and internal audit should also be educated on how risk can be used as the basis for allocating economic capital. Business staff should also learn how to utilise measures of risk as a basis for pricing transactions. Finally, as illustrated in the upper right corner of the figure, one should educate business managers and risk managers on how to utilise the risk measurement tools to enhance their portfolio management skills.

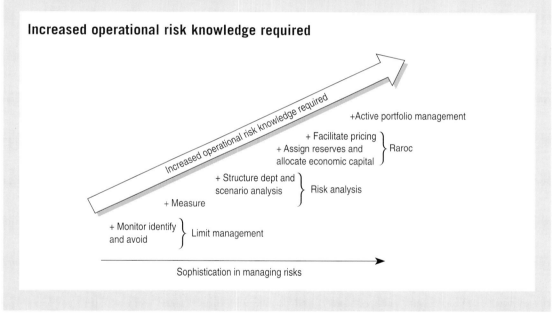

Increased operational risk knowledge required

methodologies such as the JP Morgan CreditMetrics offering, and CreditRisk+ from Credit Suisse Financial Products. Similarly, vendor-led credit VAR packages include a package developed by a company called KMV (which is now in use at 60 financial institutions).[6] All this suggests that, in time, the banking industry will sponsor some form of operational risk VAR methodology.

We can push the parallel a little further. The financial community, with the advent of products such as credit derivatives, is increasingly moving towards valuing loan-type products on a mark-to-model basis. Similarly, with the advent of insurance products we will see increased price discovery for operational risk. Moreover,

just as we see an increasing trend toward applying market-risk-style quantification techniques to measure the credit VAR associated with products whose value is mostly driven by changes in credit quality, we might also expect to see such techniques applied to develop an operational VAR.

A major challenge for banks is to produce comprehensible and practical approaches to operational risk that will prove acceptable to the regulatory community. Ideally, the integrated risk model of the future will encompass market risk VAR, credit risk VAR and operational risk, and be able to calculate *both* regulatory capital and economic capital.

15. Best practice risk management

Concluding comments

The developments we discussed above and new, integrated risk management system technologies are enabling more effective risk management for institutions. Increasingly, institutions will be able to gain a competitive advantage by monitoring and managing all of their risks on a global basis – although to achieve this the firm has to confront some fundamental infrastructure issues discussed in Panel 5.

Infrastructure aside, an integrated goal-congruent risk management process that puts all the elements together, as illustrated in Figure 15, will open the door to optimal firm-wide management of risk. "Integrated" refers to the need to avoid a fragmented approach to risk management – risk management is only as strong as the weakest link. "Goal-congruent" refers to the need to ensure that policies and methodologies are consistent with each other.

For example, one goal is to have an "apple-to-apple" risk measurement scheme so that one can compare risk across all products and aggregate risk at any level. The end product is a best-practice management of risk that is also consistent with business strategies. This is a "one firm, one view" approach that also recognises the complexity of each business within the firm.

In this chapter we have stressed that operational risk should be managed as a *partnership* among business units (along with their business infrastructure groups), corporate governance units, internal audit and risk management. We should also mention the importance of establishing a risk-aware *business culture*. Senior managers play a critical role in establishing a corporate environment in which best-practice operational risk management can flourish. Personnel will ultimately behave in a manner dependent on how senior management reward and train them (Panel 6).

Indeed, arguably the key single challenge for senior management is to harmonise the behaviour patterns of business units, infrastructure units, corporate governance units, internal audit and risk management and create an environment in which all sides "sink or swim" together in terms of managing operational risk.

1 *Operational risk in financial institutions is not a well-defined concept. The academic literature ignores it or, more precisely, relates operational risk to operational leverage, ie to the shape of the production cost function, and in particular to the relationship between fixed and variable costs.*

2 *See Step 3.*

3 *These categories are consistent with the typology introduced earlier in this chapter.*

4 *A list of the sources that drive the headline categories of operational risk exposures should be developed to help identify a common taxonomy of the drivers of risks.*

Sources should be added to (or removed) from the list as business circumstances evolve or as other sources of greater operational risk are identified.

5 *The corollary to severity in the credit risk model would be "exposure" – ie the total of all loans in the portfolio. Similarly, the "value-at-risk" of a credit portfolio is the potential loss that may be realised out of those exposures by combining exposure with the probability of the default net of recovery.*

6 *The KMV model is based on an expanded version of the Merton model to allow for an empirically accurate approximation in lieu of a theoretically precise approach.*

4

Defining and Aggregating Operations Risk Information

Applications in Risk Mitigation and Capital Allocation

Jonathan Davies, Matthew Fairless, Sonia Libaert, Jason Love, David O'Brien, Peter Slater and Tim Shepheard-Walwyn
Warburg Dillon Read

Risk exposure is an essential part of a bank's business and we at Warburg Dillon Read (WDR) foster a business culture that accepts risk-taking as a fundamental component of our activity. This extends beyond credit and market risks to include funding, operations, legal and liability risks, as well as business risks in general.

While we accept risk-taking as essential for us to achieve our objectives, we actively manage our exposures in the interest of our shareholders and are committed to applying the best market practices for risk management. In particular, we consider risk identification, risk quantification, and risk management to be crucial for the continuing strength of the bank.

This chapter covers two primary topics, these being:
❑ the determination of operations risk – the identification and management of operations risk; and
❑ operations risk and the allocation of capital.

The determination of operations risk

This involves the identification and management of operations risk. To determine the overall risk portfolio that we are required to understand and manage we have identified 10 risk categories. This constitutes our "risk envelope", as shown in Figure 1.

This is not a fixed list, and the relative importance of each component may change. However, in order to assess the relative significance of these different risks, there is a need to develop a framework that can be used to assess these risks on a consistent and comparable basis.

Each of the risk categories, of which operations risk is one, is clearly defined and

specific responsibility exists for policy development, monitoring and measurement in each. Our approach to operations risk is fivefold:
❑ define operations risk;
❑ clarify the boundary events with other loss categories;
❑ aggregate operations risk information;
❑ measure and mitigate operations risk; and
❑ allocate capital to business units.

The first four steps will be covered in depth here, and the fifth, allocation of capital, will be covered in the second half of this chapter, with a discussion of the regulatory environment.

DEFINE OPERATIONS RISK
To clarify what we mean by operations risk we will use the following definition of *operational* risk:

> The risk that deficiencies in information systems or internal controls will result in unexpected loss. This risk is associated with human error, system failures and inadequate procedures and controls.[1]

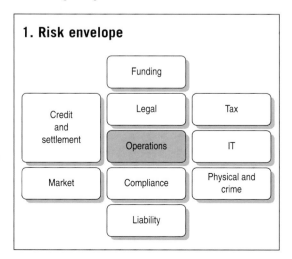

1. Risk envelope

A HISTORY OF OPERATIONS RISK

The growth of the industry

The banking environment has changed radically in the last 30 years. The shift has been from predominately small, less-sophisticated clients to a broader range of clients. This now also includes sophisticated multinational corporates and fund managers. In order to meet the challenges of the new world, there has been a significant expansion in the product range, from basic cash products to a broad range of both exchange-traded and over-the-counter derivatives.

Highly complex and flexible technology is now available to enable organisations to manage the increased volume of information that exists in the new world. Greater deregulation and increasingly sophisticated clients have led to significant increases in cross-border transactions, with substantial increases both in values of transactions and volumes in general.

To enable the banks to risk manage this expanded product range, they have moved away from risk managing on a single-product/single-location basis, to risk managing globally, on an open portfolio basis. It is only logical that many of these changes have had an impact on the operations environment.

The growth of "operations"

In the early 1970s, the support functions of investment banks were generically called the "back-office". This is an appropriate term, generating connotations of administrative, and clerical type activity, with significant levels of paper processing. The back-offices tended to provide support on a very localised basis and to individual

A. Banking from the 1970s

1970s	1980s	1990s
• Inflexible environment • Local approach • Unsophisticated products • Embryonic technology	• Deregulation • Increased sophistication of the client • Increased complexity of products • Era of mainframe • Improving communication • Initial globalisation	• Continued deregulation • Globalisation of clients • Explosion of emerging markets • Technology revolution • The global village • Consolidation of investment banks

B. Timeline

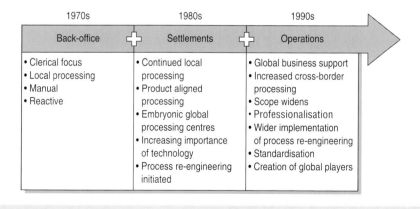

1970s	1980s	1990s
Back-office	Settlements	Operations
• Clerical focus • Local processing • Manual • Reactive	• Continued local processing • Product aligned processing • Embryonic global processing centres • Increasing importance of technology • Process re-engineering initiated	• Global business support • Increased cross-border processing • Scope widens • Professionalisation • Wider implementation of process re-engineering • Standardisation • Creation of global players

The key points to draw out from the Basle definition are:

❑ the risk arises from deficiencies in information systems or controls;

❑ the key causes of the risk are associated with human error, systems failure, or inadequate procedures and controls.

product lines. Overall, there was a reactive approach to business support.

The 1980s saw the name change to "settlements" and the beginning of a shift in the understanding of the true value of the function. Although "settlements" continued to be largely product aligned and generally locally based, it started to become more proactive. In the 1980s it was recognised that there were significant opportunities for organisations to make improvements in both efficiency and client service through process re-engineering. At the same time, some investment banks started to develop global centres of excellence for certain core processes.

In the 1990s the function is now named "operations". There has been a very definite move to professionalise "operations". For many major investment banks, the function works in partnership with the business, proactively assisting business development, while still recognising that a core objective is to provide efficient and effective support.

The core objectives of "operations" are as follows:
❑ to manage the trade/transaction settlement process;
❑ to act as an independent control check on the activities of salesmen/traders;
❑ to work with clients/counterparties to ensure that a trade, once booked, is correct and correctly settled; and
❑ to manage and control the logistics and operations component of change.

However, in more recent years, there has been a growing recognition that, as a cross-product function

managing a major part of the business process, it also has a key responsibility for managing operations risk.

The growth of operations risk

As the industry has grown it is not surprising that, given increased complexity, rapid growth and the breakdown of both regulatory and technology barriers, there has been a significant increase in the focus on developing and implementing risk management tools, policies and techniques.

Credit or counterparty risk was the first area of risk management to receive a high level of attention, with the eventual development of sophisticated models to manage and measure the risk exposures.

With the creation of sophisticated derivative products, and the need to risk manage across broad portfolios, market risk became the next target area, closely followed by settlement risk, particularly across the foreign exchange business, after the Herstatt failure.

It has only been over the past few years that the industry has realised that one of the major challenges in the new millennium will be to understand and manage operations risk. Losses amounting to billions of dollars have been incurred over the past few years due to the failure of banks to do this.

Operations has developed to meet these new challenges, by becoming a proactive, professional partner of the industry.

C. Risk development

However, in our definition of operations risk we have restricted this to risk of losses associated with the processing of business-related transactions. It is important to note that the risks arising from areas such as payroll and disaster recovery, are not covered by this definition of operations risk. This definition restricts operations risk to breakdowns in the bank's business transaction processes. It is a somewhat narrower definition than those offered in other chapters of this book.

The use of a component breakdown of residual risk (ie the risk unaccounted for once credit and market risk have been assessed) allows the individual risk components to be measured and thus managed more effectively than by considering them together as a "risk bucket".

CLARIFY THE BOUNDARY EVENTS WITH THE OTHER LOSS CATEGORIES

The scope of operations risk

To determine the scope of operations risk, and thus to define its boundaries with other loss categories, we have defined the operations risk environment.

In Figure 2 it can be seen that the component parts of the environment act upon and influence each other. Thus an external event (an event in the external environment), such as the introduction of the euro, has an impact on the process environment.

The process environment ultimately controls the quality of data integrity. This includes both static data (eg data concerning customers and instruments) and transaction data (eg data

concerning trades and positions). The principle of operations risk that we have adopted is that *transaction integrity* is key to successful management of operations risk.

Operations risk can arise at any part of the process, from order capture to the recording of the transaction to the general ledger. Operations risk is therefore not limited to operations, the function, but within the *process environment* can be defined by three major activity groups:

1. Set up
❏ The set up of new instruments and counterparties.
❏ New business process, to control the migration of new products into the process environment.

2. Pre-settlement activity
The capture and agreement of trade data and details of settlements with third parties:
❏ trade capture;
❏ confirmation/affirmation;
❏ balancing to exchanges; and
❏ maintenance events, eg rates refixes and expiries.

3. Post-settlement activity
The movement of, and control over, cash and physical assets:
❏ processing of the movement of assets, eg cash and stock;
❏ inventory management, eg custody and corporate actions processing;
❏ reconciliation of internal records to custodians and agents.

In terms of specific boundary issues with the other risk components, the major boundaries for consideration are between operations risk and credit and settlement risk, and between operations risk and market risk.

Credit and settlement risk boundary issues
Specific boundary issues would include losses arising from:
❏ collateral management;
❏ inadvertent credit exposure; and
❏ sundry settlement differences/write-offs.

The definition of the credit risk category is based on the assumption of perfect counterparty and transaction data. Any breakdown in the control process around the credit risk management application would be considered an operations loss.

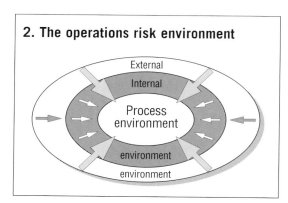

2. The operations risk environment

External
Internal
Process environment
environment
environment

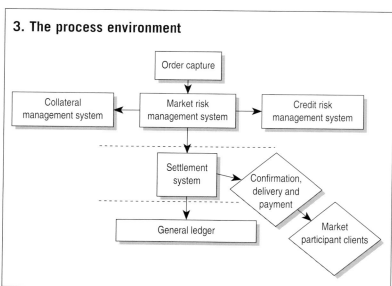

3. The process environment

Order capture

Collateral management system

Market risk management system

Credit risk management system

Settlement system

Confirmation, delivery and payment

General ledger

Market participant clients

Market risk and funding risk boundary issues
Some other specific boundary issues would include losses arising from:
❏ incorrect valuation parameters; and
❏ incorrect market risk models.

Again the underlying assumption is of perfect transaction data; any breakdown in the control process around the market risk management application would be considered an operations risk loss.

Both the internal environment and the external environment affect data integrity within the process environment. The key elements of the internal environment are:
❏ Human resources, including the turnover and the skill set of the staff. It is essential to have trained and motivated staff in order to minimise the risk.
❏ Information technology infrastructure, including the technology production infrastructure and development environment. The stability of the production environment, including the number of systems, platforms and development activity all contribute to the level of risk.
❏ Organisational structure. Clarity regarding responsibilities (including the segregation of duties) is essential for risk management. The rate at which the structure changes as well as the level of matrix management also contribute.

The external environment acts upon the internal environment and thus also upon the data integrity within the process environment. The key factors here include:
❏ The various different markets in which an organisation operates. Contributing factors include the level of development of the markets and the sophistication of the market-settlement mechanisms, together with market activity levels (volumes and the degree of commoditisation of products, for example).
❏ The agent bank infrastructure that a bank uses. Its flexibility, overall quality and speed of response.
❏ The type of clients and counterparties the organisation deals with, including their level of automation and their experience and maturity with products.
❏ Mandatory changes, such as the introduction of the euro and preparation for the "millennium bug" in the year 2000.

Thus an event in the external environment, such as the introduction of the euro, will have a profound effect on all operations risk environments. Such events are likely to put significant stresses on most organisations, their people, their processes and their infrastructure.

AGGREGATING OPERATIONS RISK INFORMATION
The third key stage in our approach to operations risk is the aggregation of operations risk information. This has two stages:
❏ formalise the capture of operations risk measurement data; and then
❏ define and monitor a series of key control indicators (KCIs).

In order to take this approach we must first determine exactly where the risks are within each environment. We can start by looking at the process flow of a single trade and see where the risk occurs and how it can be measured.

Example – a foreign exchange process flow
Figure 4 shows a foreign exchange process flow. Key parts of this process include reconciliation and the use of nostro, depot and suspense accounts. Throughout this simple transaction process, there are a number of risks:
❏ Trades may not be captured, or may be captured incorrectly. Therefore the reported profit and loss could be wrong. In addition, if positions are incorrect, traders may trade off the wrong position. Furthermore, such errors can damage the organisation's reputation with its clients.
❏ Settlement errors may be made. This could lead to interest claims, loss of assets and damage to the bank's reputation.

Therefore a series of key controls is required to prevent these errors from occurring or to pick them up as soon as possible after they have occurred. In order to pick up the errors the capture of operations risk has to be formalised.

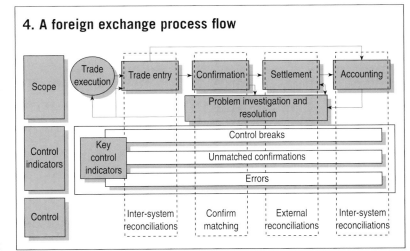

4. A foreign exchange process flow

5. Trade data integrity

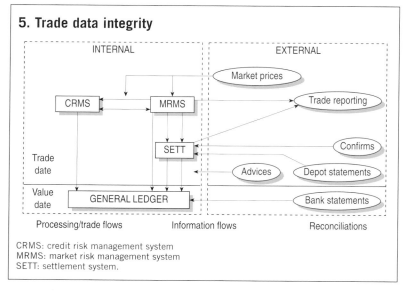

INTERNAL | EXTERNAL

Market prices

CRMS | MRMS

Trade reporting

SETT

Confirms

Trade date

Advices | Depot statements

Value date

GENERAL LEDGER

Bank statements

Processing/trade flows | Information flows | Reconciliations

CRMS: credit risk management system
MRMS: market risk management system
SETT: settlement system.

Accordingly we define the key controls and then put in place a structure to report when the controls fail.

We then define the key control indicators, which show where the data have become flawed. The pre-settlement KCIs to be measured and monitored are:

❑ unconfirmed trades;
❑ front-office/back-office reconciliation breaks;
❑ exchange reconciliation breaks;
❑ back-office/general ledger reconciliation breaks;
❑ inter-company/intra-company reconciliation breaks;
❑ late trade reporting fines.

Post-settlement KCIs to be measured and monitored are:

❑ nostro/depot reconciliation breaks;
❑ fails;

❑ physical holdings count breaks (safe versus system);
❑ transitional, control and suspense account reconciliation breaks; and
❑ collateral movements not actioned/adequacy of coverage against limits.

These KCIs are then fed into the reporting structure through the control process (see Figure 6). The control process contains a regular, "day-to-day" control mechanism where key control indicators are reported to management at various levels, culminating in an executive summary for senior management.

When there is a failure in the integrity of the data, a key control indicator will show that this has occurred. The next step is to translate this failure into monetary terms. This is achieved by examining the actual losses that are incurred through operations risk. The losses measured can be classified under four categories:

❑ Interest claims and fines – claims against us after use of funds; external fines from exchanges etc.
❑ Operations write-offs – losses of principal, payment errors.
❑ Profit-and-loss adjustments – cost of restatement of market and/or credit risk positions.
❑ Cost of correction – investigation, reconciliations.

This information along with the KCI information is then fed into the operations risk reporting structure as shown in Figure 7. Using this structure, an error can theoretically be traced from a nostro break to the eventual cost to the bank of the error (such as an interest claim).

MEASUREMENT

The penultimate stage in the approach is to measure operations risk as a whole. A consistent approach to measurement must be taken across all defined risk categories. For this reason the bank has developed three primary types of losses to measure risk categories. These are *expected loss, unexpected loss* and *stress loss.* These loss types are presented as a frequency distribution in Figure 8. From the distribution we can determine the losses that must be assumed to arise, on a continuing basis, as a consequence of undertaking particular businesses. This is the *expected loss,* not a forecast of the actual loss in any particular year, but the average amount we expect to lose every year. In order to keep this figure the same each year, a provision is used. If in one year the actual losses are below the expected losses, the excess funds will be put in

6. The control process

Qualitative
• control environment
• IT systems infrastructure
• key indicators

Quarterly risk report

Monthly executive summary - qualitative/quantitative

Quantitative
• provision
• exposure
• write-offs

Graphical summary of exceptions

Prepare minutes and action items

Documentation of weekly meetings

Formal weekly scheduled meetings

Review action items and current control

Analysis by risk/control team

Why? responsibility resolution date

Produce daily exception report

a provision. This provision will be used to average out the losses in a year where the actual losses are above the expected figure.

The extent to which the actual loss is likely to differ from the expected value in any one year can also be determined. This amount consists of the unusual but predictable losses that the bank should be able to absorb in the normal course of business.

We need to determine how much that may differ by over a period of time, and how much worse the actual loss could be, in any one year, over and above the expected loss. This amount is the *unexpected loss* it can be determined by measuring the standard deviation of the distribution.

The distribution, however, also has limitations which must be understood. It can predict under normal circumstances, but it cannot predict losses under unusual circumstances. These are referred to as *stress loss* – losses in a possible, although improbable, worst-case scenario. The bank must be able to survive such losses.

This approach is already in use for credit risk. The approach will be the basis for the formulation of an efficient operations risk model. In operations risk, the initial step of the measurement process, the collation of actual loss information, will provide the expected loss. The unexpected loss will be derived from this information. Scenario analysis is used to identify potential stress losses.

Through the monitoring of the risk indicators, and the collation of information for the measurement of operations risk, it can be seen that positive behavioural change can be encouraged. An effective continuous improvement loop has been created.

The final step in the approach to operations risk is the allocation of capital. However, success in implementing effective management of operations risk comes from mitigation against the risk occurring in the first place. This can be achieved through the efficient use of the key resources available to operations management, that is the internal environment.

Mitigating operations risk – the internal environment

The four key fundamental resources and mechanisms of the internal environment are:
❑ people;
❑ organisational structure;
❑ technology; and
❑ the control environment.

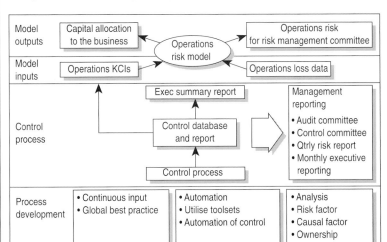

7. Operations risk reporting structure

8. Frequency distribution

9. The internal environment

PEOPLE
Human resources and people are one of the most important assets. The culture of an organisation and the people who work within it enables an operations risk policy to be carried through.

Emphasis has to be placed on risk management as a core competency. There has to be a high level of understanding of the types of risks that are inherent within the business, and how to manage them. In addition, it is essential that the corporate philosophy has a truly global perspective.

Employees must have a broad skill set, and high development potential. Key skills required include communication, teamwork and leadership, problem solving, analysis and judgement, and the ability to manage projects. They must have a thorough understanding of the business and products as well as a developed awareness of the implications of risks across the entire process, including cross-border processes.

Attracting and retaining the best people is difficult throughout the industry. It is essential to implement a standard performance measurement and management process to meet this objective. This begins with the setting of clear strategic objectives for the group. One of these includes the implementation and ongoing management of risk. These objectives affect each individual's objectives, which are then monitored through the people-management process. This process drives career planning, promotion, compensation and training. The core competencies defined in this structured people management process are directly sought during recruitment.

STRUCTURE

A key enabler within an organisation is its structure. It is imperative that the structure meets the business needs of the organisation. The WDR structure is functionally driven.

The main focus of the regional managers is to ensure that the day-to-day operations activity runs effectively and efficiently, that local regulatory requirements are met and that specific local implementations are successful.

It is the role of the global functional managers to develop the strategic plans for their functions and to ensure the global implementation of a consistent infrastructure and common applications, together with process and control standards and best practice.

Global functions comprise both production and production-support functions. There must be a consistent global approach for each product-related function and for the cross product support functions. Hence, within WDR, the existence of operations risk, data control and programme management as defined global functions.

It is essential, in any matrix structure, that clarity of responsibility exists.

TECHNOLOGY

Technology has become increasingly important in the modern environment. The effective use of technology is an essential part of managing operations risk. The business process environments are very complex and most are still plagued with excessive fragmentation of processes, multiple systems, high levels of manual intervention, a lack of standards, and multiple databases requiring high levels of data movement. This significantly increases the level of operations risk to which banks are exposing themselves. The key requirements of technology are:

❑ Common data depositories, both for transactional and static data. Data movement is reduced thereby increasing data integrity. The target must be to capture data once and, where possible, electronically.

❑ Flexible functional modules that can become standard global applications utilising the common depositories.

❑ A greater level of standardised, electronic market and client interfaces to lower the level of operations risk.

❑ As a prerequisite to any technology development, core functionality should always include the development of appropriate diagnostic tools, so that information exists to permit the assessment of control breakdown, operations efficiency and data flows.

Historically, banks have not had total discipline when defining data standards. It is thought that the imposition of standards can create an excessively rigid structure, which is then too brittle in the fast-changing environment.

---

10. People – the process

However, more often it is a lack of standards that creates the least flexible environment.

THE CONTROL ENVIRONMENT

As mentioned above, the high levels of data movement and fragmented systems result in multiple representations of trade data throughout the transaction process. These representations must be consistent and must satisfy the requirements of each stage of the process. For example, a market risk system must represent the correct market risk, whereas in an operations system the emphasis must enable settlement.

Inconsistencies in these trade representations will raise operations risk levels. To ensure a high level of integrity in these data a robust control environment must be in place. Key features of an effective control environment are:

❑ Automated reconciliation tools. Transaction reconciliations should be performed on a daily basis. The automatic performance of reconciliation increases the time available for investigation and resolution of discrepancies.

❑ Automatic reporting of reconciliation output (statistics). Timely, accurate and transparent reporting of the number of discrepancies and their age profile to management is a prerequisite for good risk management decisions.

❑ Timely implementation of audit points (both internal and external). Risk issues identified by the audit function should be dealt with as soon as is practicable. Many such issues will identify control weaknesses that will increase operations risk levels. An effective audit function process is therefore vital.

❑ A high level of control over the profit and loss and balance sheet is required. All accounts should have designated owners and be reconciled on a regular basis.

OVERALL CONTROL AND MITIGATION OF OPERATIONS RISK ENVIRONMENT

The requirements for the control and mitigation of operations risk are:

❑ Clear standards across both core production functions and product support functions. Global best practices across business processes and global standards for control and programme management.

❑ Clear definition of key control indicators. Transparency of control information across all major locations can be gained through the implementation of a standard control reporting process. This information can then be accessed from an internal Web site.

❑ A standard control tool set is important to manage multiple systems and a high level of data movement. This should include a standard internal match engine, a standard cash-management and funding-analysis tool and an external reconciliation tool. These should be implemented globally.

❑ Clarity of responsibility, both within operations, and between operations and other functions. Lack of clarity of responsibility always significantly increases the level of operations risk.

The responsibilities of all individual functions should be determined at group level.

Operations risk and the allocation of economic capital

Banks and financial service firms have recognised for some considerable time the important role that risk-based capital allocation techniques play in the overall management of their business. In the case of banks, much of the original impetus for such an approach originated with the work of the Basle Committee on Banking Supervision through the 1988 Basle Accord, which established for the first time a common international standard for setting regulatory capital for banks. However, the original Basle standard, which was established at a time before most of the recent developments in modern risk management theory and practice, was extremely simplistic, effectively requiring banks to hold a minimum of 8% of capital as backing for all their unsecured commercial lending, whatever the quality of the borrower. Moreover it was based solely on the risks in a bank's credit portfolio, and made no attempt to capture the other risks that a bank faced. As a result of this, when the Basle Committee moved on in the early 1990s to consider the introduction of a capital requirement for market risk, the banks made a strong case to be allowed to use internal risk measures based on their value-at-risk (VAR) models as the basis for assessing the regulatory capital requirement for market risk.

The agreement by the regulators to allow firms to use internal models for market risk, which was incorporated in the 1996 market risk amendment to the Basle Accord, has set in train a process of re-evaluation of the appropriateness of the Basle standards for credit risk, as the simple 8% requirement is widely recognised to be a poor measure of the true credit risk in a bank's portfolio. This, in turn, is forcing banks to recognise that their own internal capital

IMPACT OF THE EURO

In this panel we present an illustrative example of the possible impact of the euro on operations risk in the external, internal and process environments.

The euro (part of the external environment) will affect the process and internal environments both as a result of any ongoing procedural changes that will be required to support the euro and the changes that will occur over the conversion weekend itself.

In a "normal" operating environment there are:
- low levels of error;
- low levels of reconciliation breaks that would be short dated;
- low levels of unmatched confirmation that would be short dated;
- low staff stress levels;
- timely resolution of issues;
- a relatively robust and stable system infrastructure;
- and low levels of expected losses.

Under these circumstances there would be a low operations risk assessment.

When the euro conversion weekend arrives, a huge volume of transactions will be rebooked/ amended by all the market participants and by many other organisations going through the conversion process simultaneously. This external event will put stress on the internal and process environments.

The new euro-stressed environment will consist of:
- a large amount of work in conversion with limited resources, potentially resulting in significant levels of conversion and matching errors;
- new euro nostro accounts opening on the January 4, 1999, at the various domestic clearing agents throughout the European countries going into monetary union;
- extended resolution time; as a result of all the conversion activity there will be an overload on the system of nostro, depot and confirmation matching breaks;
- increased reputation risk because of the potential errors that may occur on conversion;
- risk of standard settlement instructions being incorrect if the static data have not been set up correctly.

To demonstrate the effect that the stress on the environment will have on operations risk we can take as an example the rebooking process of the DM German government security into euros. (A generous five-business-day resolution time has been assumed in this example rather than one day in the normal operating environment. This could be optimistic given the sheer quantity of change over this weekend and the immediate period after the conversion weekend as organisations get used to new processes).
- *Error one* – in the new stressed environment a rebooking error occurs while redenominating a DM bond, resulting in an inflated position of EUR 5,140,938.8.

Euro scenario

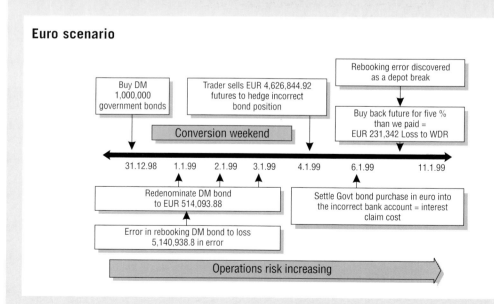

❏ *KCI pickup* – this type of error would lead to a depot and confirmation matching break as well as a potential profit and loss account restatement when the trade is rebooked.

❏ *Error 2* – the incorrect position is traded. The trader will think that he has not hedged this government bond correctly and puts an order in the market to sell the equivalent of EUR 4,626,844.92 (EUR 5,140,938.8 – EUR 514,093.88) futures to hedge this exposed position.

❏ *Error 3* – the purchase is settled into the incorrect nostro account and it takes a further five days to correct as a result of the backlog of nostro breaks.

❏ *Loss* – this will mean that we have a five-day interest claim on the settlement price.

❏ *KCI pickup* – five days later, on January 11, 1999, the rebooking error is discovered as a depot break by monitoring one of the key control indicators – depot reconciliations. The price of the futures position that we were using to hedge the bond has increased by 5% as a result of sharp interest fluctuations that may possibly occur over this conversion period.

❏ *Loss* – we correct the bond position in our book to reflect the true position of EUR 514,093.88 and at the same time buy back the portion of the future that we should not have sold on January 4, 1999, for EUR 4,858,187.17 with a resultant loss of EUR 231,342.21 on the transaction. This leads to a significantly higher level of loss.

The conversion will have an effect across the remainder of the rates, equities, FX and money markets business. The risk of error and loss is therefore extremely high. The following, then, is an assessment of operations risk in the new "stressed" operating environment of conversion weekend:

❏ increased level of errors resulting in increased profit-and-loss account adjustments;

❏ increased funding costs and liquidity risk as a result of an increase in fail trades resulting from the change in nostro accounts;

❏ an increase in interest claims both against Warburg Dillon Read as well as clients/counterparts as a result of the increase in fail trades resulting from the large number of standard settlement instructions (SSIs) that need to be changed;

❏ increased credit risk as positions with counterparties/clients may be incorrect, thus not accurately reflecting whether their credit limit has been reached or not;

❏ an increased number of reconciliation breaks – and they will be getting older;

❏ an increased number of unmatched confirmations – and they too will be getting older;

❏ extended issue resolution times;

❏ staff working excessive hours;

❏ systems becoming less stable.

There is a shift in the overall operations risk rating from low to high. A major shift in operations risk.

Impact

The advent of the euro will have a significant impact on all areas of operations risk:

❏ in the external environment, virtually all aspects of the trading world within the euro zone will be affected;

❏ in the internal environment, where banks will be coping with the euro as well as preparing for computer problems in the year 2000;

❏ in the new process environment, where changes will be made to internal processes, systems and procedures leading up to, during and after, the conversion weekend itself.

In order to meet these challenges and minimise the operations risk arising from the euro, WDR has set up a Euro Operations Risk Stream within the bank-wide euro project.

Its key objectives are:

❏ to provide a transparent reporting mechanism (Euro Operations Risk Report) that provides a complete and accurate picture for each business stream, on its conversion approach, volumes of positions and open trades converting, and data integrity levels of the key control indicators that are supported, with an analysis of the effect on operations risk;

❏ to analyse and report (Euro Conversion Control Report) on whether the conversion controls and conversion processes are working effectively prior to conversion and thereby provide a secure control environment for the conversion weekend;

❏ to calculate a euro operations risk provision to assess the financial impact the euro will have on operations risk. The purpose of this provision is to achieve cost smoothing and, more important, to identify key factors affecting operations risk and then monitor and manage the status of each of these factors going into conversion;

❏ to ensure that any reconciliations required to support the euro, both in the ongoing euro production environment, and specifically over the conversion weekend itself, are euro compliant – built and tested to cope with the euro.

allocation processes need to be aligned more directly on their own internal risk measures rather than on the regulatory requirements. In this context they need to consider how risks other than market and credit risk, which are the only risk factors directly addressed by regulatory capital requirements, should be incorporated into these methodologies. Moreover, the regulators, in considering the possibility of a revision to the capital requirements for credit risk, are themselves looking to the industry for ideas about how risks other than credit and market risk should be incorporated into an overall revised regulatory capital framework. These developments put the onus on the financial industry to develop a clear view of how these other risk measures should be developed and could be incorporated into an integrated firm-wide risk capital process.

THE ROLE OF RISK CAPITAL IN FINANCIAL FIRMS

In considering how we can approach this challenge, it is important to start by asking ourselves why a financial firm needs a methodology for allocating risk or economic capital to its business areas, and why this requirement is different from the requirements of other firms that also seek to optimise risk and return in the interests of their shareholders. The reason is relatively clear. In the case of a manufacturing firm, the key question that management has to answer is whether a particular activity or investment adds to, or detracts from, shareholder value. It can approach this decision by comparing the expected rate of return from the activity with the cost of the funding that is tied up in the business. If the firm knows the average cost of its capital, which is made up of the cost of equity and the cost of debt, it can then work out a hurdle rate for the required return on the investment concerned. If the return exceeds the weighted average cost of capital then the activity is one that will enhance shareholder value. Moreover, because the cost of funds to the firm, in terms of both equity and debt, will reflect the market's assessment of the "riskiness" of the firm's earnings, this is automatically a risk-adjusted process. So a firm that is judged to have a riskier earnings, profile will find that it faces a higher cost of capital and will have to achieve a higher hurdle rate on its investments in order to meet the market's requirements for an adequate risk-adjusted rate of return.

The problem for a financial firm is that for a number of reasons it is almost impossible to apply this same methodology when trying to work out which activities add to or detract from shareholder value. In the first place, many activities in finance that are clearly risky, such as a forward foreign exchange deal or a written option, do not require funding. Indeed they may even generate cashflow at the outset. But no one would dispute that they are risky and need to be assessed to determine whether they will provide a risk-adjusted return that is in the interest of shareholders. Secondly, even if a transaction such as a loan or the purchase of an outright cash position needs to be funded, it is difficult to judge in isolation whether it adds or detracts from shareholder value. Management needs a lot more information about the overall portfolio effects and the impact on the operating environment before it can make this decision in a meaningful way. The same transaction can, in one portfolio, add to the overall "riskiness" of the firm at one time and at another act as a hedge that reduces the risk. Thirdly, and perhaps most importantly, the way in which financial firms fund their activities through the wholesale markets, and through instruments such as repos where a market rate is set that is almost totally independently of the firm, means that the average cost of funds is not the same as the cost of capital to the firm. Indeed the average cost of funds to the firm provides little if any meaningful information about the market's hurdle rate for the required return on the capital funds of the firm or of the marginal effect on that hurdle rate of any particular investment decision.

Faced with this challenge, we have to think again about how senior management can take consistent and meaningful decisions about which businesses and transactions are most likely to add to shareholder value. In summary we are looking for a decision-support tool that will substitute for the standard capital asset pricing model (CAPM) that most non-financial firms can use in one form or another to assess their contribution to shareholder value. This recognition brings us to the first important conclusion about capital allocation procedures in financial firms which is:

Principle 1: capital allocation techniques in financial firms are a decision-support tool for senior management to enable them to assess each business area's contribution to shareholder value – they have nothing to do with how a business area is funded.

DESIGNING THE RISK CAPITAL METHODOLOGY

If we recognise that a risk capital methodology is essentially a decision-support tool to assist management in deciding between different investment decisions in a way that systematically enhances shareholder value, we now need to determine how this tool should be designed. In order to answer this question we have to start by asking ourselves what shareholders value most from any equity investment. The clear message here is that what investors value most is a predictable and healthily growing income stream. Put another way, shareholders put the highest value on a firm that has a high expected level of earnings with a low expected volatility attached to those earnings. So our decision support tool must be designed to enable management to assess not only the contribution of an investment to the expected earnings of the firm but also its contribution to the expected volatility or "riskiness" of those earnings.

If we consider this issue further, we can see that, at the simplest level, the expected earnings stream of a financial firm in any period has three key components: the change in value of its portfolio of credits and traded instruments, its income stream and its costs. We can express this as follows:

$$E(Rp_{t+1}) = E(\Delta P_{t+1} + Y_{t+1} - C_{t+1})$$

Where:

$E(Rp_{t+1})$ is the forecast value of earnings in time $t + 1$

ΔP_{t+1} is the change in the value of the firm's portfolio of assets in time $t + 1$

Y_{t+1} is the value of the firm's new business revenues in time $t + 1$, and

C_{t+1} are the costs that the firm incurs in time $t + 1$.

We could, of course, expand this term to identify the different business activities and trading books within the firm, but that is not necessary at this stage. The critical question that we need to address here from the risk management perspective is how we assess the risk in this expected income stream. Again, thinking about this from the perspective of the shareholder, this means that we need to consider the expected variance of the expected income stream, and we can derive this quite readily from our expected income terms:

$$\sigma^2{}_{t+1} = \sigma^2 \Delta P_{t+1} + \sigma^2 Y_{t+1} + \sigma^2 C_{t+1} \\ + 2(Cov(\Delta P_{t+1}, Y_{t+1}) \\ - Cov(\Delta P_{t+1}, C_{t+1}) \\ - Cov(Y_{t+1}, C_{t+1}))$$

Where $\sigma^2{}_{t+1}$ is the expected variance of $E(Rp_{t+1})$.

This is the term that, for any given level of expected income, management should be seeking to minimise in order to maximise shareholder value, and so our decision-support tool must be designed with reference to this term.

If we now look at this term more closely, we can draw some important conclusions with respect to capital allocation methodologies in general and for operational risk management and the measurement of all risks of an operational nature.

❑ Firstly we can see that, to the extent that current capital allocation models concentrate almost exclusively on credit and market risks, they really only capture the first of the terms in the equation relating to the portfolio elements of risk.

❑ Secondly, we can see that the factors that affect the variance of the revenue stream need to be given greater attention, and that this applies to all aspects of the revenue stream including businesses such as corporate finance, fund management and private banking, which have not been traditionally regarded as requiring any risk capital to be allocated to them as they did not assume credit or market risk.

❑ Thirdly, we clearly need to be able to measure all the risks that contribute to the variance of the cost base, which is where operations risk management is likely to make a significant contribution to enhancing our economic capital methodologies.

The need to be able to measure the covariance between these elements of the firm's revenue is just as important as the ability to measure the variance of each of these elements, and here it is interesting to note that we find the cost–income ratio as an element of the firm-wide risk term. It has been known for some time that banks that have a firm control of their cost–income ratio consistently outperform the market, so it is reassuring to find that this is clearly confirmed by our risk model.

So we can now reach our second conclusion about capital allocation, which is:

Principle 2: the risk capital allocation methodology should be as complete as possible, including risks such as operations risk which affect the variance of revenues through their impact on the variance of costs, and recognising the effects of covariances between the different elements of the firm's costs and revenues.

DETERMINING THE CAPITAL ALLOCATION METHODOLOGY

Having determined why we need a risk capital allocation methodology based on earnings volatility in order to assist management in maximising shareholder value, the next question to consider is what risk measures we need and how this should relate to the overall capitalisation of the firm. This will enable us to determine how much capital we should allocate to the business areas for each of the risks that have been identified.

The central question here is whether the methodology we need to use should be a capital allocation methodology, which seeks to allocate all the firm's equity to one or other of the business areas, or whether we should be using a risk-based allocation methodology, which need not necessarily add to the total capital. In thinking about this question, we need to go back to the recognition that the purpose of our risk capital allocation process is to help management to take business decisions based on the risk implications of the particular business line, and has nothing to do with funding. Consequently, the exercise is not designed to work out which businesses are actually using the capital on a day-to-day basis – only which businesses are more or less risky than others. So the only reason why we would need to try to allocate the whole of the firm's capital through the risk capital allocation process would be if the total capital of the firm were itself a useful measure of the actual risk in the business as seen by the shareholders and, moreover, if changes in the risk profile resulted in changes in the cost of capital in a systematic way.

In practice, it is relatively easy to see that financial firms have very different capital structures and levels of gearing for similar risk profiles. From this observation, we can conclude that the capital structure per se reflects a management decision about the acceptable level of gearing within the firm rather than about the totality of the risk. In other words, it is a management decision about the extent to which the firm wants to provide assurance about its risk cover. In this context it is interesting to note that the market seems to allow quite wide ranges in the acceptable level of gearing within financial firms for similar risk profiles, but does not seem to accept too much capital cover, since there are very few triple-A banks left. This would seem to imply that there is a preference among investors for some minimum rate of return when investing in financial firms, even at the cost of some additional volatility.

The conclusion we can draw from this, however, is important because it suggests that there is no need to try to allocate all the capital in the firm to the different business areas, because the amount of capital that the firm has cannot be assumed to be a good measure of the expected volatility of earnings.[2] What is much more important is to be able to measure the contribution of different risk factors to the overall risk in a systematic way. In addition there is another important reason for not trying to allocate all the capital, which is that a firm can never be certain that it has correctly identified all its risk factors. Consequently, if a risk factor is material but has been missed, an allocation methodology that uses the identified risks as a basis for allocating all the capital to the business area will inevitably send the wrong signals by overcharging for the identified risks relative to the unidentified risks. Indeed this is precisely the effect that exists for firms that use the Basle capital standard as the basis for internal capital allocation, as it "overweights" credit risks relative to other risks and penalises those business areas that assume credit risk relative to those that have cost or revenue-based risk. Consequently we can reach a third important conclusion about our capital allocation methodology which is:

Principle 3: the risk capital allocation methodology should be based on internal measures of risk and does not need to be scaled to the actual capital of the firm.

IDENTIFYING THE OPERATIONAL RISK FACTORS

As we have seen, a central requirement of our risk allocation process is to be able to assess the extent to which the exposure to a risk factor increases or decreases the expected volatility of earnings. This means that we first have to be able to identify risk factors with sufficient precision to be able to monitor and control them effectively. There is no single definition of all the risks that are material to a financial firm. The Basle Committee definition from the 1994 *Risk Management Guidelines for OTC Derivatives* identifies firm categories as credit, market, settlement, liquidity, legal and operational risk.

Unfortunately this definition of operational risk leaves a wide variety of diverse factors such as liability risk, tax risk, compliance risk, IT risk, physical security risk as well as operations risk itself, under the broad umbrella of operational risk.

Thus the first requirement for a firm that is looking to develop a risk capital allocation process for risk at the group level is to undertake a risk identification process that analyses to a significantly greater degree of specificity, which of these different risks are material to its business. This will inevitably vary from firm to firm but the critical issue here is to be able to distinguish between different risk factors in a way that enables the firm to understand the dynamics of the individual risk factor, and to control and measure the risk in a way that is relevant to its business. As discussed earlier, at WDR (and indeed UBS AG), the risk categorisation currently includes the 10 risk categories in Figure 1.

We believe that these categories are sufficiently specific and distinct to require separate risk management and control for each class of risk. However, we also recognise that the process of risk identification is a dynamic process and that this can never be an exhaustive list, which leads to a fourth conclusion about the risk measurement and allocation process, which is:

Principle 4: it is always necessary to keep the risk factors under review in order to ensure that the most important risk factors are being captured on an ongoing basis by the risk process.

MEASURING THE RISK FACTORS
This brings us to the final part of our process, which is the need to determine how we should measure our different risk factors using a measurement methodology that is consistent across all risks. In doing this we need to be clear that the purpose of this exercise is not to find a single risk measure that is designed to give us a complete handle on the exposure to the risk. The requirement is very specific. The objective is to find a measure that is most appropriate for the purpose for which it is required. In this case, it is to provide a best estimate of the contribution of a defined risk factor to the expected volatility of earnings as perceived by the shareholder.

Other measures, such as the results of stress tests and scenario analysis will almost certainly be required for broader risk management and control purposes and no risk manager should rely on a single aggregate measure as a basis for understanding the full extent of a firm's exposure to a risk. But this still does not invalidate the effort to attempt to normalise risk measures for capital allocation purposes. Indeed, there is no alternative to such normalisation if we are to attempt a consistent risk capital allocation process. The question we have to resolve, however, is "what is the most appropriate basis for this normalisation?"

In this context it is also important to note that what we are seeking to measure is not the expected value of the firm's exposure to a risk factor over the relevant period, but rather the variance of that value. This can be a significant distinction, even in relation to operations risk, because the expected value and the actual cost of exposure to a risk may vary significantly from period to period.

It is therefore necessary to ensure that once the expected cost of a firm's exposure to a risk factor has been quantified – for example the risk associated with over-the-counter (OTC) derivatives – this should be provided for on the basis of an expected value even if the cost does not actually accrue in the period concerned. This ensures that it is only the expected variance of that expected loss – which we have termed unexpected loss – that is seen as the "true" risk associated with the risk factor.

The consistent quantification of unexpected losses can, however, only be achieved once we have addressed two related issues that are of critical importance in achieving a satisfactory degree of normalisation across risk factors. These are, first, the time period over which the risk should be measured and, second, the confidence interval that is appropriate to the exercise. For example if we measure the variance of one risk on a daily basis using a 99% confidence level, this implies that we regard it as acceptable to have an exception once every 100 days, whereas if we measure another risk on an annual basis with a 95% confidence level this implies that we regard one exception every 20 years as acceptable. As we have no means of knowing how large the exception might be, these two different measures would imply very different risk tolerances on the part of the shareholder, and both cannot be right at the same time.

The critical issue here is to recognise that, although there may be no right or wrong answer, the system does require consistency in order to be reliable. Moreover, bearing in mind the purpose of our risk capital allocation

YEAR 2000

Internal risks

The potential problems associated with the year 2000 challenge may give rise to significant operations risks as a result of outright systems failure or incorrect processing due to date-related issues. Steps must be taken internally to ensure that these risks are mitigated through a sound internal testing programme.

The following factors are likely to have the greatest impact on operations risk:
❑ deficiencies occurring in information systems;
❑ human error – particularly as the hours worked will be long and stressful.

As with many other firms, Warburg Dillon Read has given the work required to prepare for the year 2000 the highest level of priority and this work has been placed under the control of senior managers. All critical IT applications and non-IT equipment that uses date-dependent computer chips will need to have been put through a programme to assess and undertake the modifications required.

External risks

A number of external risks associated with the year 2000 problem are difficult or impossible for a firm to mitigate individually. External operations risks are many and varied, ranging from power or transport failure to agents and major counterparties being affected. The recognition of these external risks led to the formation of an industry-wide Global 2000 Co-ordinating Group.

Warburg Dillon Read has been extensively involved in the establishment of this group.

The co-ordinating group consists of various members of the global financial community who have joined forces in an effort to address the year 2000 challenge. The group's aim is to identify and resource areas where co-ordinated initiatives will facilitate efforts by the global financial community to improve the readiness of global financial institutions to meet the challenges created by the year 2000 date change.

Risk management in the context of year 2000

The Global 2000 Co-ordinating Group's work on year 2000 contingency planning is based on a risk management philosophy, with contingency planning forming one part of the approach. Given the current limits on available information, and the number of permutations and combinations, it is felt that the use of a rigorous scenario approach may be premature. In addition, scenario planning is test developed on an institution-by-institution basis according to each institution's size and scope.

The group is therefore currently working on strategies that are applicable across different sizes of organisation and can be used as a basis for discussion. These include:
❑ definition of a year 2000 business planning timeline that stages events based on the likely availability of information;

---

process, it helps to think about the issue from the perspective of the shareholder. In general the shareholder will obtain information about changes in earnings on at most a quarterly basis, so we should try to align our risk measure to this frequency of data. Moreover when thinking about the acceptable frequency for exceptions we should take a sufficiently long view, which suggests that we should probably operate somewhere between a 99% confidence level for quarterly data (ie an exception once every 25 years) or a 95% interval for annual data (ie an exception once every 20 years). This then leads to our final conclusion about our risk capital process, which is:

Principle 5: the time period and confidence interval for risk aggregation should be consistent across all risk factors and be determined with reference to the shareholder's time horizon and risk tolerance.

CONCLUSION
In this section we have attempted to set out a framework that would allow us to incorporate operations risk into a risk capital allocation process in a consistent way. Without question, this remains a conceptual framework at this stage. Few, if any, firms yet have the quality of data that would allow them to measure the unexpected loss of operations risk, even at an aggregate level. Moreover, if the risk capital tool is to work effectively it will have to be possible to go beyond the aggregate level and to measure operations risk and allocate capital at the level of the individual desk or business area, as it is only when a business area is able to have an influence over its capital charge that the risk capital tool will really have the effect of "incentivising" behaviour that maximises the risk–return trade-off effectively. This implies a level of disaggregation and data integrity about operations

❑ engaging the industry in a process of building broad awareness and taking practical steps through a business readiness checklist;
❑ development of comprehensive "day zero" plans and a command centre structure to manage them;
❑ creation of a well-defined crisis management process.

The introduction of the euro and the problems of year 2000

The operations risks associated with the year 2000 are slightly different from those associated with the euro. The year 2000 problem is less of a "big bang". Many of the problems may occur when the systems have been remedied and when they are gradually brought back on line during the first and second quarters of 1999. The timescale is therefore different and there will be concentrations of changes, both internally and externally. The risk associated with the euro can be seen as

one peak, however the risk associated with the year 2000 can be seen as a series of smaller peaks, with the larger peak in the first half of 1999. The exact shape of the curve (small peaks, bell-shaped with a long tail or other) will in fact probably be different for each firm.

Figure B demonstrates what will happen if we do not control our operations risk sufficiently and do not "clean up" after each major impact.

This diagram highlights the most crucial element of these factors. The introduction of the euro and the change to the year 2000 cannot be thought of as stand-alone events. Their effect is not on just one weekend, but on the whole of the next two years. It is therefore essential that operations risk is correctly understood and controlled in all areas of the business and at all times.[1]

1 Further information is available from the group's web site: www.global2k.com

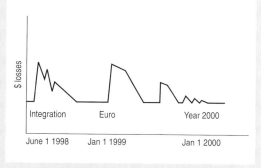

A. Tidal wave series syndrome with operations risk controlled

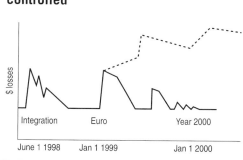

B. Tidal wave series syndrome when operations risk is not sufficiently controlled

risk, as well as the other risks in our risk categorisation, at the business area level, which in most cases goes well beyond what has been collected previously. Nevertheless, it is a goal that is certainly worth exploring as it offers the possibility of determining the true balance between

risk and return in a financial firm, where the risks to the quality of earnings are increasingly recognised to be related to factors such as operations risk as well as to the more traditional areas of credit and market risk.

1 *This definition is taken from the Basle Committee's 1994 Risk Management Guidelines for OTC Derivatives (Guidelines, Vol. 16).*

2 *For a more formal proof of this point, see the Annex to Tim Shepheard-Walwyn and Robert Litterman, 'Building a coherent risk measurement and capital optimisation model for financial firms', Federal Reserve Bank of New York, Economic Policy Review, October 1998.*

5

Measuring and Managing Operational Risk within an Integrated Risk Framework

Putting Theory into Practice

James Lam and Greg Cameron

Enterprise Risk Solutions; Fidelity Investments

Measuring and managing operational risk is one of the most important risk management issues facing corporations and financial institutions today. In the past, risk managers have focused on financial risks, which include market risks (ie exposures to price changes in the equity, interest rate, foreign exchange, commodity and real estate markets) and credit risks (ie exposures to the risk of default by borrowers, counterparties or key vendors). While advances in financial risk management have produced new tools such as value-at-risk (VAR) and credit migration models, several factors clearly demonstrate the need to include operational risk in an overall risk management framework:[1]

❑ The most significant and well-publicised losses over the last few years (eg Barings Bank) have resulted primarily from operational risks.[2]

❑ Leading corporations and financial institutions are establishing enterprise-wide risk management programmes that encompass all aspects of risk, and these programmes often identify operational risk as one of the most significant risks that the firm faces.

❑ Investment banks and insurance companies have begun to offer cost-effective integrated risk solutions such as catastrophe bonds and multi-risk insurance policies.[3]

In response to all this, risk managers are broadening their definition of risk management to include operational risk – often as a core component of an integrated risk management framework.

The purpose of this chapter is to discuss, by means of five key themes (Table 1), how operational risk management fits into just such an enterprise-wide risk management programme, and to show how we attempted to make this a reality at Fidelity.

Establishing an integrated risk management framework

An integrated risk management framework is intended to provide a unifying conceptual methodology that can be used to address any risk in any business unit, as well as the overall risks faced by the corporation. It should tackle three main issues:

❑ What are the major sources or components of risk faced by the company?

❑ What are the critical questions that senior management should ask?

❑ What are the key levers that management can use to manage risk?

COMPONENTS OF RISK

Within our broad definition of risk, which includes but goes beyond financial risks, we identify five major components:

❑ market risk;

Table 1. Five key themes

1. Establishing an integrated risk management framework
2. Developing the basic components of operational risk management
3. Implementing advanced applications in operational risk management
4. Leveraging the key trends in enterprise-wide risk management
5. Implementing enterprise-wide risk management: the Fidelity case study

---

MEASURING
AND MANAGING
OPERATIONAL
RISK WITHIN
AN INTEGRATED
RISK
FRAMEWORK

❑ credit risk;
❑ operational risk;
❑ business risk; and
❑ organisational risk.

Market risk includes client investments and our own balance-sheet and proprietary trading. Credit risk includes counterparty, settlement and lending exposures, as well as exposures to the default of critical business partners and vendors. Operational risk involves mainly "back-office" operations such as transactions processing, fund pricing, cash and securities movement, and systems. Business risk includes "front-office" business issues such as strategy, client management, product development and pricing, and distribution. Finally, organisational risk involves the company's reputation, people and skills, as well

as incentives and other aspects of the control environment.

KEY MANAGEMENT QUESTIONS
It has been said that a major element of effective management is asking the right questions. The second dimension of our framework comprises the four key questions that senior management should ask about any risk-taking activities in any business unit. We used the acronym "RISK" as a simple way to prompt these questions, which are illustrated in Figure 1 and presented in more detail in Panel 1.

LEVERS OF CONTROL
There are three levers that management can use for firm-wide risk management: increase awareness (risk awareness); mitigate risk (risk management); and increase risk transparency (risk measurement).

A high level of risk awareness should prevent many problems from occurring in the first place. In this regard, it is very important for management in any company to "walk the talk". For example, business managers will always *say* that they are committed to risk management, but what happens when a top revenue producer repeatedly violates risk management policies? Management's commitment to risk management must be communicated through words and demonstrated through actions. Programmes focused on the other two levers, risk management and risk measurement, will be discussed below.

The confluence of the five components of risk, the four key management questions in Panel 1, and the three risk management levers represents what we call the "risk framework" (Figure 2).

Develop the basic components of operational risk management

Since the late 1970s, a great deal of effort has been expended throughout the financial services industry on the measurement and management of credit and market risk. One would have difficulty finding a financial institution that believes it is unable to quantify its credit and market exposures, or which is unaware of the various tools available to reduce or modify those exposures. (This does not guarantee success in managing these risks, of course). Risk professionals are presently searching for tools to measure and modify operational risk with the same analytical objectivity that has been applied to market and credit risk.

1. The "RISK" questions

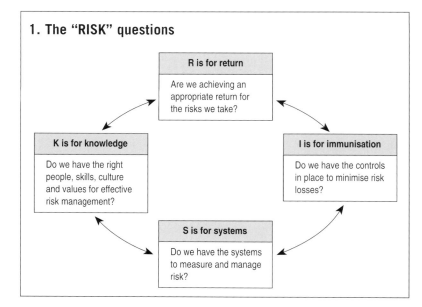

2. Risk framework

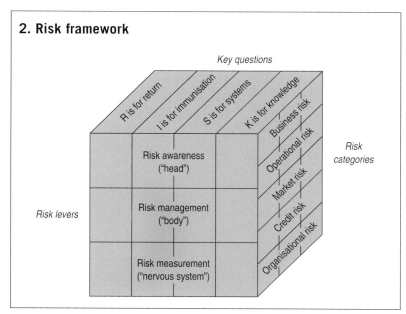

83

MEASURING
AND MANAGING
OPERATIONAL
RISK WITHIN
AN INTEGRATED
RISK
FRAMEWORK

PANEL 1

KEY "RISK" QUESTIONS FOR SENIOR MANAGEMENT

❏ *R is for return* The first question is "are we achieving an appropriate return for the risks we take?" Tools that can be used to answer this question include risk-adjusted return measurement, risk-based reserve and capital allocation, and risk-adjusted pricing models. Importantly, this question should also be asked backwards: "If we are experiencing extraordinary return or growth, what underlying risks are we assuming?" Industry problems are often preceded by periods of high profits and growth.

❏ *I is for immunisation* The second key question is "do we have the controls and limits in place to manage downside risk?" Methods used to answer this question include setting risk limits, and establishing escalation and response procedures. Market risk limits include stop-loss limits (maximum mark-to-market losses), factor sensitivity limits (the "Greeks" of the options risk manager such as delta risk), scenario limits (maximum event-dependent losses), and VAR limits (maximum loss within a specified probability interval). Credit risk limits include counterparty (actual and potential exposures), industry and country limits. Operational

risk limits involve error or exception levels beyond which management would deem the operational performance to be unacceptable. For example, some Fidelity business units establish goals and MAPs (minimum acceptable performances) for all of their key operational risk measures. In addition to setting limits for all types of risk, management should develop clear escalation procedures and risk mitigation strategies. As such, risk limits will function as "trip wires" for management communication, decision and action.

❏ *S is for system* The third key question is "do we have the systems to measure and report risk?" This question raises the need to develop the data, systems and reporting processes for firm-wide risk measurement. Issues relating to data integrity and information security should also be addressed.

❏ *K is for knowledge* The fourth question is "do we have the right people, skills, culture, and incentives for effective risk management?" This question is focused on human capital and how individuals are organised, motivated and deployed for risk management.

Some of the tools we discuss below are versions of tools that have long been applied to financial risk management, while others come from outside of the traditional risk management area.

TRANSFER BEST PRACTICES FROM QUALITY MANAGEMENT

An overall quality programme is focused not only on the delivery of product to the customer, but on the process used to generate the product. Evaluation criteria for the Malcolm Baldrige Quality Award, the US government's award for organisations with world-class quality management programmes, include several facets of the product creation and delivery process. The award's criteria are grouped into seven areas: leadership, information and analysis, strategic planning, human resources, business results, customer focus and satisfaction and process management.

These areas have long been the focus of corporations as they try to enhance profitability and growth through a disciplined approach to continuous improvement. Through their focus on

improving process performance, organisations have developed tools that can be applied to measuring and managing operational risk. Analytical tools such as process maps, histograms, Pareto analysis, and fishbone diagrams are applied regularly by quality engineers in both manufacturing and service environments – and they can be applied in financial services companies. These tools can be used to identify variables and determine causes of variation.

However, in order to use these quality tools, data must be gathered on operational performance and on key trends that could point to areas for improvement. As we describe below, our risk management programme at Fidelity gathers information both through monthly risk reporting and annual self-assessments.

CONDUCT AN ANNUAL CONTROL SELF-ASSESSMENT

The annual risk assessment (the global risk review) is our opportunity for gathering data about the known risks throughout the company. The data we require include reports of losses and incidents that have occurred over the past

MEASURING
AND MANAGING
OPERATIONAL
RISK WITHIN
AN INTEGRATED
RISK
FRAMEWORK

year, as well as an infrastructure survey, which tells us about the policies and procedures that each business unit had in place during the year to react to an incident. The infrastructure survey also provides information about the business unit's risk management staff and their escalation procedures.

We decided that the most efficient way to gather these data was to allow each business unit to conduct a self-assessment, because this also gives the businesses an opportunity to re-evaluate their risks.

Our biggest challenge when devising the global risk review was to create a set of universal questions that were general enough to apply to all business units, but specific enough to gather meaningful risk information. We did not want to provide an opportunity for a business to say that the question was not applicable. We also learned throughout our three-year programme to ask only for the information we truly needed. (Over three years, we reduced the number of survey questions by 50%).

We have also become more efficient in collecting the survey results. Originally, we sent out word processed documents and asked each unit to complete a form. Now, we use intranet technology to collect the information and to download it directly into a database for analysis. We have found that this saves time, and the information is also more relevant and fresh, since it can incorporate organisational changes or the introduction of a new product or service. We are also able to use this information to perform year-over-year analysis as a measure of our progress.

ACCOUNT FOR OPERATIONAL LOSSES
The global risk review initiated the gathering of data about actual losses across all of Fidelity's business units. However, since this was done at the end of the year, and relied on ad hoc processes, this method probably captured only about 70–80% of the losses that were actually occurring. And since all losses affect the firm's profitability and, more importantly, provide valuable lessons to be learned, we decided it was vital to create a more efficient way to record and track these data.

We worked with our accounting department to establish one section of the company's general ledger to track market, credit and operational losses (Table 2). We established a process of accounting that captured only economic losses as they were incurred. Reserve provisioning, or any other type of "smoothing", was accounted for outside of the loss accounts. There is an accounting discipline for reserving for bad debt as the revenue is declared but, for our purposes, we only wished to capture the account write-off when it was an economic loss. As one can imagine, this created some additional accounting entries in order to remain compliant with accounting principles, but it allowed us to segregate accounting expenses from economic loss. As we will see later, these data are valuable in forecasting loss reserves and allocating capital because they reflect the volatility of loss.

ESTABLISH A MONTHLY REPORTING PROCESS
Once we created and set into motion our annual reporting process, we decided it would be advantageous to collect risk information on a monthly basis. Considering the diversity of Fidelity's businesses, we again needed to establish a reporting method that was general enough to apply to each unit, but standardised enough so that we had a consistent reporting format that could be easily reviewed by senior management.

The result was a two-page template (Figure 3a–b). Page one consisted of three elements. The first was gross losses, in which the loss numbers from the general ledger were reconciled. The second provided details on all material risk incidents, based on that business unit's escalation procedures. The third was a management assessment – a discussion by the unit's management of its major risk issues. We wanted a way to quantify the answer to the question: "What was keeping them up at night?" This format was self-enforcing because if the management assessment did not correlate with the first two items on the page, it told us that the management team was either being dishonest about its risk incidents or did not understand the business well enough to respond and plan appropriately.

The second page of our template was mainly quantitative. It established our core risk measures – the risk indicators that we had determined should be tracked on a monthly basis. This page also highlighted our key risk trends, or trouble indicators. This area changes each month, as different problem areas become apparent. For example, reconciliation might have been the big problem in January, while by February the trade errors across several business units might be creating many operational losses. This area of the report is also used to update the operating

85

MEASURING
AND MANAGING
OPERATIONAL
RISK WITHIN
AN INTEGRATED
RISK
FRAMEWORK

Table 2. Loss categories and descriptions

Operational losses

As-ifs – general loss	Actual loss incurred for delayed processing of instruction to buy or sell a mutual fund share or other security. Losses result if the current price is different from the price the transaction was to be processed at, ie trading errors
As-ofs – systems loss	Actual loss incurred for as-of transactions required due to disruption in trading and support systems that made processing the transaction in a timely manner impossible.
Billing errors loss	Actual loss incurred for incorrectly calculated bills or items not billed in error.
Fines loss	Actual loss incurred (ie payment) for regulatory and civil fines imposed due to an unlawful Fidelity action.
Fraud	Actual loss incurred for fraud perpetrated by a Fidelity employee or a party external to Fidelity, ie customer, vendor, etc.
Goodwill adjustments loss	Actual loss incurred for reimbursing for what the customer claims occurred due to Fidelity's error.
Legal settlement loss	Actual loss incurred as part of the settlement of a legal action or customer arbitration. Does not necessarily need to be a judgement against the firm, action may be settled between the involved parties.
Other unspecified loss	Actual loss incurred for other figures not described by the submitting business unit.
Pricing errors loss	Actual loss incurred for incorrect pricing of shares due to errors in the valuing of the underlying assets. If transactions occurred on the mispriced shares the firm could be responsible for reimbursing the funds.
Reconciliation errors loss	Actual loss incurred resulting from inaccurate or untimely reconciliation of bank and ledger accounts.
Theft loss	Actual loss incurred for company assets stolen.
Operational loss recoveries	Recoveries for operational losses previously recognised. Could include compensation from third parties or insurance claims. Recoveries may be from a different accounting period than that in which the loss was recorded.

Credit losses

Bad debt charges – direct loss	Actual loss/write-off due to a debtor's inability or unwillingness to repay money owed to Fidelity.
Miscellaneous bad debt loss	Actual loss/write-off of small balances in which the company/person owing the money was not recorded or maintained.
Service provider losses (external)	Actual loss/write-off of an investment or loan Fidelity has made to a vendor that will not be recovered.
Bad debt recovery	Money recovered from accounts previously written-off. Recoveries could include money or assets recovered from the original counterparty, but could also include third-party payments, including insurance. Recoveries may be from a different accounting period than that for which the loss was recorded.

Market losses

Foreign exchange loss	Actual loss due to relative changes in currencies where a change in the value of the firm's assets was required and charged to operations.
Principal trading loss	Actual loss incurred for differences in value between the purchase price and the sale price (or market value) of a security which was held in the firm's trading account. Examples include: OTC market making, fixed income trading.
Underwriting losses	Actual loss on positions held as part of underwriting an issuance.
Market loss recovery	Recoveries for market losses previously recognised. Could include compensation from third parties or insurance claims. Recoveries may be from a different accounting period than that in which the loss was recorded.

committee about an earlier trouble sign that has been brought back to an acceptable level.

SET OPERATIONAL RISK GOALS AND MAPS

Collecting data about past incidents taught us a lot about each business unit's risks and the collective risks for Fidelity. However, without the establishment of goals to work towards, the data might not have improved future performance. For us, an operational goal is defined as the "stretch target" that we are trying to achieve for a particular process. We also establish a

minimal accepted performance (MAP) for each measure. We then apply the concept of goals and MAPs to a set of operating metrics, establishing the optimal and minimal performance standards for each operation.

For example, when looking at a trade process, the error rate should be no greater than our established MAP, which for this example we will set at 0.2%. Our goal may be 0.1%, so if the unit is operating within 0.1% and 0.2%, its process is acceptable. If the error rate rises above 0.2%, we know there is a problem and

86

MEASURING
AND MANAGING
OPERATIONAL
RISK WITHIN
AN INTEGRATED
RISK
FRAMEWORK

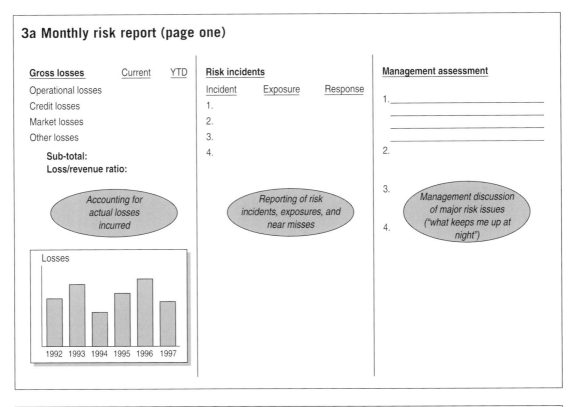

3a Monthly risk report (page one)

Gross losses	Current	YTD
Operational losses		
Credit losses		
Market losses		
Other losses		
Sub-total:		
Loss/revenue ratio:		

Accounting for actual losses incurred

Risk incidents		
Incident	Exposure	Response
1.		
2.		
3.		
4.		

Reporting of risk incidents, exposures, and near misses

Management assessment

1. _____
   _____
   _____
   _____
2.
3.
4.

Management discussion of major risk issues ("what keeps me up at night")

Losses

1992 1993 1994 1995 1996 1997

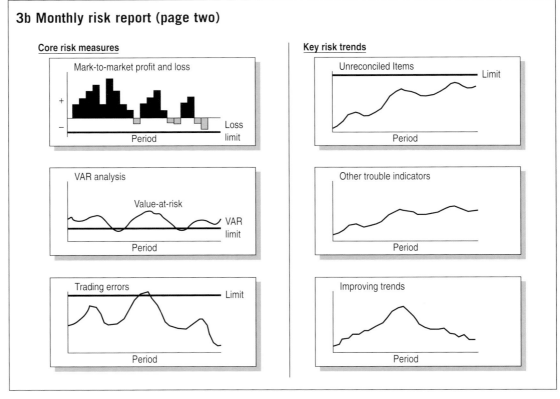

3b Monthly risk report (page two)

Core risk measures

Mark-to-market profit and loss
+
−
Period
Loss limit

VAR analysis
Value-at-risk
VAR limit
Period

Trading errors
Limit
Period

Key risk trends

Unreconciled Items
Limit
Period

Other trouble indicators
Period

Improving trends
Period

we must investigate its root cause and set up action plans to fix it. If a business unit is continually performing better than the goal it has set, it will most likely need to raise the bar, so that the unit can focus on improving its process over time.

ORGANISE CONSULTING AND/OR "TURBO TEAMS"

A consulting or "turbo team" is a group that is called into action when a unit is performing below its MAP. The team is cross-functional, meaning that it includes a representative from

87

MEASURING
AND MANAGING
OPERATIONAL
RISK WITHIN
AN INTEGRATED
RISK
FRAMEWORK

CALCULATION OF LOSS RESERVES AND CAPITAL

Suppose that over the last few years a business has incurred the losses and revenue shown in the table.

From the table we can estimate a distribution based on our few data points. Although the number of data elements is small, this example will work for illustrative purposes. The distribution from our sample would look something like the figure.

Now, this all suggests that if the same business had forecasted revenues of $175 million for 1999, a reserve of 5.8% or $10.15 million might be established to cover *expected* operational loss. Additionally, capital of $16.8 million ($2\sigma$ [2 * 4.8%] * $175 million) would be allocated to cover *unexpected* losses. Altogether, this business would have $10.15 million in reserves and $16.8 million in capital, giving it a total of $26.95 million to cover expected and unexpected loss.

In other words, based on history, we can say with a confidence level of 97.5% that the business will be able to cover its potential losses during 1999. (The 97.5% figure represents two standard deviations; the level of confidence we desire for our upper boundary of reserves determines the number of standard deviations from the mean).

These calculations comprise only the required reserves and capital for operational losses. We would also need to calculate the capital required for credit and market risk exposures. The limitation in our method is it does not reflect correlation between these exposures. A more precise method would identify these correlations and reflect them in the calculations.

Revenue and operational losses: an illustrative example

Year	Loss $ million	Revenue $ million	Loss/revenue (%)
1994	15.4	120.3	12.8
1995	2.3	135.5	1.7
1996	8.2	138.9	5.9
1997	1.6	142.7	1.1
1998	12.3	153.8	8.0

Weighted average	*5.8%*
Standard deviation	*4.8%*

Loss distribution: an illustrative example*

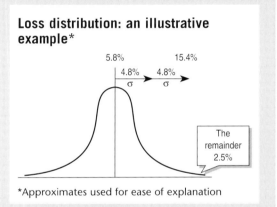

*Approximates used for ease of explanation

different disciplines across the organisation. For example, a team may include a person from operations who is involved with the process, a sales/client services agent who understands the customer impact, and a finance or risk management consultant who can work within the framework of controls and metrics. This "turbo team" is set up to address a specific issue in a short time frame of about one to two weeks. Once it has investigated the operational problem and the risks it is posing for the company, the team reports back to the business management and recommends a solution.

Implement advanced applications in operational risk metrics

After the data has been collected, and resources have been mobilised to analyse and understand how the exposures might affect our operations,

one can begin to think how else one might use the information to run the business.

If operational risk exposure can be measured, then this information must be incorporated into the kind of integrated risk framework that we discussed above. If operational losses are to be expected, at least in the short run, then planning for those losses through reserves will decrease the volatility in earnings. If the volatility of loss can be measured, it can also be employed when assigning capital to the firm – an illustrative example of this is provided in Panel 2. Business performance can then be measured taking into account the capital deployed. By applying this type of approach, operational risk can begin to be managed in the ways in which credit and market exposures are currently measured and managed within the integrated risk framework.

88

**MEASURING
AND MANAGING
OPERATIONAL
RISK WITHIN
AN INTEGRATED
RISK
FRAMEWORK**

ESTABLISH LOSS RESERVES

After loss information that can be trended over a series of periods has been collected, it can then be compared to revenue or transactions. This ratio can then be applied to forecasted revenue (or transactions) and capital can be reserved to cover these losses over the period. This capital is, in effect, being set aside to cover "expected loss".

The degree of segregation that is established in the loss accounts determines how specific the reserve is to each different type of loss. When deciding how detailed the segregation should be in loss reserves, it is important to remember the operational impact of creating specific reserves for each type of loss. Since the reserve will be created using average loss based on historical relations, the more specific the reserve categories the greater chance that each loss reserve category will deviate from the losses that are actually incurred. These deviations will need to be analysed and reconciled to explain the differences. Put simply, the fewer reserve accounts that are established, the less book-keeping and entry correction will be required at the end of the period.

The variation of loss-to-revenue that the firm has experienced historically will determine how much of the loss exposure can be covered using reserves, and how much additional capital will need to allocated.

ALLOCATE OPERATIONAL RISK CAPITAL

If the loss-to-revenue has traditionally been very consistent, the "expected loss" reserves should be large enough to absorb losses over the period. If, however, losses have been lumpy or experienced rarely, capital may need to be dedicated to absorb the unexpected loss.

Variation can be measured in the deviation around the historical loss-to-revenue ratio. Measuring the dollar value of loss only may be misleading, especially in a growing or contracting business. Basing the loss calculation on revenue, and calculating the mean and standard deviation of the loss-to-revenue, allows the risk manager to apply the figure that is output regardless of any growth that might occur in the business. After calculating the standard deviation, capital can be allocated based on the confidence level that the management requires. For example, a single-tail 97.5% confidence level would be two standard deviations larger than the mean.

To the extent that it is applied to an entire firm, or to a whole business, the approach we have outlined above represents a high-level attempt to quantify operational risk exposure. Depending upon the nature of the business, it may be useful to bring the analysis down a level and to apply this methodology to individual business processes, as opposed to the aggregate business.

There is also the question of how to cope with the "tail" of the probability curve, that is, the 2.5% of the distribution that is not adequately reserved for using this methodology. It is unlikely that it would make sense to increase our standard deviations to incorporate more of the tail. On the other hand, management might, quite sensibly, be concerned about the kind of improbable but severe losses that occur every 40 years or so. In order to ensure that the firm is adequately protected against this kind of "tail risk", we should prepare liquidity lines that would allow the business to remain in operation even after a catastrophic loss. These liquidity lines can be arranged as self-insurance, through pre-secured credit lines, or through more expensive catastrophic insurance. Of course, establishing bank credit lines will not smooth out any of the income volatility. However, they would allow the business to remain in operation and meet customer commitments.

INTEGRATE OPERATIONAL, MARKET AND CREDIT RISK

In recent years, market and credit exposures have come to be measured in most financial institutions by means of a value-at-risk calculation. For example, based on historical price movements, the financial exposure of a firm to a market position can be calculated to a given confidence level. Using the process demonstrated above, a reserve and capital allocation can also be calculated for operational exposure. The three exposures – market, credit and operational – can be calculated separately and then incorporated into a single capital allocation for the business enterprise. (To do this in a sophisticated way will eventually involve factoring in the correlation effects of the overall portfolio of risks). Limits may be established for each exposure, but a limit exception process might also be established to allow management the ability to exceed those limits, within certain guidelines.

MEASURE RISK-ADJUSTED PERFORMANCE

After establishing exposure limits and assigning capital to cover exposure, performance can be measured in relation to risk capital. The net

89

MEASURING
AND MANAGING
OPERATIONAL
RISK WITHIN
AN INTEGRATED
RISK
FRAMEWORK

income of the operation can be measured as a percentage of risk capital. Similar to a return-on-investment calculation, return-on-risk capital is the return divided by the assigned capital.

This process allows business managers to differentiate between business opportunities based on their ratio of risk to reward. For example, if two opportunities offer the same relative return on investment, the business manager might be indifferent about which to invest in. Alternatively, if after measuring returns on a risk-adjusted basis a material difference between the opportunities becomes apparent, the manager will naturally select the investment that offers the highest return on his risk capital. In many banking businesses, opportunities that *seem* highly profitable may not turn out to be nearly so attractive when the volatility of loss is accounted for in terms of capital reserves.

ESTABLISH RISK-ADJUSTED PRICING
After measuring business opportunities based on risk-adjusted returns, a firm may decide that it needs to review the pricing of its products. The best way to begin this task is to establish the target levels of returns that the firm expects each product or process to achieve. If these are not achieved in terms of the risk-adjusted returns, the firm is faced with two main options:
❏ price the product more appropriately; or
❏ take steps to reduce the risks associated with the product.

Interestingly, if the returns are much *larger* than expected, this may indicate that the market is inefficient and that over time there will be downward price pressure. Alternatively, this result might be a warning sign that the risks have been understated through some weakness in the data or methodology.

BENCHMARK "PEER GROUP" PERFORMANCE
A significant amount of loss information can be found in a public company's financial statements. In the footnotes that provide information about the calculation of the bad debt loss reserves, write-offs by year will be detailed. Although the footnotes generally do not include operational losses, assumptions can sometimes be made from information that is available through trade organisations. As a result, a loss-to-revenue number can be approximated for businesses that lie within the "peer group" of any company.

Another valuable number to calculate for any "peer group" analysis is the operating margin of

these businesses, which will also be available in the financial statements. The operating margin and the loss-to-revenue can then be compared, and one can even create a relationship matrix graphically. An efficient frontier can then be generated for the "peer group" similar to that described in Panel 3.

Leveraging the key trends in enterprise-wide risk management
The management of operational, market and credit risks within an enterprise-wide risk management framework is one of the most important topics in the field of risk management today. A number of leading organisations developed this vision years ago and have already put in place the people, systems and processes to implement enterprise-wide risk management. They are, in many ways, ahead of the game.

Three key trends seem likely to reshape the risk management landscape in the years ahead:
❏ *Integration of control functions* The integration of operational, credit and market risk management can be thought of as simply the first step towards integrated risk management. Logically, the next step would be the integration of other control-oriented functions within an organisation, including audit, compliance, security, legal and finance. These other functions have important oversight responsibilities as well as powerful tools that are complimentary to the tools used in risk management. For example, the audit function conducts extensive and detailed examination of financial and operational controls, but their presence is episodic (eg annual or bi-annual reviews). On the other hand, risk management provides ongoing risk monitoring and reporting of risk exposures against policy limits, but their investigations do not usually go very deeply into operational issues. Therefore, the coordination and/or integration of risk management and audit activities, along with other control functions, is likely to improve the efficiency and effectiveness of an organisation's control environment. Such improvement may include more accurate risk identification and assessment, more concise risk management reporting and, most importantly, more effective execution of risk mitigation strategies.
❏ *Integration of financial and insurance products* As companies integrate their risk management and control activities, there is a corresponding integration of the kind of products offered by investment banks and insurance firms to help them solve their risk

90

MEASURING
AND MANAGING
OPERATIONAL
RISK WITHIN
AN INTEGRATED
RISK
FRAMEWORK

RISK/RETURN ANALYSIS – IDENTIFYING THE NATURE OF A BUSINESS

The graph below depicts the "risk versus return" of various corporations, based on the premise that the return of a corporation can be measured by means of its operating margin and that its risk can be measured in terms of loss-to-revenue. If we accept this premise we can begin to construct an "efficient frontier" model similar to that used for investment portfolio evaluation.

For our example we have captured the operating results and losses from publicly released financial statements and corresponding footnotes. Without exception, each of the highlighted companies' losses was comprised exclusively of credit losses, since operational losses are not detailed in the financial footnotes. In the future, however, companies can look forward to similar expressions of their risk/reward profile that are based on all sorts of risks, including operational risks.

Graphs such as these will point up some interesting questions for corporations, similar to those faced by portfolio managers. Do I want to be in a business that

enjoys large margins (return) or do I want to be in a business with low percentage of loss (risk)? Most business managers would wish to be in a business that enjoys large margins and low losses, but in an efficient market that scenario is unlikely. Businesses should make an informed decision on their appetite for risk and make an explicit statement of the losses they are willing to incur to achieve a desired return.

These loss expectations, generated using methodologies such as that described in Panel 2, can be used to create loss reserves to reduce income volatility. These statements also empower management to operate their business within the prescribed loss and return boundaries. If the business operates within these boundaries, than it should be achieving an adequate return base on its perceived risk. If either the risk or the return is materially better or worse than expected, than management should re-evaluate its loss/return statement.

Risk/return analysis*

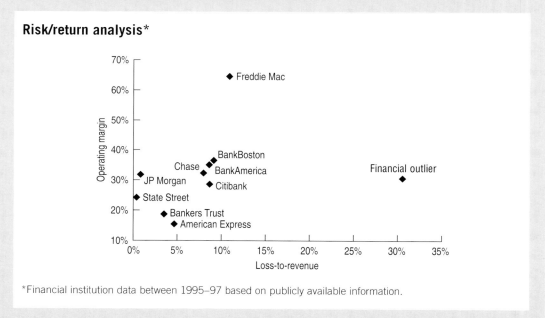

*Financial institution data between 1995–97 based on publicly available information.

problems. Such integrated risk management products include multi-risk insurance policies, hybrid derivative products, and catastrophe bonds. The trend towards integrated risk products is hastened not only by the demands from clients for enterprise-wide risk solutions, but also by the consolidation of commercial banks, investment banks, mutual funds companies and insurance firms. True, the market for integrated

risk products is at a very early stage, and before it can mature and grow, a significant amount of client education and product standardisation (both in terms of structure and pricing) is required. Nonetheless, over time the integration of financial and insurance products offers risk managers significant opportunities to manage their risk profiles in a comprehensive and cost-effective manner.

91

MEASURING
AND MANAGING
OPERATIONAL
RISK WITHIN
AN INTEGRATED
RISK
FRAMEWORK

❏ *Integration of risk management and business management* Beyond the integration of control activities and risk management products, we believe the greatest opportunity for risk managers to add value to their companies will be the application of risk management to business management. In the past, risk managers have focused on hazard or "downside" risk management, including the purchase of insurance and the reduction of significant financial risk exposures. Today, risk managers are also focused on reducing the volatility of business performance by using techniques such as risk limits and value-at-risk calculations. In the future, we believe best-practice companies will apply risk management to the overall business management of the firm. For example, senior management will use their risk management tools to answer critical strategic and business questions such as:

❏ What business strategies should we pursue given our core competencies in risk management?

❏ How should we structure and price our products and services given the underlying risks and the required risk capital?

❏ How would potential acquisitions affect our overall risk profile, and what risks of the acquisition should we retain and what risks should be mitigate by means of the insurance and/or capital markets?

❏ What organisational and technical skills do we need to successfully execute our business and risk management strategies?

As a result of these trends, risk management as a function is likely to evolve from a defensive mechanism to an offensive weapon. More importantly, senior management will be able to maximise the return on their significant investments in risk management staff and systems.

In closing our general discussion, we would like to leave you with a final thought. Over the long term, the only alternative to risk management is crisis management. In risk management, you are managing your risks. In crisis management, your risks are managing you. More importantly, the latter is much more painful, time consuming and expensive.

A case study: implementing enterprise-wide risk management at Fidelity

The purpose of this section is to discuss in more detail the steps that we took at Fidelity Investments to implement a firm-wide risk management programme.

The global risk management organisation at Fidelity Investments started as a new corporate function at the end of 1995, with the objective of building a firm-wide risk management infrastructure and ensuring that best practices are in place for managing all types of risk across the company.

In the first 30 days, we drafted a three-year plan that included the following components:

❏ Assess management requirements and expectations.

❏ Promote risk awareness among senior management.

❏ Develop an integrated risk management framework.

❏ Identify firm-wide risks and implement risk mitigation plans.

❏ Increase risk transparency through reporting systems and processes.

Below, we discuss how we implemented each of these ambitions.

ASSESS MANAGEMENT REQUIREMENTS

As a new corporate risk management function, one of our first objectives was to ensure that the firm-wide risk management programme met the requirements and expectations of senior management. There is no "one size fits all" risk management programme: the approach at each firm must be consistent with that company's culture and business practices.

To better understand the company culture and management's expectations, we met with the top 100 executives in one-on-one meetings during the first three months of operations. These executives included company presidents, CFOs, and senior risk managers, and represented the key stakeholders of the firm-wide risk management programme. In these meetings, we discussed business strategies, past problems and current risk issues, and exchanged ideas for risk management. These meetings resulted in two tangible benefits. Firstly, we gained a greater appreciation of Fidelity's decentralised business culture and, because Fidelity business units are ultimately accountable for business and risk performance, we realised that the firm-wide risk management programme must have the support and participation of this group of key stakeholders.

Secondly, these meetings also provided senior management input into the final three-year plan for global risk management. This plan included not only the major components for firm-wide risk management that we want to put in place

MEASURING
AND MANAGING
OPERATIONAL
RISK WITHIN
AN INTEGRATED
RISK
FRAMEWORK

over the three-year period, but also the specific milestones by quarter for the first year. For example, in the first quarter of 1996 we accomplished four key milestones:

❑ we obtained support for the three-year plan from the operations control steering committee (OCSC), a group of eight of the company's most senior executives organised to sponsor the firm-wide risk management initiative;

❑ we organised a small but highly experienced global risk management team made up of internal and external hires with skills in market risk, credit risk, operational risk and systems project management;

❑ we established the global risk oversight committee, which includes the senior risk executives from the businesses and the heads of other control functions such as audit, compliance, finance, legal and security; and

❑ we developed a formal programme to promote risk awareness among senior management.

PROMOTE RISK AWARENESS
The cornerstone of the risk awareness programme is the global risk forum, a regular meeting of the group of 100 key stakeholders. The first meeting was dedicated to discussing the lessons learned from the well-publicised problems experienced by other financial institutions. We reviewed case studies of what happened at these companies, analysed some of the common themes and underlying root causes, and concluded with a discussion of key lessons learned.

In subsequent global risk forum meetings, we discussed lessons learned from our internal risk management problems and how we went about fixing them. Also in these meetings, the business units discussed their risk management programmes, initiatives, and systems so that best practices could be shared across the company. To gain an external perspective, we invited senior executives and recognised industry leaders from other financial institutions for round-table discussions of their risk management approaches. Two agenda items are regularly included in the global risk forum. One is opening remarks made by a senior executive, such as Fidelity's chairman or an OCSC member, to set the tone from the top regarding senior management's commitment to the risk management process. The other regular agenda item is an update on firm-wide risk management initiatives to show progress against the three-year plan and to ensure continued support and participation by the key stakeholders.

In addition to the global risk forum, we organised awareness programmes for individual business units and corporate functions such as finance, compliance and human resources. We also worked with business units and human resources to ensure that the individual accountabilities for risk management were understood and that incentives were appropriately linked to those accountabilities. One of the key objectives of the global risk forum and other awareness programs is to educate and train senior managers on an integrated framework for risk management, including specific tools, methodologies and applications.

DEVELOP AN INTEGRATED RISK MANAGEMENT FRAMEWORK
We reviewed the various risk management frameworks developed by consultants and industry groups (eg G30, COSO, etc) but decided to develop our own – as described in some detail earlier in this chapter. Essentially, the framework was designed to address the risk management issue from a business management perspective and, at the same time, to unify the key principles advocated by the other frameworks.

The development and implementation of our "risk framework" enabled us to accomplish the following objectives:

❑ Establish a common methodology and language about risk.

❑ Apply a disciplined approach to ensure all risks are being addressed.

❑ Provide a consistent set of tools for risk assessment and training purposes.

IDENTIFY AND MITIGATE RISKS
To identify firm-wide risk, we developed the global risk review, an annual self-assessment process completed by each of 40 business units. In the global risk review, business units are asked to define their "top 10" risks, as well as the existing controls and planned initiatives to manage those risks. They are also asked to quantify and analyse their risk losses and incidents. The individual assessments are then compiled to produce a firm-wide analysis of major risks, risk losses and trends, and actual incidents. The firm-wide risk results are reviewed with independent corporate functions such as finance, audit, and compliance to ensure the quality of the information.

Based on the results of this firm-wide risk report, the global risk management team would focus on specific business units or shared risk issues. These projects include more in-depth risk

93

MEASURING
AND MANAGING
OPERATIONAL
RISK WITHIN
AN INTEGRATED
RISK
FRAMEWORK

PANEL 4

RISK MANAGEMENT PROJECT RESULTS

In 1996 Global Risk Management teamed with a Fidelity business unit to perform a detailed risk assessment and provide recommendations on how to manage these risks. The project scope included all facets of the business from market strategy to operations and included input from all functions, business partners and external clients.

From this assessment, documents were constructed detailing business processes, recommendations and action plans. These documents were reviewed with senior management, and the "ownership" of them was then passed on to the business risk managers.

The project identified a number of best practices gathered from inside Fidelity and from our business partners. These were shared with management and many were included in the final recommendations. Some of the most notable included the documentation in a log of losses greater than $5,000. This log included root causes and the controls required to prevent similar incidents in the future. Senior management began to review these logs monthly.

Also included in the recommendations were improvements that needed to be made to risk reporting. This meant not only the documentation of incidents but also tracking operational and system exposures through daily flash reports. This reporting led to a greater awareness of key risks, and losses have decreased substantially (see Figure). Using 1995 as the base year, losses declined 85% for 1996, 1997 and 1998. This reduction of losses represents a saving of over a million dollars a year for the business unit.

Risk event log

Event	$ loss	Root causes	Controls needed

Gross losses

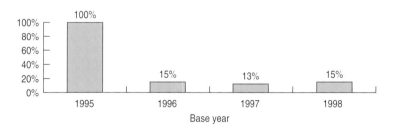

assessments, as well as specific action plans and accountabilities to mitigate risk for the targeted business units and risk issues. Panel 4 provides a specific example.

While the global risk review provided us with a disciplined firm-wide process for risk assessment, we needed to develop more timely risk information and reporting for senior management.

IMPROVE RISK REPORTING SYSTEMS AND PROCESSES
One of the key issues we needed to address was how to establish a consistent risk reporting framework for 40 different and diverse business units. These units range from mutual fund and brokerage operations to venture capital and international businesses. With the objective of reporting consistent high-level risk information

to senior management, we developed the two-page monthly report template described earlier in this chapter (see Figures 3a–b).

To support firm-wide risk measurement and reporting, we are implementing two major risk systems. One is the global risk MIS, a Web-based intranet application that will automate the firm-wide risk reporting process and provide real-time information on risk exposures, losses and incidents. We are also incorporating databases for best practices and lessons learned into the global risk MIS because we want to facilitate interactive communication of risk issues and approaches. Finally, we will apply "push technology" so that significant losses, exposures and incidents will be communicated to senior executives via the intranet without requiring them to log into the global risk MIS.

MEASURING
AND MANAGING
OPERATIONAL
RISK WITHIN
AN INTEGRATED
RISK
FRAMEWORK

The second system is GRIP (global risk information platform), which is a financial risk aggregation and reporting system. Many of the business units have developed their own financial risk systems designed for their businesses. However, to aggregate firm-wide financial risk, we must establish consistency across these systems, such as common data conventions, VAR methodologies, and counterparty and security mapping rules. The GRIP system is designed to establish a common linkage across these systems so that we can aggregate and report firm-wide financial risk. The global risk MIS and GRIP represent the core technology infrastructure for firm-wide risk measurement and reporting.

1 *Operational risk is often defined as exposures to a failure in people, process or system. While some define operational risk as all risks that are not market or credit risks, we break risks down into five key categories: business risk, operational risk, market risk, credit risk and organisational risk.*

2 *See detailed descriptions in Chapter 9. Some losses involve two or more contributing risk factors. In these cases, it is useful to identify the "first order" risk, or the primary root cause.*

3 *See "Who Needs Derivatives?", Forbes, April 21, 1997.*

6

Minimising Operational Risk in Financial Conglomerates

Thomas C. Donahoe

Metropolitan Life

Operational risks cannot be avoided. They are inherent in virtually every business environment, and some types of operational losses are a daily occurrence. The common pitfalls of operational risk often build up over a long period. Transaction errors, for example, tend to occur quite frequently and the losses are usually small.[1] Like other operational errors, they are typically the result of human nature – lack of oversight or inattention – or a structural gap in controls. Their frequency lulls managers into a false complacency. Often, insufficient attention is paid to near misses. The true risks a business has been running only become apparent in a crisis situation.

The underlying causes of operational risk range from insufficient staffing and training to untested processes and lack of reporting, feedback and escalation procedures. It is difficult to guard against moral hazard and it is virtually impossible to prevent a conspiracy of two or more individuals; this is usually detected *post facto*. Serial bungling and managerial inattentiveness are also typical factors in the run-up to a large operational loss.

In the current environment of value-at-risk numbers and risk toolkits, clichés and buzzwords have often substituted for serious, reflective thought about operational risk. There are no magic solutions to the problem it poses. Instead, it is necessary to focus attention and management effort on the less glamorous but highly vulnerable aspects of the financial services business: transaction processes, legal agreements, compliance, credit standards, disclosure, and corporate governance.

Each organisation is unique but financial conglomerates share many common risks. This enables us to create a consistent analytical framework for controlling risks. This chapter focuses on minimising operational risk in a financial conglomerate, with a special emphasis on maintaining adequate controls during a merger. It presents practical solutions to common operational risks, focusing on specific problem areas, and has four main themes:

❑ review of the recent operational environment: mega-bank mergers;
❑ the nature of operational risk;
❑ the proposed framework for operational risk control (see Panel 2);
❑ identification of problem areas and some practical solutions.

The reader should come away from this chapter both with practical suggestions on how to minimise risk and, equally important, a more thorough understanding of the relevant issues and a framework to guide the process. Naturally, each organisation will need to tailor its own solutions from the recommendations made here and in other chapters of this book.

Review of the recent environment: mega-bank mergers

Large banks have been uniting domestically in mega-bank mergers throughout the 1990s. In 1998, the top five US banks held a quarter of all domestic commercial banking assets, double the amount held in 1980. The top 100 US banks held three-quarters of domestic bank assets in 1998, up from one half in 1980.[2] This "urge to merge" has expanded from the US to Europe – witness the intra-country merging of Swiss banks and German banks.

The financial world is now poised to move beyond the mega-bank merger. This trend is likely to lead to cross-border mergers, including mergers across political and linguistic boundaries, following the lead of the drug and automobile industries. There are also likely to be cross-industry mergers involving a combination of banks, insurance companies and retail brokers in the style of the Citigroup merger.

The melding of commercial and investment banking, retail brokerage, insurance, and money management into a single corporate family heralds a new age of the financial conglomerate – the age of the so-called "financial supermarket". Sceptics might regard it as a false dawn, however.

Arguably the US has experienced analogous combinations before, notably the Shearson/Lehman/Amex and Sears/Dean Witter/Allstate alliances. In the late 1980s these firms tried to combine credit card, retail brokerage, banking, insurance, and consumer marketing to harness perceived synergies and cross-selling potential. These combinations failed to achieve their ambitious goals for a variety of reasons. Chief amongst them were differences in corporate culture, internal conflicts, regulatory hurdles, consumer resistance and general economic conditions. Had these combinations been less ambitious in scale, and had they occurred in a different environment and with a more receptive client base, the results might have been far different.

WHY ARE THEY MERGING NOW?
The main reasons offered for this new wave of "financial supermarkets" are:
❑ the globalisation of markets;
❑ the need for advanced technologies;
❑ the quest for economies of scale;
❑ stiff competitive pressures;
❑ a belief that you cannot "grow into" these businesses;[3] and
❑ the abundance of stock options and the "empire building" mentality that exists in US executive suites.[4]

What is different today? Today, technology is commonplace and widely accepted by the investing public. Investors are widely involved in world markets, reaction times are faster and trading volumes are enormous. Workers have become more financially sophisticated and are responsible for planning their financial future to a greater extent. The stock of financial assets is now larger than that of tangible assets for the first time in history.[5]

Regulators are actively accommodating evolving industry structures. Given the confluence of these special factors, the likelihood of success for organisations such as the new Citigroup is greatly enhanced. One key problem remains:

how to deal with operational risks both before and after the merger.

In the event of a merger, the short-term solution to risk control is often merely to increase the size of the risk management unit or the frequency of reports. This only reinforces managers' and regulators' illusion that risk management is just a case of the status quo writ large. In fact, this is not the case. Risks may be less transparent because they may be reported on a consolidated basis without sufficient detail or without sufficient information about their context. In some cases, hedging activity is reduced as employees worry about being "second guessed" by new management. Proper internal control often does not really start until business managers sit down with the new departments and lines of business and start to experience the work processes.

REGULATORY CONSIDERATIONS
Financial conglomerates operate in uncertain regulatory environments. Conflicting oversight and competing regulatory controls could impose burdens on merged companies. Regulators may feel their turf is threatened by an entity that crosses over into different regulatory areas. Data become less transparent as the giants in industry extend beyond state and national borders and as information is reported in an aggregated fashion. Disclosure is complicated because it often occurs on a consolidated basis and is presented by legal entity and not by risk exposure. One recommendation is for "ongoing improvements in cross-border information sharing ... and it should be paired with a focus ... on risk types rather than on corporate entities."[6]

The Securities and Exchange Commission (SEC) generally focuses on the adequacy of disclosure, the Fed and Office of the Comptroller of the Currency (OCC) on banking safety and soundness, and insurance regulators on solvency. When a crisis hits, however, regulators are not averse to taking an expansive view of their area of purview. When Bankers Trust settled legal actions with Proctor & Gamble, the bank paid a fine to the SEC as well as to the Commodity Futures Trading Commission (CFTC). One leading legal commentator expressed scepticism about whether the CFTC had clear jurisdiction in the sale of OTC derivatives in that case.[7]

OPERATIONAL CONTROL AND MERGERS: TYPICAL PROBLEMS

Personnel

❑ After a merger: "Turmoil at the acquired bank is inevitable, as executives fire some workers, reassign others, reorganise management and indoctrinate a work force to a new corporate culture".[1] Steps need to be taken to identify and address operational risk exposures arising from this.

❑ The winning side in a merger may not value advice from the losing side or short timers. This was exemplified by a famous fiasco in a major railway merger. Engineers from the acquired firm cautioned against using the main track to sort trains instead of using train yards. Traffic delays skyrocketed, perishable foodstuffs spoiled on sidings and it took days to locate shipments. The fact that the company insisted on carrying out routine track maintenance while this was occurring simply compounded the crisis. In the end the government had to step in.

❑ Rationalising competing compensation schedules within a combined entity can be extremely difficult. Pay discrepancies occur at many levels. In the Daimler–Chrysler merger, the compensation question is proving to be one of the thorniest issues. At the time of the merger, Chrysler's chairman was earning eight times as much as the head of Daimler.

Culture

❑ There is always a problem in melding the differing cultures of the organisations involved in a merger. When one firm buys a portion of another firm, the problem is compounded. "Dividing up the pie" is easier when one firm triumphs in a merger. In the words of one ex-Chase executive, "in a good merger, one company will inevitably be dominant".[2]

❑ One additional issue is likely to be that of the precise people, products, systems, or assets that have actually been purchased. Often the negotiation starts after the final contract is signed and it can be very complicated.

❑ There is the danger that if a firm that has been growing internally for a long period of time makes a large acquisition, it may be ill-prepared culturally to adapt to the merged environment.

❑ Even if integration is largely successful, it is often the case that, as a result of human nature, years later employees are still known by the institution from which they came and there remain remnants of an "us-versus-them" mentality.

❑ Risk appetites vary. In the case of a merger, the resulting entity may not wish to pursue certain established lines of business even if they have performed well over time. This is exemplified by Travelers' closure of several trading units such as the Salomon US Bond arbitrage group (Salomon Brothers Inc had long enjoyed a reputation as one of the leading trading firms on Wall Street, known for making big risky bets in the bond and stock markets) and a stock risk-arbitrage unit. Despite the units' success, the volatility of earnings was higher than the intestinal fortitude of the resulting entity.[3]

❑ Approaches to risk taking vary in other respects. A recent book co-authored by Goldman Sachs and Swiss Bank made mention of the contrasting centralised and decentralised approaches to risk taking of these companies. For example, at Swiss Bank the foreign exchange traders can take foreign exchange risk, but the foreign equity traders would not take a stand-alone foreign exchange risk. Goldman Sachs, by contrast, allows a greater latitude for cross-product trading.[4] Neither approach is necessarily better. What is important is that, within an institution, the new approach is widely understood and followed.

❑ The risk vocabulary of the merged organisations may be different. Some institutions use primarily duration measures and others use more sophisticated measures such as convexity and gamma measures. Senior management must be conversant with the assumptions and implications of various measures. The worst danger is that there may be an appearance of sophistication or control when none in fact exists. Duties can be delegated but ultimate responsibility rests with senior management.

Clients

❑ In a typical merger, sales efforts come to a halt as salespeople decide who stays. Unless client coverage issues are resolved quickly, clients may move if they perceive a lack of focus. Banks like First Union, which have had prior experience with consolidation, estimate that there is a six-to-eight-month window of opportunity for rivals.[5] This is typically the most vulnerable time for clients to be poached from the outside. Difficulties in reconciling computer systems and coordinating sales efforts can easily lead to a significant loss of clients.

❑ Cross-selling may generate resistance as clients object to data mining and possible dissemination of credit card or medical histories. Regulators are especially concerned with this aspect of combined firms as witnessed in the extensive documentation that they compiled as they approved the Travelers/Citibank merger.[6]

❑ Multiple branding may cause further confusion. When large firms merge there must eventually be a rationalisation of the products that remain.

❑ Failure to overcome compliance hurdles early represents a common delay for merged entities, preventing them from maximising their post-merger sales efforts. Selling a product approved by the SEC on a nationwide basis may not be that cumbersome. Going nationwide in the United States with an insurance product implies approval from every state regulator, which may be time-consuming.

Valuation

❑ When a merger occurs, two competing valuation systems often need to be integrated. The party that is effectively "selling" its assets will want to reduce asset valuations – with "lowballed" numbers, future performance should naturally be enhanced. It might be helpful to perform a sampling analysis to validate the numbers. Take comparable liquid securities and compare mark-to-market valuations and value-at-risk estimates. There may be a level of comfort obtainable in terms of the methodologies used by the two organisations and you may be able to focus reconciliation efforts on more exotic trade valuations or limited classes of transactions. You should be able to "bracket" the range of errors or disputes. Valuation should always be performed using "sealed models".

Business strategies

❑ Business strategies are often developed over a short time horizon and this frequently places different business units in conflict. In the Bell Atlantic merger with GTE, the deal "came together so quickly" that there had been no opportunity even to pick a name for the resulting organisation[7] (the name has still to be finalised as this publication goes to press). A merged entity should first focus upon establishing business strategies. Consider, for example, a mission statement that gives a company's mission as to "sell investment and insurance products to middle-class individuals in all major international markets". It sounds simple. Implicit in that mission statement is the need to rationalise client databases, cross-selling literature, credit

and underwriting standards, internal communications, risk allocations and pricing of capital, to name a few major issues.

Leadership

❑ Delegation of duty is doubly challenging when a new chief executive is unfamiliar with the new staff and whether they will work together. Sometimes the control approaches of new chief executives are different from those of their predecessors. Sometimes they just do not know about certain aspects of the company.

❑ Implementing strategy calls for execution and integration skills. These are very different from sales and trading skills. The surviving organisation is ill served if the actual task of integration is given to the dealmakers because they forged the deal. A different set of skills is required.

Process controls

❑ Disaster recovery is typically an afterthought and breakdowns can be especially severe if they occur in the early stages of a merger. Given the increased reliance on technology and just-in-time inventory management, the likelihood of needing back-up capacity has greatly increased. Changeover to a new system should not be permitted until a workable recovery process is already in place. System backup is not sufficient by itself. In the event of a disaster like the World Trade Center bombing, other firms will be affected. Assuming the firm recovers quickly, its regular customers may need to do more business and it will need its credit people available to approve the requests. Supporting staff and infrastructure need to be pre-placed.

❑ One likely result of the merger of companies in unrelated industries is a lack of consistency in reporting and difficulties in evaluating and standardising the measure of capital usage and return rates across the entities.

Credit

❑ It can be especially difficult for a merged entity to achieve consistency in credit standards.

Technology

❑ A common systems platform should be implemented as soon as practical after a merger.

Cost cutting

❑ The recurring refrain in support of mergers is that they lead to economies of scale and cost cutting. The reality is often that cost cuts equal control cuts.

1 Wysocki, Bernard Jr., 1998, "After Big Bank Merger, CoreStates Customers Prove Ripe for Taking", Wall Street Journal, July 2, p. A1.

2 Interview with Jeff Larsen, Derivatives Strategy, May 1998, pp. 37–9.

3 Raghavan, A. and P. McGeehan, 1998, "Travelers Reins in Risky Stock, Bond Plays by its Salomon Unit", Wall Street Journal, August 25, pp. C1–C2.

4 Goldman Sachs and SBC Warburg Dillon Read, 1997, The Practice of Risk Management, Euromoney Publications plc, London, p. 61

5 See note 1 above.

6 Wells, Robert, 1998, "Traveller, Citicorp merger must wait for Fed, U.S Congress", Bloomberg News, August 9, p. 2.

7 Cauley, Leslie, 1998, "Bell Atlantic – GTE Deal Boosts Executives Anxiety", Wall Street Journal, July 29, p. B4.

In the new environment, regulatory concerns have already surfaced with regard to the following operational risk areas:

❏ unlicensed salesmen marketing SEC-registered products to inappropriate, unsuited customers;
❏ customer lists being provided to a different legal entity without authorisation or regard to customers' privacy; and
❏ transfer of assets between member companies at non-market prices.

Regulators continue to request more detailed information and quicker turn-around times. Banks need to provide holdings by industry, by country and by currency. The need to respond quickly to regulators was evidenced by the fact that the regulators' request for data during the 1997/1998 emerging markets crises was measured in hours. Regulators are likely to become even more demanding in future.

MEGA-MERGE EQUALS MEGA-RISK?
When mergers are involved, there is often a perverse synergy in the resulting "mega-firms" that are created. Some risks are intensified rather than diversified. This is especially true if both partners focus on the same markets. The attendant risks are greater than the sum of the risks present in the separate businesses, and they are of a different nature. Rapid growth and a headlong rush into new markets can exacerbate the typical integration challenges of these large mergers.

In smaller, specialised institutions, management tends to be more nimble and response time is quicker. Businesses can be more focused and more flexible. Within a "mega-firm", particularly one resulting from a merger, however, there are often many unrelated specialised forces that force standardisation and impose a corporate rigidity that may inhibit controls or force ill-suited controls on a particular business. The Wall Street Journal referred to this as the creation of a "bureaucratic mastodon" with all its attendant consequences.[8] Issues such as sales coverage, corporate culture, compliance, technological support, capital allocation, and related categories of concern are proving to be especially intractable. These areas receive a special focus throughout this chapter, while Panel 1 spotlights issues that are particular to mergers.

The nature of operational risk

One definition of operational risk is "the potential for loss caused by a breakdown in information, communication and settlements systems. This risk is mitigated by the maintenance of a comprehensive system of internal controls…"[9]

Operational risk exists in most businesses and is primarily associated with internal functions, particularly how information moves within the company, how work processes are controlled and how critical tasks such as cash movement or mark-to-market methodologies are controlled. Many firms have concentrated on dealing with market and credit risk measurement and have omitted operational risk as a priority. This is changing – due in no small part to the efforts of the regulators and various reports and guidelines. Table 1 on page 102 details some of the key published sources for those trying to pin down what is meant by operational risk and how to start managing it. In Panel 2 we present a framework for building an operational risk control function that readers may like to consider before reading the rest of this chapter.

SOME UNDERLYING CAUSES OF OPERATIONAL RISK
Complacency
Complacency is a risk because operational risk is so commonplace. As we mentioned above, operational errors typically take the form of a series of small events, each having a minimal impact, and lulling companies into a false sense of security.

100

MINIMISING
OPERATIONAL
RISK IN
FINANCIAL
CONGLOMERATES

PANEL 2

PROPOSED FRAMEWORK FOR OPERATIONAL RISK CONTROL

Personnel and organisational structure

Who should control/oversee operational risk controls? On the asset side, there is an extensive overlap in the types of investments used by banks, mutual funds, and brokerages. This would suggest that asset specialists might be most appropriate. Others would argue that portfolio mangers or traders would be most appropriate, as a broader view is essential. Treasury or auditing personnel would also be possibilities. Exclusively staffing a group with financial expertise appears to be too limiting as one also needs staff with line experience and product experience.

A sensible answer is to create an enterprise planning unit one step below the corporate office. The corporate office would have to be meaningfully committed to such a unit for it to be effective. This unit would be staffed with a small core of skilled financial professionals as well as a rotating complement of "rising stars" from middle management who understood the lines of business and strategic focus of the firm. With some products, such as insurance, and with products where there are complicated liabilities, intimate knowledge of the liabilities is essential. A group of 12 to 15 professionals with adequate support staff might be appropriate.

This unit should produce monthly reports that enable readers to understand how well the company is doing and that highlight problem areas. In addition to the financial statistics, the reports should show variance from plans, should provide a narrative summary of events, should include appropriate operational data and should give a preview of the outlook for the next quarter. The important goal is to track the risk indicators that are most useful for the individual firm

and to have sufficient management support to enable the unit to obtain full information.

In order to function effectively the unit requires co-operation from line managers and explicit, public support from the top echelon of management. In order to secure committed support from line managers, they must be correctly compensated, and convinced that the controls are appropriate or workable and that meeting these controls will lead to an economic benefit for themselves and the company.

The unit needs to monitor information and the key criteria appropriate for the business. The information needs to be comparable and to cover identical time periods. It must also be reconcilable and verifiable.

There should be resident expertise at board level but the board cannot spend too much time on operational risk issues. The unit should be created around functions and not around individuals.

Methodology

The methodology we propose deals with control issues using a top-down approach. It analyses a company by industry, legal entity, management hierarchy, business unit, information processes, technological capabilities, among other factors. The approach is inspired by COSO – an internal self-assessment based on asking key questions about control – and is similar to a due diligence review.

Each company has its own special, unique style, which means that any control solution/structure should be tailor-made for that particular company. There are sufficient commonalties, however, to enable us to determine what should work and what should be avoided.

Generic organisation chart

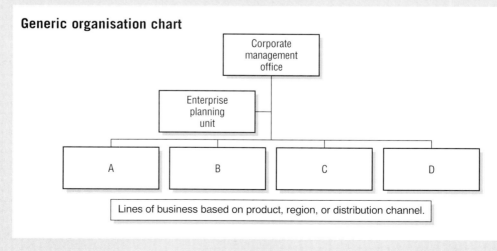

101

MINIMISING
OPERATIONAL
RISK IN
FINANCIAL
CONGLOMERATES

Key steps in building an operational risk framework

1. Create a framework for analysis – how do you compare with other similar businesses?
2. Prioritise your business goals
3. Describe the products/services you provide
4. Identify your essential customers
5. Describe your distribution systems
6. Make an inventory of your key financial measures, ie "pulse points"
7. Explain why these "pulse points" are key
8. Review how information flows through your firm
9. Identify who is responsible for evaluating this information
10. How is feedback provided from senior levels?

Identifying the nature of the company

First determine the goals of the business by reviewing similar businesses and potential competitors and determining the markets the company serves or could serve. These form the basis of the overall mission statement. Describe the company's culture and what type of risk appetite or tolerance the company wants to maintain. An appropriate risk level is a function of a company's history, its management, its corporate structure, its client base, expertise, reputation, and so forth, as well as a function of what is common in the industry and of the competitive pressures that are imposed upon the company.

Describe the products you offer and what needs these products fulfil. Which products are generic and which are customised? Determine the products that provide the best margin and have the best past trends or best potential. Rank the products in order according to use of company resources including manpower, technology, and capital.

Identify your essential customers and determine why they are buying your products/services. How loyal are the customers? Identify trends in market penetration and cross-selling of products. Determine whether the money is hot or cold – hot money is sensitive to interest rates, credit ratings, and competitive market pressures; cold money is generally associated with small, retail investors and is far less sensitive to these forces. Ascertain what alternative investments are not being bought and what effects external changes could trigger in your business mix.

Describe the distribution systems. Determine whether sales are achieved on basis of a single encounter or a courtship process. Identify the products that require licensing to sell them or need special disclosures or customer consent.

Pulse points

Inventory your "pulse points". These are *the measures that enable management to determine how well the business is performing*. Obviously certain "pulse points" are appropriate for virtually any large company. There are, however, certain measures that will be specific to an industry. Management should be able to explain why certain measures are appropriate for monitoring company performance. Return on equity and earnings per share (EPS) are probably the most significant of all measures for the financial services industry. If book yield is not important, it should not be considered as a pulse point. Pulse points will probably include:

❑ sales numbers (volumes and trends);

❑ financial measures such as earnings before interest, taxes, depreciation and amortisation (EBITDA), net interest income (NII), return on average assets (ROA) and return on equity (ROE);

❑ "people numbers" such as employee expense and turnover, compliance errors, failed trades, customer complaints, regulatory requests; and

❑ information flow (see Panel 3).

Agree on benchmarks so that employees maintain the proper targets. For each "pulse point" determine in advance what is planned, what will be acceptable and what will be considered deficient.

Given the significant leverage that is common for large financial services firms, and the enormous volume of transactions, it is paramount that "pulse points" be monitored closely.

Comparison with similar companies

Comparison with *genuinely* similar companies in the industry is a good "reality check". It provides insight into how the business is performing and how it is perceived in the market, and the process mimics the process used by rating agencies and stock analysts. One large hurdle is that competitors' figures and performance data are not always easily obtainable, especially if your business is competing against a segment or division of other companies. If a company is focused in a niche market, its price/earnings ratio and other financial ratios may not be directly comparable with those of competitors who may be active in several markets. There are always significant differences between companies. For this reason it is rare to find a perfect benchmark.

A further consideration is that management will always question why the business is not doing what others are doing. It is necessary to stay abreast of competitor activity and to understand the type of activity that would suit your own company.

102

MINIMISING
OPERATIONAL
RISK IN
FINANCIAL
CONGLOMERATES

Table 1. Information resources on operational risk

Title	Author	Details	URL
Derivatives: Practices and Principles	Group of Thirty (July, 1993)	This report is often regarded as the "bible" of risk management in financial institutions. Original full-scale risk review and guidelines	
Risk Management of Financial Derivatives	Office of the Comptroller of the Currency (OCC) January, 1997.	Review of internal controls and risk process questions used by the OCC to guide examiners of banks	
Risk standards	Risk Standards Working Group (November, 1996)	Risk standards for institutional investment managers and institutional investors	http://www.cmra.com
Trading and Capital Markets Activities Manual	Federal Reserve Board (February, 1998)	In-depth guide, emphasises global applicability and portfolio measures	http://www.bog.frb.fed.us
Internal Control Issues In Derivatives Usage	Committee of the Sponsoring Organisations of the Treadway Commission (COSO) (1996)	Self-evaluation of adequacy of integrated controls	
Framework for Supervisory Information	BIS/IOSCO (September, 1998)	Useful framework for presenting risk exposure	http://www.bis.org

Cost

The cost of implementing a meaningful and comprehensive control system is perceived as being an additional net cost. In fact, it is only through a cost–benefit analysis test that a firm can judge the appropriate level of investment in risk control. Such an analysis compares the severity of an event against the frequency with which it occurs. The cost of internal controls is not insignificant, however, these controls do provide protection against the "big hit" or disaster scenario. The cost–benefit approach recognises that the elimination of all operational risk is probably not the correct goal.

It is wrong to think that prosperous firms necessarily spend more on controls. In fact, a bull market may make it more difficult to incorporate more controls until the next crisis occurs. As the acting US Comptroller noted, "slippage in effective internals controls [is due] to complacency created by the industry's current prosperity and to cost-cutting pressures...."[10] The preferred approach is to make expenditure on operational controls a natural part of the business process, rather than trying to add them on as a superstructure.

The problem of measuring operational risk

The difficulties of measuring operational risk are dealt with in some detail in other chapters of this book. Here, let us note that even where it is possible to quantify operational risk, a single number can never give the whole picture. It is like looking at the score at the end of a ball game: it may have been nip and tuck throughout or close only at the end – you can't really tell. The challenge is to standardise the risk management measurements and supplement the numbers with prose commentary. Snapshots of data are insufficient by themselves. Rather, average numbers, highs and lows in a given period and other types of trend analysis are necessary. A noted case was a medium-sized mutual life insurance company where end-of-quarter numbers did not reflect the intra-period activities when borrowings skyrocketed between reporting periods. As decisions are made in dispersed locations, personnel and turf disputes also become more difficult to monitor.

Miscommunication

Miscommunication is a large source of operational risk. People define terms inconsistently or in different ways. Terms like "hedging", "speculation", and "leverage" have become debased by misuse of the language. One cardinal rule is to avoid jargon or "buzz words". Senior people may be very unwilling to admit that they do not understand a product. If something appears substantially similar to another process/action, it is dismissed as being just like that product. Clarity is a particularly important issue with respect to packaging and disclosure. "Libor range floater" was a popular investment in the early 1990s. It was a floating rate note that paid an additional margin as long as Libor rates stayed within a

103

MINIMISING
OPERATIONAL
RISK IN
FINANCIAL
CONGLOMERATES

preset range. If the coupon reset was outside the range, the note paid zero interest for that coupon period. Many investors saw through the "packaging" only when interest rates pierced the range.

Over-reliance on outside vendors and suppliers
Exposures to single points of failure have become more common as reliance on outside vendors and suppliers increases. One need only to think of the transportation strikes in the United States (United Parcel Service, railroad industry and General Motors) in the late 1990s and their negative effect on companies dependent on "just-in-time" supply systems. The Galaxy IV satellite malfunction that disrupted paging and telecommunications throughout the United States in 1998 is another example. The satellite's control processor and back-up both failed and an estimated 13 million customers lost paging services for several days.[11]

Incompatible systems
Incompatible systems are an area of concern, especially legacy systems feeding into return and attribution systems. Errors such as deletion of sinking fund schedules and stale market pricing occur too frequently. Additional factors compound these problems. The programmer/systems people servicing these systems might lack a thorough understanding of the underlying markets. Conversely, those reading the reports on the business side might have a reflexive adulation of any output or reports emanating from "the system".

As companies feel compelled to change, they frequently venture into new asset categories. Emerging market bonds and new ABS classes are fraught with danger of inexperience as they may be subject to different risk factors and historical price data may be non-existent. The market may also be dominated by a handful of players or several brokers.

Decentralisation
Risk in financial conglomerates has become highly decentralised. Instead of a single chief trader taking positions, product specialists on many desks take risks. The new risk may be "managing the risk managers" rather than managing the underlying risks directly. The likely outcome for most "financial supermarket" risk management is a decentralised risk control process. This has its dangers. Expertise is diffused throughout the organisation and risks may be

taken with less knowledge of the marginal impact on the entire entity. Correlation assumptions become more important and may receive less scrutiny. Decentralisation might be prudent on a smaller scale, but when aggregated it may actually increase risk. Decentralisation requires more reliance on formalised reporting and scripted encounters and underlines the importance of the information flow issues discussed in Panel 3.

Organisation-specific factors
Each business unit has its own market, product lines, and customer base – its own special characteristics that distinguish it from other businesses. Problems arise because they *appear* superficially similar; it is easy to overlook such technical issues as licensing, regulatory issues, customer suitability, and sufficiency of disclosure.

The level of risk tolerance is also often dramatically different in different companies. Investment banks are often market makers and may run extensive proprietary positions as they interact with an institutional client base. For such companies, operational risk problems can compound other risks due to high asset turnover. At the opposite end of the spectrum are traditional multi-line insurance companies servicing individual clients for life insurance and annuities and focusing on safety and protection for their clients.

In part the organisation-specific factors in a diverse business simply have to be tackled by devising organisation-specific strategies. However, as a starting point it can be useful to look at the generic risks and solutions that we discuss in the next section.

Special areas of risk and some practical solutions
This section identifies some special areas of risk in conglomerates and ongoing businesses, in contrast to the particular operational risk issues associated with mergers that we looked at in Panel 1. The areas that require special attention can be divided conveniently into
❑ people;
❑ processes;
❑ finance; and
❑ technology.

In Table 2, these areas are divided into subcategories. This listing serves as a guide and is not intended to be an exhaustive listing of all potential problem areas.

104

MINIMISING
OPERATIONAL
RISK IN
FINANCIAL
CONGLOMERATES

INFORMATION FLOW – A KEY "PULSE POINT"

Information flow is an example of a "pulse point" that needs to be monitored within any company.

First, determine whether information is widely disseminated within the company. Pay particular attention to information flow in situations where many processes overlap, where procedures are not written down, or where there is a high turnover or a large number of reassignments in middle management.

Accurate information is often available but personnel who can understand and interpret the data are often lacking. The individuals who report to the board of directors, or who distil the information in prose form, must have a thorough understanding of the underlying markets and products. They are a crucial link and can act as an early warning system to highlight problems.

Feedback may come directly from senior levels or it may be filtered down through the management hierarchy. If it is filtered, it might not arrive in its original form.

In firms where profit is not the primary motivator, another currency will become the coin of the realm. In those instances, information often becomes the currency of choice. Such firms are especially difficult environments in which to effect control. Information, even in the best of situations, is often incomplete. In an environment where essential information is not widely disseminated not only are sub-optimal decisions made but the energy devoted to second guessing (and the attendant dissension) rises to high levels.

Finally, remember that there is always a reluctance to provide full information. This is driven by territoriality, job insecurity, or an inability to generate the information.

PERSONNEL

Training should be carried out on a formalised basis to ensure consistency and sufficiency. Desk manuals and databases should be updated and distributed. (A risk manager has opined that guidelines should be "force fed" to sales staff). One bank uses laminated risk place mats on each trading station that outline key requirements and/or regulatory guidelines cross-referenced to a source compliance policy document. This is a handy and reliable reference tool that fosters adherence to policies.

Employees' business and market experience are important assets. Sometimes narrowly averted catastrophes are not written down but reside in the memories of the risk managers/operations managers. Turnover and "downsizing" result in a loss of this institutional memory. They eliminate an important control whereby employees know how to respond to crises, what worked in previous situations or, equally important, what did not. A database of "near misses" would be instructive.

Integrity is the cornerstone upon which all financial products are sold. Each sales position should have a mandated minimal skill or experience level, should fulfil all relevant licensing requirements, and should be subject to active supervision. Employees selling SEC-approved products or derivatives salesmen should have a special human resource code to better track their sales activity. Each year, a supervisor should acknowledge in writing the individuals for whom he is responsible and the supervised employees should acknowledge that relationship. Sales by unlicensed salespeople or salespeople using misleading/inadequate disclosure, or recommending products that are not in their clients' best interests (mis-selling) continue to cost companies millions of dollars in fines and restitution payments each year. Witness the many life insurance sales settlements that have occurred since the early 1990s where companies have been accused of using misleading sales practices.[12]

To ensure proper motivation by competing units, the firm may need to credit multiple parties for selling the same product or for providing referrals.

CULTURE

Decision making in a commercial bank has historically been collegial or by committee. Given the decentralisation of risk that is occurring in many institutions, decision making is now taking place at the subsidiary and department level. It is incumbent upon senior management to be specific when delegating duties and with regard to the limitations placed upon the authority of staff. Ultimate responsibility and fiduciary liability rests with senior management but it is important to obtain input from all parties that can provide insight into management decisions, rather than limiting input. Junior members of

105

MINIMISING
OPERATIONAL
RISK IN
FINANCIAL
CONGLOMERATES

Table 2. Areas requiring particular risk-control attention

Problem areas	Issues
Personnel	training experience compensation integrity
Culture	risk appetite decision-making process in-house expertise organisational chart
Clients	identification cross-selling distribution compliance
Leadership	business strategies, the "vision thing"
Merger execution	dividing up the pie delegation of duty strategies/ challenges
Risk policies	identify the risks written risk policies valuation/attribution audit review
Products	design disclosure pricing new products
Process controls	inventory processes written reports reconciliation disaster recovery
Legal/regulators	authorisation ISDA/IFEMA guarantees regulatory oversight
Market	exposure inventory risk decentralisation risk testing attribution/performance
Capital	returns leverage liability structure rating agency liaison
Credit	standards concentration netting collateral
Technology	data requirements disaster recovery system platforms crisis response

staff and operational people may have valuable insights and consulting them will certainly help the *esprit de corps*.

An additional danger is that, when specialists handle large transactions, they focus on only a piece of the transaction. Only a few people view the transaction in its entirety and so the aggregate impact of certain actions may not be fully evaluated.

Even with in-house expertise, some projects should not be done internally. A large

company does not have to do everything itself just because it is big. It may be inefficient to use valuable in-house resources for non-income-producing tasks.

CLIENTS

Identifying which particular sales staff cover which particular clients often involves a turf battle. Where these issues arise, as is often the case with newly merged companies (see Panel 1), they should be resolved quickly.

Compliance requirements may necessitate higher levels of disclosure to certain clients. In addition to appropriate disclosure, the salesman may need to examine the client's needs and assess whether the type and volume of the product sold is appropriate to the client given its size and its sophistication. A risk place mat guide would help here! The common adage goes, "if a client loses a little money, he calls his banker; if he loses a lot of money, he calls his lawyer". Disclosure and suitability checks go a long way towards minimising operational risk.

Companies may also need to protect themselves from the customer as well as to protect the customer from himself. It is becoming increasingly common for credit losses to arise from the client's unwillingness to pay, rather than its inability to pay.[13]

RISK POLICIES

A complete inventory of risk positions is needed to properly identify risks. Risk controllers need to be especially alert for compilations that show all "operating" portfolios or "unused" credit lines: Portfolios may be "investment only" and not "operating" and so would be omitted from the report. Oversized credit lines may hide large exposures. It is important to ask open-ended questions when assessing risk controls in order to obtain all relevant information – just asking about new clients does not necessarily provide information about long-dormant clients who have suddenly become very active.

It is important to look beyond the counterparties and understand where the market is laying off the ultimate risk. In the mid-1990s foreign investors purchased large amounts of Russian Treasury bills (GKOs). These same investors then sold roubles forward with Russian banks to hedge the foreign currency risk. On paper, it was a perfect hedge. The reality was that when the 1998 crisis occurred, the risk remained within the economy. Russian bank defaults and exchange controls led to the rude awakening

106

MINIMISING
OPERATIONAL
RISK IN
FINANCIAL
CONGLOMERATES

PANEL 4

CHARACTERISTICS OF EFFECTIVE CONTROLS

The various kinds of controls a firm might implement include:

❑ preventative controls;

❑ managerial controls;

❑ advisory controls; and

❑ escalation controls.

Whichever type is used:

❑ Good controls are logical, sequenced, intuitive, focused and verifiable. This is easy to say but the real challenge is to create and apply controls that meet these standards.

❑ Controls should complement the business and should be part of the operational process. They should be appropriate both to the industry and to the company's internal processes and should incorporate its risk philosophy and reflect its culture and history.

❑ Controls need to be arranged in a hierarchy and a logical sequence.

❑ Controls are only effective if timely and accurate information is available, and if it is reviewed and acted upon.

---

that country risk had been underestimated on a massive scale.

Written risk policies must be clear and well disseminated. Controls should be escalated for new exposures, or exposures that are larger or longer than normal. This focuses attention on riskier transactions so that the firm can review whether it is being adequately compensated for a higher-than-normal risk. It is not a preventative control; rather, it is an informational and management control.

Controls will never be "airtight" or anticipate every possible situation. Panel 4 gives some characteristics of good controls.

It is necessary to appoint a final arbiter or "designated worrier" to make the tough risk decisions. Senior management should show strong support for the risk policies. As one observer noted, if the corporate treasurer takes large, speculative positions, his underlings are unlikely to be reprimanded for engaging in their own smaller, speculative trades.

Audit reviews are often not tough enough. External auditors often treat a large client deferentially. Consistently attractive EPS numbers may lull auditors, analysts and management into false complacency.

The opposite problem also occurs. When a firm's problems mount, auditors may go to the other extreme and reject nearly everything, even common, accepted practices in the industry.

If the external auditors also act as outside consultants, they can exert tremendous leverage within the audited firm. The audit firm has information sources within the bank and informal information sharing may occur amongst employees of the outside audit firm.

Internal audits can be a truly meaningless exercise unless the audit staff are experienced and line management sees the benefit of working with them and implementing their recommendations. In the infamous Barings case, internal auditors made several recommendations that might have prevented or severely limited the scope of the resulting debacle, including strict segregation of duties between trading and back office. A properly utilised internal audit review should be a dry run for the external auditors and regulators and an opportunity to refine reports and procedures.

Companies that dramatically increase in size or make major changes to their structure may find that the controls that worked effectively before are inappropriate to the new entity and that the risks incurred are materially different.

PRODUCTS

When products are designed in-house they should be accurately described. This is essential both for monitoring purposes and to address compliance concerns. The life insurance industry would have saved itself much grief had more control been exercised over sales illustrations and related literature.

Providing common hardware platforms and software to sales forces helps ensure product consistency. In early 1998, a major US insurance company announced that it was spending $100 million to establish just this goal. All the field sales force will be equipped with identical tools to ensure consistency and accuracy.

The legal department must review all sales materials and periodically spot-check the sales force to ensure adequate disclosure. Here the

107

**MINIMISING
OPERATIONAL
RISK IN
FINANCIAL
CONGLOMERATES**

"10-80-10" rule applies. The top 10% of salesmen may be too aggressive and evade the rules and the bottom 10% may be too desperate to follow the rules. The middle 80% performs as expected. Another concern is when a product is sold via an outside sales force and less control over the sales process is obtainable. If an outside vendor were to sell a US dollar annuity to a foreign investor, it is important to ensure that the annuity holder knows that the annuity payments are fixed in US dollars and not the foreign currency amount.

Product pricing can be as dynamic as the changing price of airline seats. Airlines now have the ability to target price levels with much greater accuracy to the customers' willingness to pay. Given the technology that airlines have developed, it is not difficult to see its applicability to the financial service world.

One should be alert for hidden options given to clients by salespeople. As an enticement, clients may be given a verbal promise of a refund of fees if they do not receive the promised tax or accounting treatment on a transaction. Your firm may have to honour that unwritten promise. New products may be truly new or they may be a repackaging of old products. Products can be described in a variety of ways, so it is important to obtain a full understanding of the essence of the product. The process of approving product descriptions should be comprehensive but not so cumbersome that it inhibits innovation or slows the product design process.

Products sold to a new client base or a book of business that has remained static for years could both be areas of fruitful exploration for a company. A new client base could raise additional compliance issues. The risks to which an existing block of business is exposed might have changed considerably if the underlying market has changed structurally in the interim.

PROCESS CONTROLS
An inventory of processes and controls is a first step to ensure independence and conformity with the standards of the Committee of Sponsoring Organizations of the Treadway Commission (COSO). This is an organisation that helped to create questionnaires to guide companies in reviewing their internal controls.[14]

These resources are particularly valuable as they give companies the ability to carry out self-evaluations.

In order to establish and create an inventory

of appropriate controls, one must first review the business plan and the process within each individual unit of the consolidated entity. One needs to review a clear, current organisational chart and process flows. Check for exceptions, duplicate processes, gaps or manual interventions. These are likely problem areas. One firm discovered that it had two competing systems for portfolio management. One system was a settlement-based system and was corrected and updated. The other was an inventory system that relied on initial input with no updates. Unfortunately, the portfolio managers were using the inventory system to monitor their portfolios until a control review highlighted the error.

Written reports must include all relevant data. Reports should be expandable and sent to all appropriate decision makers. If a company has built a steady profit and reputation from certain lines of business, dramatically increased volume and new large ticket trades may be signs of a greatly increased risk profile. Significant changes in activity are also often harbingers of *future* risks. Trends in line usage are as critical as line overage reports. The reports must be comprehensive; you cannot manage risks if you do not have information about them. Dead or unused fields should be deleted as they may distract from the important data. Internal communications (e-mails) should be standardised to simplify identification of important policy changes and action times.

Reconciliation is often carried out on the basis of output or summary reports and not at the source. Manual intervention often leads to an omission at a later date. Extra effort should be made to match data entry with source documents. Exception reports are a key control for this. It should be easy for approved individuals to make changes in records but these should be closely tracked via a real-time audit trail. Reconciliation should be done on the same day and sufficient personnel should be trained to perform this task. Some businesses are more prone to errors in this respect than others. "Firms with large emerging market operations are particularly under the spotlight ... given the less sophisticated trading conditions in those markets".[15]

One major bank lost millions of dollars in its emerging markets trading because a trader was evading limits by entering false trades into the computer system, indicating sales of an emerging market currency. The trader was under strict limits to fully offset customer trades and

108

MINIMISING
OPERATIONAL
RISK IN
FINANCIAL
CONGLOMERATES

not to have an open position. The currency devalued and the phantom trades came to light.

LEGAL CONSIDERATIONS

Legal risk management should occur before an entity enters into a transaction. Essentially, it means that the proper homework must be done. An entity's legal counsel should develop the policies and procedures in consultation with its risk management personnel.

Many expensive lapses in legal risk management have involved *ultra vires* activity – transactions that were not allowed by municipal charter. In the famous case of the London borough of Hammersmith and Fulham, the municipal entity walked away from $175 million in losses by successfully claiming that the swap contracts were not permitted investments of the legal entity. The contracts became effectively void.[16]

An especially insidious practice is the creation of written agreements that do not reflect actual terms and are actually used as a false benchmark for outside clients. An additional concern would be a joint purchase of an asset where one firm carries out the analysis and another is somehow reliant upon that same analysis.

The use of a company's guarantee and recourse loans is an area of special concern. It is necessary to control and monitor who has signing authority, for what purposes, and in what magnitude. If outside managers, working for a fee, have the authority to extend a blanket guarantee, what incentives exist to ensure that they maintain the best interests of the company?

On the other hand, it is essential to avoid the situation where only the chairman or president can extend the guarantee. Obtaining a response from them may be a time-consuming process and business opportunities may evaporate in the meantime.

This leads us into the more general area of the legal responsibilities of senior executives (see Table 3).

Careful liaison with regulators is needed given the magnitude and complexity of regulatory oversight. "Regulators have been wrestling with the task of keeping this kind of financial conglomerate on a leash..."[17] Companies need the ability to co-ordinate responses and minimise duplicative efforts. Quick accurate responses to regulators' requests are needed.

We mentioned above that whenever a regional or global crisis is rumoured or occurs, the regulators often demand to see exposures at short notice. It is important to build flexible data-sorting systems into risk management systems. "Concepts of financial soundness vary widely between industries, and calculating a consolidated capital adequacy ratio for an amalgam like Citigroup will not be easy".[18] Similarly, regulators may consider that selling a bond to an individual has quite different requirements in terms of disclosure and suitability from selling the same bond to an institution.

Companies should be wary of situations in which one entity controls another and the legal separation is determined to be a "sham". Creditors often can reach back into the controlling entity in that situation. Another frequent infraction involves "musical assets": as an alternative to recognising a loss, one company may sell a distressed asset to an affiliate at par, the selling company receives a cash infusion and has a clean balance sheet over the end of a reporting period, the asset can then be sold back in a new reporting period or to another affiliate.

Enterprise financing is another area of concern. In the case of longer term borrowings, make-whole provisions, prepayment conditions, posting of collateral and other covenants should be carried out in conformity with similarly situated borrowers outside the corporate family.

Table 3. Executive responsibilities and legal duties: a framework

	Board of directors	Senior managers	Line management/operations
Duty of care	Legal duty to understand the businesses and how they interrelate. They must review all major actions and controls.	Responsible for adequately trained personnel and proper segregation of duties. "Delegate and forget" is not a protected approach.	Monitor individual transactions to ensure conformity to corporate charter, corporate authorisations, and full range of internal controls.
Duty of loyalty	Ensure that major undertakings are evaluated as to shareholders' best interests.	Responsible for creating and implementing policies to safeguard the financial and legal interests of the corporation.	Must act consistently with corporate policies and within authorisations. Cannot direct trading to counterparties/brokers in an inappropriate fashion.

109

MINIMISING
OPERATIONAL
RISK IN
FINANCIAL
CONGLOMERATES

A comfortable, informal agreement covering long-term debt is an imprudent approach given the many instances where firms have sold off member companies and purchased other companies in their stead. It is incumbent on each member company to protect its shareholders, as a sister company may become a rival.

International Swaps and Derivatives Association (ISDA) swap agreements and International Foreign Exchange Master Agreement (IFEMA) foreign currency agreements should be standardised amongst counterparties to ensure conformity. If agreements vary as to netting, choice of law, or credit triggers it will be difficult to measure legal exposure. This may be an arduous and time-consuming process but it will minimise the chance of any lurking exposures. Special attention should be paid to the exact name of the legal entity and any deal-specific collateral provisions. In the case of a merger, if the survivor organisation has two ISDA swap agreements with one counterparty, then it can usually determine which ISDA is appropriate.

MARKET

An exposure inventory of all assets held and any contingent liabilities should be taken. Given the complex holdings and highly structured investments that exist, often only individual product specialists can determine whether all exposures have been captured and understood. Risk data collection cannot be cursory or formalistic. The data assemblers must understand the data. Sometimes the mere gathering of data provides the best control.

The growing tendency towards risk decentralisation implies that senior management is now several steps removed from managing the underlying risks directly. Oversight must be consistent and thorough. It is highly advisable that a surprise transaction-by-transaction review of new trades or large positions should be performed three times each month if feasible.

The strength of risk testing is based in part on the accuracy of the underlying model's assumptions. Given the idiosyncratic nature of some measures, it is important to obtain an accurate listing of assumptions or an explanation of the methodology used in order to determine whether comparable information is being provided or whether data are merely being forced into a template. A risk system (VAR) may provide risk estimates for a portfolio of US treasuries and a portfolio of emerging market bonds. The treasury estimate may be based on

two years of actual trade history and the emerging market estimate may be based on a one-year history of illiquid prices. Backtesting, a method of validation where historical data are fed into the model and results are compared to actual observed results, can be an important validation of the risk management process and resources should be devoted to this area from the outset.

Another important consideration is that risk should be measured over time and not simply measured at start of the trade and estimated holding period. Interim measures are essential as one often cannot choose when to sell an asset.

Performance attribution system results are often edited or altered in order to reflect different assumptions or to adjust for timing differences or internal performance measures. These types of adjustments can be especially insidious when a trader leaves and another takes over management of a book of business.

CAPITAL

Returns are often reported on a gross basis. Ensure that agreed and analytically valid proper targets are being used and that the proper risk-adjusted return on capital measure is used. Bankers Trust helped pioneer the concept of risk-adjusted return on capital (Raroc).[19] Portfolio managers are notorious for highlighting returns achieved and ignoring the risk taken to achieve those returns.

Leverage should not be prohibited automatically. Certain levels of leverage may be appropriate and prudent depending on the nature of the business. Simply taking more risk to obtain more income is obviously not prudent. Regulators are typically concerned about double leverage – the same capital being used to backstop multiple exposures in different legal entities. Borrowings by sister companies can often be sidestreamed, downstreamed, or upstreamed. Depending on tax and legal considerations it may be advantageous for one corporate entity to issue debt in the market and lend the funds to another entity within the same corporate family. The funds can go up, down, or sideways within the related entities and hence the terminology.

Liability structure can be quite flexible and there should be agreement on a company's priorities. Maintaining certain financial ratios, minimising cost of funds and avoiding concentration of funding are all valid guidelines. At times, however, one of these objectives must predominate. Risk-based capital (RBC) can be a rather crude measure for determining appropriate capital levels but it is a measure that will probably remain for the foreseeable future. In the insurance industry, RBC is a proxy for measuring the equity required as a safeguard in the event of asset defaults. Despite its imprecision, RBC does permit a comparative analysis of diverse risk positions.

Rating agencies may force companies to behave in sub-optimal ways. Rating agencies are especially sensitive to perceptions. Acceptable ratios may change simply due to a competitor experiencing a problem. Regulators may reorder their priorities or a company's business mix may change rapidly and a new standard may be in order. The most obvious example is the changing nature of the insurance industry in the US, where new annuity sales have bypassed the sales of life insurance and now represent the majority of new sales for many large companies.

CREDIT

Credit concentration is typically limited by industry regulators, company charter, or prospectus, yet violations of these restrictions have probably been the most frequent causes of financial company crises. One need only to think of certain debacles in the US insurance industry.

Enforceable netting is a concern for the legal department and not simply the back office. It cannot be delegated like other operational issues because there are often multiple layers of complexity. An individual with bankruptcy law expertise is often needed to ensure a thorough review.

Posting of collateral and its valuation must be monitored frequently. Collateral is often forgotten or not properly perfected. Assets might not be included in lists of holdings as a trustee may hold them. The opportunity to exchange collateral and optimise the use of the repo market in reducing cost of funds may also be lost with inadequate monitoring. It should also be made clear whether collateral can be rehypothecated.

ASSETS

The range and variety of assets available to investors continues to grow dramatically. Securitisation of assets is growing exponentially. Some of these assets are too new to have experienced a complete economic cycle. Investors do not know how these assets will fare in the event of economic crisis.

Some categories of assets may be appropriate for certain business units but not for others. Although an asset may well be a prudent investment, internal investment guidelines or general authorisations must specifically allow for the purchase of the asset class. Failing that, a special review by the board of directors may be needed to ratify a purchase.

A related concern is whether the company has sufficiently trained people and adequate systems in house or on loan to analyse the purchase of all assets that are held. Asset names are sometimes irrelevant or misleading in that they do not reflect the underlying nature of the investment or exposure.

TECHNOLOGY

The data needs of a centralised system require uniformity of data, measurement and presentation format. It is probably only possible to achieve this in the longer term. Data and systems expertise is often centralised and the field offices and outside managers/departments feed into headquarters. The central office may not be alert to subtle differences in data coming from multiple sources or to whether items are being "force fitted". A related issue is whether a particular business segment (such as the mergers and acquisitions advisory unit) lends itself to ratio and mathematical processes and monitoring.

A particularly important issue where technology is concerned is that of disaster recovery. Pre-crisis planning is the only safe way to address this. "Financial institutions are now heavily reliant on their technology and face huge consequential liabilities in the event of systems failure."[20]

Given the romance with outsourcing, even the reliability of essential tasks may be beyond one's control. One should ensure that if the back-up mode is engaged during a disaster, new activities should be recorded in a way that allows them to be re-input electronically when conditions return to normal.

Systems implementation is difficult as the rate of technological change appears to be growing at an extremely fast pace. The human capital needed to support further technological innovation is often underestimated. Technical skills vary widely and integration skills are also more in demand. The pace of work frequently does not allow users sufficient time to learn new programs adequately. Employees often use

111

MINIMISING
OPERATIONAL
RISK IN
FINANCIAL
CONGLOMERATES

technology to the minimum extent necessary and do not take full advantage of its capacity.

When a "legacy system" (an older computer system, often not year 2000 compliant) is terminated, it is important to ensure that the new backup system is sufficiently tested. Testing should take place across a range of transaction volumes and a variety of market scenarios. One should inventory hardware in use and software reliability and review the maintenance schedules and downtimes. Computer programs are often not fully documented in such a way that all their model assumptions are known. These assumptions include calculation methodologies, logic and data checks and default processes. In addition, the program may only be understood by a small cadre of personnel.

A strong crisis-response capability is evidence of adequate controls and staffing. The risk manager must be able to satisfy senior management, the rating agencies and regulators that such a capability exists. These constituencies do not have future needs – they only understand immediate response.

The human factors and effort involved in using technology have been vastly underestimated. The supply of highly trained (or sufficiently trained) individuals to monitor and master the technology is simply inadequate.

Summary

The financial service industry is a people-to-people business that requires substantial investment in staff and reliance upon technology. The dependence on technology and the interaction between people and technology has created many new control issues. Often employees become so specialised that they are unaware of legal, accounting, tax or related issues triggered by business activity. Several layers of control are often required and it might be prudent to escalate controls as risks become larger.

The competitive environment and investor demands for performance have created an atmosphere that focuses on short-term consequences. The workforce is much more diverse and commonality of values has consequently been reduced. What is required is senior management commitment to the risk-control process and acceptance of the additional managerial time required and of the cost of limiting operational risk.

American-style economic rationalism (or, as cynics would term it, economic Darwinism) is spreading with the likely result that the market environment will become even more competitive. The dominant firms will be those with better technology, better people, better products, or better cost structures. The dominant firms will also be the ones that best implement a comprehensive framework of controls.

The financial services industry faces a truly overwhelming torrent of information. Management's task of obtaining essential information has been likened to trying to sip water from a fire hydrant. The volume and magnitude of transactions continue to rise dramatically – one need only to look at the NYSE, with weekly volume in 1998 approaching four to five billion shares, which is several times the volume just a few years earlier. "Financial supermarkets" must be able to handle these massive amounts of "throughput".

With the advent of the "financial supermarket" there are new and qualitatively different risks. Foreign exchange, political risks, and technology risks will remain with us, but operational risk is often the true "Achilles' heel" of an organisation. The goal and the challenge is to master existing risks in the context of a dynamically changing industry, global markets that continue to become more treacherous, and the need to react ever more quickly to competitive challenges.

1 *Parsley, M., 1996, "Risk Management's Final Frontier",* Euromoney, *September pp. 74–9.*

2 *Brimelow, P., 1998, "Merger Mania", Forbes, August 10, pp. 102–3.*

3 *Rockett, J., 1998, "The Urge to Merge: Trends in Bank Mergers", Financial Institutions News (Practice Group of the Federalist Society), 2(2), (Summer) pp. 1–6.*

4 *See note 3 above.*

5 *Guildman, Till, 1998, "Changing Industry – Changing Risks", keynote conference address at Risk 1998, Arlington VA.*

6 *Institute of International Finance Inc., 1997,* Report of The Task Force on Conglomerate Supervision. *Washington DC, Institute of International Finance, p. 11.*

7 *Donald L. Horowitz, 1996, "P & G v. Bankers Trust: What's all the fuss?"* Derivatives Quarterly, *Vol. 3(2) (Winter), pp. 18–23.*

8 *Chernow, Ron, 1998, "The Birth of a Bureaucratic Mastodon",* Wall Street Journal, *April 9, p. A22.*

9 *Credit Suisse,* Credit Suisse Financial Products Annual Review, 1996, *p. 22*

10 *Williams, J. L.,* Acting Controller of the Currency, *August 24 1998, Press release announcing new internal control handbook.*

11 *Sykes, Rebecca, 1998, "Satellite Fails, U.S. Paging Systems Crash",* PCWorld, *May 20, p.1.*

12 *Throughout most of the mid-1990s, large life insurance companies and affiliates have paid out hundreds of million of dollars in fines and restitution. Many of the major insurance companies have been implicated.*

13 *Chew, Lillian, 1996,* Managing Derivatives Risks. *Chichester, John Wiley, 1996, p. 134.*

14 *COSO is composed of five trade groups including the AICPA (American Institute of Certified Public Accountants), located in Jersey City, NJ, USA.*

15 *Bray, Nicholas, "ING Barings See Trade Mismatches in New Markets."* Wall Street Journal, *Section B, September 22, 1997.*

16 Hazell v. Hammersmith and Fulham London Borough Council, *2 W.L.R. 372 (H.L. 1991).*

17 *Graham, George, "Big and Bigger", April 7 1998,* Financial Times, *p. 13.*

18 *See note 17 above.*

19 *Wee, L. and J. Lee, 1995,* Raroc and Risk Management, *Bankers Trust, New York.*

20 *Parsley, Mark, 1996, "Risk Management's Final Frontier",* Euromoney, *September, pp. 74–9.*

7

Operational Risk in Retail Banking

Promoting and Embedding Risk Awareness Across Diverse Banking Groups

Chris Rachlin
The Royal Bank of Scotland[1]

This chapter looks at ways to build operational risk-aware business practices across a diverse retail banking group. We start by considering some of the changes in retail banking in recent years that may have an effect on operational risk, and continue in Panel 1 by looking at the typical processes, systems and people skills that support a retail bank. An understanding of these areas is important, as they are often the areas that "go wrong" and give rise to operational risk incidents.

Having investigated where operational risk arises, the chapter considers six key concerns that must be addressed to ensure good business management of operational risk (Table 1). Unless otherwise stated, the examples provided did not necessarily occur at The Royal Bank of Scotland, but were derived from the author's experience at a large number of banking organisations while working as a consultant.

Recent changes in retail financial services – and future directions

To understand many of the operational risks that may arise in banks as retail financial service organisations, it is important to understand the nature of changes in the industry in recent years. These changes include:

❑ an increase in the range of services and products provided by banks as they try to accommodate the diverse needs of their customers;

❑ an increase in the number of delivery channels used by banks to provide their services, including telephone and PC banking;

❑ a greater use of technology to streamline processes, provide access to data and reduce manual errors;

❑ new ways to market bank services, including targeted mailing;

Table 1. Six key concerns in managing operational risk

1. Establishing *clarity* of people's roles, responsibility and accountability

2. Gaining *acceptance* that managing operational risk is good for the bank and its management and staff, therefore embedding it into everyday processes

3. Making certain changes to the bank's culture to help the management and staff *participate* and carry out better operational risk practices

4. Providing the necessary specialist *expertise* to help management

5. *Co-ordinating* operational risk initiatives with other related initiatives

6. Building the necessary level of *understanding* in management and staff through training

---

❑ new entrants to the marketplace, such as supermarket banks and Virgin, with a heavier focus on the branding of products;

❑ an increase in the geographic spread of the marketplace; and

❑ an ever-increasing rationalisation of the industry with an exceptional level of merger and acquisition activity.

All of this puts pressure on managers to perform and on technology systems to deliver. There is also ongoing pressure to achieve reductions in costs by making the best use of these innovations.

In Tables 2 and 3 we look at two areas of change – delivery channel and branding – in more detail. From Table 2, it is clear that the use of technology to deliver services has become increasingly important over time. The security of this technology and the availability of systems to meet the risks associated with fraud, error and the impact of service failure are likewise increasingly vital.

At the same time, all this technology must not overburden the customer with an excessive

Table 2. Evolution of delivery channels

Past	Present	Future
The branch outlet has been the traditional delivery channel for retail bank services. It was important to have the branch located as close to the customers as possible, to make it convenient for them to access their accounts. Customers tended to use the branch on a frequent basis and staff would often know the customer. The branches contained a wide range of staff with knowledge of many areas of banking. In many ways, each branch was a mini-bank in itself.	While the branch outlet remains the main channel for face-to-face delivery of many services, the telephone is increasingly used to deliver services together with automatic teller machines (ATMs). Branch staff have a greater sales focus to their job. Knowledge of the customer is likely to come from the profile of recent transactions and there is less face-to-face contact. More recently, the supermarket and even the Internet have started to be used as delivery channels.	It is likely that an increasing variety of distribution channels will be required, including the branch outlet, the travelling banker, telephone, supermarket and Internet.

Table 3. Evolution of branding

Past	Present	Future
In the past, a customer's perception of a bank's brand was linked to the branch they visited. In Victorian times impressive branches were built to signify the bank's financial strength. People tended to select a bank based on recommendations from family or friends. Once a relationship had been set up, it was rare for someone to change their bank.	People are still very likely to choose their bank according to which bank their parents or close relatives or friends use. However there is a greater propensity to "shop around" for certain financial products. There is also evidence (such as the success of the supermarket banks and Direct Line) that people are willing to place their money with a strong brand rather than an organisation with a long history in the business.	In the future, the branding of financial services will be very important. Banks will need a strong, distinctive brand, and it may form the key distinguishing factor between the different organisations offering a financial service. Technology is likely to make it increasingly easy to switch between banks and, therefore, the expectations created by the brand will need to be met.

number of passwords, PINs and other authentication methods. Increasingly, electronic profiling of transactions and neural networks, such as those used by a number of credit card companies, will replace branch-level manual checks and improve the level of control.

It is clear from Table 3 that the potential losses associated with reputational impact, and the need to provide a high quality of service in terms of accurate and timely processing, are also likely to increase over time as the use and importance of branding increases and as customers are able to swap banks more easily.

Identifying operational risk in a diverse organisation

For the purposes of this chapter, we will adopt a reasonably wide definition of operational risk: it is all risk other than credit, market and actuarial risk.

One of the problems when trying to compare operational risk data from other organisations is that operational risk events are almost always unique to an organisation, and to the circumstances affecting the organisation at that time.

Therefore, in order to understand the operational risks that can arise in the kind of generic retail bank sketched in Panel 1, it is important to start by gaining an understanding of the unique nature of the particular bank under investigation. This will include the bank's:

❑ goals;
❑ culture;
❑ structure;
❑ businesses;
❑ services delivered;
❑ manner in which it delivers those services (especially the processes, systems and volumes);
❑ global spread; and
❑ customer profile.

Next it is important to understand where the operational risks might arise. While this might sound straightforward, it is often an area that causes confusion because managers focus on the *effect* rather than the *cause* of risk. As a result banks often try to reduce the symptoms rather than trying to rectify the underlying problems.

For example, a bank finding itself "snowed under" trying to clear reconciliations is often

| PANEL 1 |

RETAIL BANKING BUSINESSES: PEOPLE, PROCESSES AND SYSTEMS

The businesses of a retail bank are very diverse and include the retail and corporate activities set out in Table A.

In the past, the majority of bank staff would have been generalist career bankers. To provide the range of services listed in Table A, however, a bank must have a diverse range of employees – increasingly, many will be specialists in a narrow field.

The Royal Bank of Scotland Group is an example of how diverse the range can be. Here, paint sprayers and panel beaters are employed in the accident management subsidiary of Direct Line, train engineers are employed in Angel Trains, the train leasing subsidiary, whereas other group companies employ bond traders and corporate financiers. A diversity of staff also implies many different levels of motivation, training and experience. Any group-wide approach to operational risk needs to take account of all this diversity.

Apart from a wide range of people, retail banks also require a wide range of processes and computer systems to support their businesses. It would be difficult to produce a fully comprehensive list – the system atlas alone at The Royal Bank of Scotland runs to over 200 pages. Some of the more important ones are listed in Table B.

In the case of the processes, there is a strong trend towards computerisation and, in some cases, straight-through trading (ie minimal human intervention). Even so, many processes still require a significant amount of manual intervention or are by their nature manual processes – and are therefore open to human error.

Table A. Banking activities

RETAIL ACTIVITIES	CORPORATE BUSINESS ACTIVITIES
retail banking	corporate and commercial banking
private banking	correspondent banking
mortgages	payment services
funds management	treasury services
insurance	private trust and executory
credit cards	structured finance
share dealing	custody
	leasing

Table B. Some key processes and systems

PROCESSES	SYSTEMS
payments	deposit
cheque clearing	loans
cash handling	foreign exchange
credit analysis	customer relationship
documentation	management
account opening	information systems (MIS)
mortgage applications	general ledger
interest charges	claims
deposits	customer payment
loans	data warehouses
foreign exchange	custody
insurance claims	credit card
insurance premium collection	CREST interface
custody processes	
credit card transactions	
recruitment	
marketing	
payroll processes	

tempted to direct all its resources towards clearing the reconciliations rather than investigating why the reconciling items are appearing in the first place.

At a bank such as The Royal Bank of Scotland, it is important to ensure that any classification of risks can be easily understood by as wide a variety of people as possible. Something that is easy to understand should, in theory, be easy to use. As Figure 1 illustrates, The Royal Bank of Scotland considers operational risk as arising from five areas:

1. The *processes* operated by the bank.
2. The *people* in the bank who help operate and manage the processes.
3. The *systems* used to support the processes.
4. The impact on the people, processes and systems that the *business strategy* adopted may have.
5. The risks resulting from the *external environment* that the bank operates in.

PROCESS RISK

As Panel 1 describes, banks operate a large number of processes in order to deliver their services. These include processes for making payments, accepting deposits, clearing cheques and so on. Risks can arise at all stages of the transaction processing – including the marketing stage. In a recent case, children as young as five were sent marketing information and application

The Figure illustrates how changes notified by customers by post, are made to static data, such as the customers' names and addresses.

In the case of the computer systems, large mainframes are still used for much of the bulk processing, and the systems running on them were often written many years ago. A large number of value-added systems have been bolted on to the core processing systems, and consequently the size and complexity of the entire set-up makes changing a system difficult. Increasingly, data warehousing and data mining technology are being used to overcome the deficiencies of core systems.

Historically, banks have not considered in any great depth the operational risks incurred when considering building or acquiring new businesses, or the changing profile of the people, processes and systems needed to support them.

Process: changes to static data

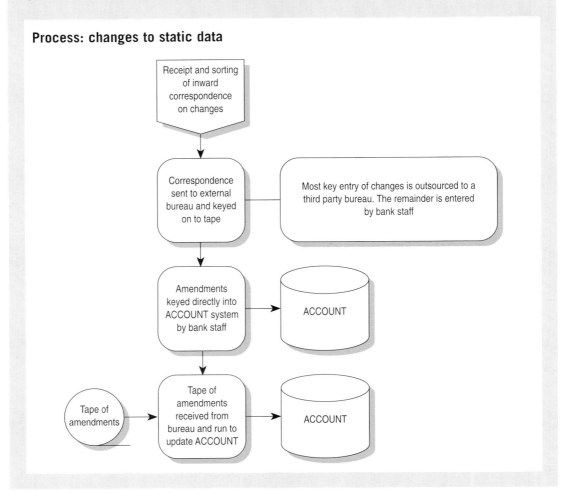

forms for a particular credit card. It turned out that the credit card company had accidentally acquired a childrens' book club members database, and was busily mailing the club's members.

Process risks can arise through, for example, the selling process, such as the problems arising from the pension mis-selling issue in the United Kingdom. Here, following tax and other changes in the UK providing increased incentive for people to change from their employer's pension to an independently supplied pension, financial institutions launched a huge drive to sell personal pensions. However, the complexity of the pensions and the limited training provided to sales staff in some institutions resulted in a large number of people being sold pensions that put them in a worse financial position than if they had stayed with their employer's pension scheme. The total industry cost to rectify this is expected to be in excess of £11 billion. The level of fines and costs incurred as a result of this mis-selling underline the seriousness of this kind of risk.

Risks can arise when making a new connection with a business customer, particularly if the authenticity of the new customer is insufficiently established – with regard to both money-laundering and fraud. Errors can creep into transactions at most stages. For example, even if

1. Five key areas of operational risk

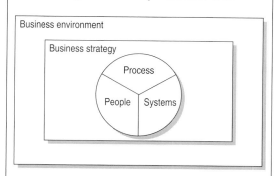

the transaction is processed accurately there are risks concerning the soundness of the documentation and the legality of the contract. An example occurred when the courts decided that swap contracts entered into by the local authority of Hammersmith and Fulham were invalid because the the local authority did not have the legal authority to enter into the contracts. As a result, banks who had entered into swap transactions with Hammersmith and Fulham and other local authorities were forced to take the losses on the contracts (at the time thought to be in the region of £500 million to £600 million) or to reach out-of-court settlements.

A bank's capacity to process transactions can be an issue, particularly with regard to unexpected volumes. An example of this was provided in the United Kingdom by one of the first bank accounts launched by a supermarket. The huge success of the savings account offered by Tesco Personal Finance took all involved by surprise. Processing volumes had been expected to be 2000 a day, but turned out to be 15,000. Not surprisingly, problems were encountered trying to keep the transaction processing up to date.

PEOPLE RISK

Although many operational risk incidents are put down to major internal control failures, it is often the case that they are the failings of people. With many bank branches evolving into largely sales operations, and general banking skills greatly reduced, issues can arise with regard to the integrity and competence of staff and management. A recent example occurred at a branch of a bank, where a customer walked in off the street and asked for five million Italian lire to be transferred from his US dollar account in the UK to his account in Italy. The bank clerk who took the request transcribed the order as five million US dollars instead of five million lire and, despite various checks and call backs to confirm

that this was the right amount, five million US dollars (approximately £3.1 million) instead of five million lire (approximately £1,800) was transferred!

SYSTEMS RISKS

Almost all aspects of banking now depend on IT systems to deliver processes and services. (It will be interesting to see at the turn of the millennium whether, if any bank systems do fail, the banks involved can still manage by using manual processes). Problems can arise from the corruption of data stored on the system, whether accidental or deliberate – eg programming errors or fraud.

In a recent case, a bank switched its payment systems off overnight to correct a problem that it was having with its decimal points. The system went up the next morning without any testing and added two zeros to the end of each payment. One million pounds worth of payments had gone out as £100 million before the error was discovered. Breaches in IT security are another area where, although losses appear to be rare to date, the potential for loss is huge. The large number of changes required to make ready for the introduction of the euro and the problems associated with year 2000 are also cause for concern. The sheer volume of these changes may result in testing being carried out less thoroughly and security relaxed to allow developers easier access to make changes.

BUSINESS STRATEGY RISK

Business strategies in the form of mergers, takeovers and re-engineering projects can have an important effect on processes, systems and people. It is important that operational risk issues, including those of change and project management, are considered when deciding on business strategy. As we discuss in Panel 2, an analysis of operational risk losses at banks found that most occurred at a time of major change in the business units.

EXTERNAL ENVIRONMENT

The external environment in which a bank operates can give rise to operational risks. This is an area where the bank itself tends to have little control over the source of the risk. The risks could arise from compliance, legal and litigation issues, unanticipated tax changes and the physical threats the bank faces, such as robbery. It would also include the effect of natural disasters such as earthquakes, flooding, and tornadoes.

WHERE DOES OPERATIONAL RISK ARISE IN PRACTICE?

Analysis carried out by the author of major operational risk incidents at a number of organisations indicated that, while the types of losses varied considerably, as did the direct causes, there were two common themes.

First, most major incidents arose during a period of change within the business unit. This may have been a re-organisation of staff, a significant increase in volume of business through purchase of a second business, implementation of a new computer system or the selling of a new product. In effect, staff and management had taken their "eye off the ball" for the period of time in which the incident arose.

Second, in many cases, problems were not identified in a timely manner because key reconciliations had either not been carried out or because reconciling items were not cleared promptly. In some cases this made it more difficult to retrieve the money lost from third parties or from fraudsters.

It follows that senior managers and operational risk managers need to monitor for problems associated with these factors if they are to avoid an unnecessary increase in risks. As most major retail banks are going through many changes at present, the first finding is particularly important. Completing reconciliations has, of course, never been the most gripping of jobs!

Some case studies included in the author's analysis of various organisations are as follows.

A custody business in the process of preparing for share certificate dematerialisation for CREST decided to take on temporary staff to help complete the work on time. Due to time pressures, the temporary staff were not vetted and basic controls such as locking share certificates away at night, or when they were not being used, were relaxed. Over £2 million worth of share certificates were stolen and eventually sold by unscrupulous temporary staff. In the same period, also due to time pressures, basic reconciliations were not performed, which meant that the fact that the certificates were missing went unnoticed for several months, allowing the criminals more time to dispose of them.

A treasury area implemented a new back-office system. Frequent differences between the new system and the bank's accounting system and a large back-log of work (caused by the implementation) resulted in staff simply "giving up" performing reconciliations. Around the same time £500,000 was sent to the account of a US counterparty instead of to the New York branch of the bank. This error was only picked up *five months* after the event – when the counterparty requested an explanation for the funds from the bank.

A more detailed breakdown of these categories of risk is provided in the appendix at the end of this chapter.

The management of operational risk

Having set a template of where in the bank operational risks might arise, the bank needs to set up an approach to manage these risks. One approach is to follow four key steps:
❏ identify specific risks;
❏ quantify risks;
❏ decide tactics;
❏ adopt mitigation practices.

IDENTIFY SPECIFIC RISKS

The first step is to try to identify all the material risks facing the organisation. This can be difficult, as any good management will believe that it is already managing the main risks its business faces. However, it is easy to be caught out by a risk not thought of previously. Methods that help identify risks include:

❏ holding risk identification workshops;
❏ the use of risk questionnaires or risk maps/templates; and
❏ monitoring of risk indicators (eg Table 4) such as number and value of uncleared reconciliation items, errors, capacity of IT systems or internal audit findings.

At the Royal Bank of Scotland, the most successful risk identification workshops involve a cross section of staff including the business unit head, the key managers, staff at the data entry level, a technology representative and group internal audit. Staff are prompted with the help of questionnaires to highlight key risks and these risks are then debated by those present. (We have found that about 10 people is the maximum number, if there is going to be a reasonable debate.) In this way, management are made aware of the risks the business units face daily, and staff are made aware of the compensating controls elsewhere in the business. The outcome of the meeting is a list of key residual

Table 4. Example technology key risk indicators

Processor – availability

Breaches in SLAs – RBS systems

Breaches in SLAs – outsourced systems/suppliers

Incidents – volume per "level"

IT Security – successful breaches
          – attempted breaches

Percentage of contract staff to permanent staff
Actual versus budgeted headcount

Unfilled vacancies – volumes in "key positions"

Reward package versus general market norms/anchors

Absence levels

Staff turnover by skill level

Project success by time/cost/quality measures

Change management events – volumes by division

Technology customer satisfaction survey ratings

Development life-cycle process – volumes

Technology platforms – number of unsupported systems

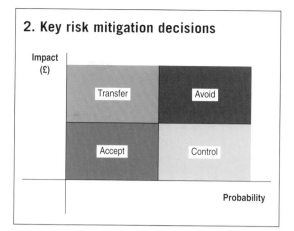

2. Key risk mitigation decisions

risks, which can be either addressed or accepted and monitored by the business.

Having identified the risks facing the business, some attempt needs to be made to analyse and understand them, and where possible to attach a number to both the economic value of their possible impact, and to the probability of the risk event occurring. There are no generally accepted approaches here, and it is probably the one area where the lack of operational risk data has held back the science of operational risk the most. However, as is discussed in more detail in other chapters in this book, techniques range from simply scoring each risk as high, medium or low, to models that consider expected loss and probability of occurrence.

The Royal Bank of Scotland, like a number of other retail financial organisations, carries out a crude quantification of operational risk at group level. The level of operational risk is calculated as 25% of operating costs. The weakness of this approach is easy to see. It penalises businesses for spending more money, even when the increased costs may have been incurred in attempts to reduce risk (eg improving control by using more staff for more checking). The strength of the technique is its simplicity. The Royal Bank of Scotland is looking to improve its quantification of operational risk and is conducting research into quantification techniques using extreme value theory.

DECIDE TACTICS

Once risks have been identified and quantified, a decision will need to be made on how to approach them. As Figure 2 illustrates, the bank may wish to:

❑ put controls in place to limit the possibility of the risk arising;

❑ accept the costs of the risk becoming an event as part of the cost of business;

❑ transfer the risk using insurance or other mechanisms; or

❑ avoid the business altogether if the cost is too high.

The tactics adopted will usually depend on the likelihood and effect of the risk occurring.

ADOPT MITIGATION PRACTICES

The practices available to management to mitigate risks, together with tools that may help with this, can be set out in a hierarchy of three levels as described in Table 5 overleaf.

In practice, risk mitigation is likely to be a combination of all three activities described in Table 5. The nature of the combination will depend on the company's philosophy – whether it is a risk adverse, risk neutral or risk-taking type of organisation. It will also depend upon an analysis of both the *costs* of putting the control in place and any *benefits* that may accrue in terms of a reduction in operational risk losses.

Establishing roles, responsibilities and accountability – including a framework

WHY ESTABLISH LINES OF RESPONSIBILITY AND ACCOUNTABILITY?

One of the key lessons from the collapse of Barings Bank in 1995 was that banks need to ensure clarity of responsibility and accountability, particularly where they operate a matrix management structure.

Table 5. Risk mitigation practices and tools

Practice	Details	Possible tools
Risk reduction	The first steps management should take are to reduce the risks inherent in the product and processes. Therefore, bank products and processes should be developed or re-engineered to minimise inherent operational risk.	A product design process that incorporates a formal risk assessment phase. A formal new product approval process where independent technical experts on operational risk areas review new products and approve their implementation
Risk control	Appropriate preventative controls (those designed to minimise an operational risk event occurring such as firewalls, passwords and authorisation processes) and detective controls (those designed to highlight that an event has occurred as soon as possible, such as reconciliations) will need to be built around the key risk areas.	Minimum control standards. Internal Audit recommendations. Risk control checklists
Risk containment	There will generally be at least some residual risk remaining, both in terms of risks without controls and the possibility of control failures. It is important that some form of risk containment is considered.	Insurance Business continuity plans Computer disaster recovery procedures Hot/cold backup sites

In particular, banks must avoid situations in which one manager wrongly assumes that a second manager is responsible for a business area or function. It is important that roles, responsibility and accountability are clearly set out for operational risk. This includes the responsibilities of the board, management, staff and specialist areas such as operational risk units, compliance, fraud etc. The way in which these functions operate should be designed to provide clarity to the entire bank, not just the functions themselves. Providing a clear understanding of who should be doing what, and when, is especially important in that it helps prevent dangerous inaction when problems arise. It is also much easier for the bank to identify where improvements are necessary when things do go wrong.

For much the same reason, the operational risk management function needs to be linked carefully to related initiatives and functions. Any bank making efforts to try to improve its overall operational risk management will need to consider very carefully other closely related initiatives that might result in a duplication of effort or confuse management and staff. While formal operational risk management may be new to many banks many aspects of operational risk will not be new. The average business unit will already have been subjected to initiatives from IT security, business continuity, quality assurance, fraud and internal controls. Without proper co-ordination, gaps in the overall management of operational risk could develop because different specialist functions in the bank believe that another function is monitoring an issue.

In order to avoid the problem, there first needs to be a clear definition of what operational risk is, communicated through a clear definition policy or statement. Next there should be defined roles and responsibilities (What is IT security responsible for? What is its role? What is business continuity responsible for? What is its role? Etc.) It may be helpful to have some form of co-ordination forum for all the relevant

3. Operational risk management practices

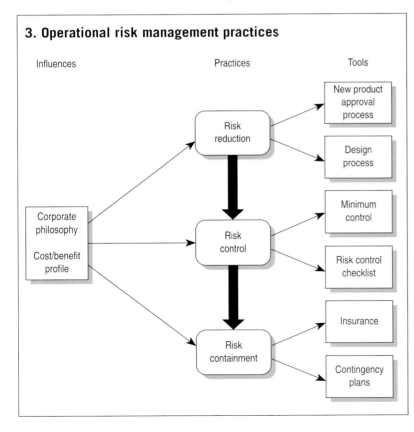

groups, possibly through a risk management committee. Alternatively, some banks structure all the risk and control functions so that they report through the same reporting line.

HOW TO ESTABLISH LINES OF RESPONSIBILITY AND ACCOUNTABILITY

Three tools help establish responsibility and accountability:

Executive sign-off

Executive sign-off of responsibilities and accountabilities must be explicit and communicated to the bank. This will help to ensure both that the board understands where responsibility lies, and that management is clear that the board understands this. In particular, the board needs to make clear that responsibility for operational risk management lies with the business management and staff at the point in the bank where the risk arises. (One problem when forming a specialist risk unit to oversee operational risk is that some business staff and management wrongly expect that they can delegate the management of the risks to the risk unit.)

Roles within a bank might be set as follows:
❏ *Board level* Deciding and setting the operational risk appetite of the bank and communicating this to the bank.
❏ *Operational risk management unit* Helping to provide management with the processes, tools and techniques to identify, assess and manage operational risk; raising awareness of and spreading best practice for operational risk management; helping ensure operational risk is managed consistently throughout the bank and monitoring significant operational risk issues.
❏ *Management* Identifying, quantifying and managing operational risks as they arise.

Policies

One mechanism for communicating executive sign-off is to put policies in place for the business to follow. These can act as a "stick" where businesses fail to operate in accordance the policy, however they work best if well communicated and explained so that the business "buys in" to them. We look at this again in the framework and training sections below.

Framework

The final aspect of understanding roles and responsibilities is setting a framework under which operational risk can be managed. At The

4. Operational risk management framework

Royal Bank of Scotland the operational risk management framework is set out under the six key areas shown in Figure 4.

Below, we first deal with the three areas that relate to the infrastructure needed to manage operational risk, and then with the three areas that relate to the processes.
❏ *Corporate standards* These include the policies, standards and definitions set by the bank in relation to operational risk. To be effective, it is important that they are appropriately communicated to the business areas and that the necessary training is provided.

One policy of particular importance is the new product approval process (Figure 5). In most banking institutions, before a major loan is made available to a customer, the bank credit committee will review and authorise the transaction. In much the same way, the new product approval process should be designed to ensure that operational risk issues are fully considered prior to the launch of a new product.

The process should include review of technical risk areas by experts and sign-off by them. As explained in the previous section, in this way new products should be launched with less inherent risk. In a new product approval process, one area that sometimes causes confusion is the name. Some business areas may take the name too literally and not submit old products delivered by new channels or processes (eg a payment service delivered via the Internet). It needs to be made clear that the process embraces any *material changes* to the risk profile of existing products.

5. New product approval process (NPAP)

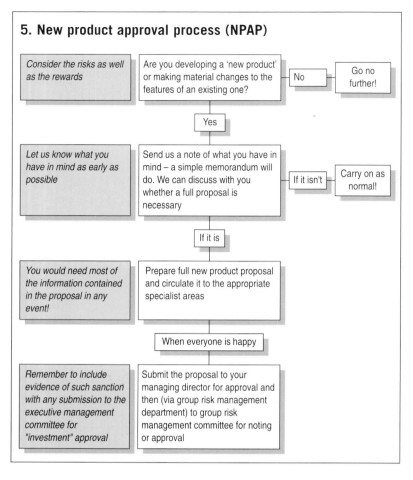

	Are you developing a 'new product' or making material changes to the features of an existing one? → No → Go no further!
Consider the risks as well as the rewards	

↓ Yes

| Let us know what you have in mind as early as possible | Send us a note of what you have in mind – a simple memorandum will do. We can discuss with you whether a full proposal is necessary → If it isn't → Carry on as normal! |

↓ If it is

| You would need most of the information contained in the proposal in any event! | Prepare full new product proposal and circulate it to the appropriate specialist areas |

↓ When everyone is happy

| Remember to include evidence of such sanction with any submission to the executive management committee for "investment" approval | Submit the proposal to your managing director for approval and then (via group risk management department) to group risk management committee for noting or approval |

❏ *Technology* Here, we mean the technology that can be used to help measure and manage operational risk. The key issues here include data standards, the risk technology architecture and strategic use of technology by the business. Historically, very few data have been collected on operational risk by organisations, and technology can help overcome this deficiency. The kind of data collected and analysed on a regular basis in business units and in group risk at The Royal Bank of Scotland is listed in Table 6.

❏ *Organisation* This aspect of the framework focuses on how the organisation is organised to

address the issue of operational risk management. It includes the lines of communication between and the structuring of the corporate committees that might consider operational risk issues (eg the problems associated with the year 2000, European monetary union (EMU), fraud and business continuity) and their relationship to the main risk committees which set and monitor risk strategy and appetite.

It is important that the committees are composed not only of people who can ensure appropriate actions are taken, but also by staff who understand the issues involved. It is easy for risk management and strategy committees to focus largely on market and credit risk issues, and ignore "uninteresting" operational concerns. The relationship and responsibilities of functions such as compliance, internal audit, any business unit operational risk functions, and indeed market and credit risk units need to be addressed under this heading.

❏ *Communication* Perhaps the most important part of the framework is communication. It is relatively easy to set policies and standards, however, without adequate business buy-in policies and procedures will be adhered to in the minimum way possible or, at worst, ignored. It is vital that the business sees the benefit of such policies being put in place. Communication also covers awareness building among the bank's personnel and the reporting of issues to the relevant departments and committees.

❏ *Tools and techniques* One way to describe this area is as the research and development side of the operational risk management framework. To date no single tool or technique seems to provide the answer that businesses have been looking for on operational risk, therefore the research continues. Piloting some of these techniques can often be a useful mechanism for establishing their effectiveness. These tools and techniques would include risk maps such as the example in Table 7, risk questionnaires, process mapping (eg the Figure in Panel 1), modelling, risk assessment tools and training.

❏ *Analysis and monitoring* This is an area where risk management functions have traditionally focused their efforts. It would include the direct identification of risk and its measurement, the development of key risk indicators as a substitute where direct identification proves difficult, and measurement techniques. Other analyses might include incident reporting and risk control self-assessment questionnaires.

Table 6. Operational risk data collected by The Royal Bank of Scotland

Risk indicator	Type of data
banking errors	value by business unit and turnover
cash errors	value by business unit
frauds	value by business limit
level/ageing of outstanding items on reconciliations	value and number
major operational risk events and related circumstances	value and number

Table 7. Example risk map – XYZ leasing business unit

PROCESS RISK

Risk type	Sub-type	Specific	Control (and residual risks)	Residual risk rating	Responsibility/ action
Transaction	Error	❏ Lease and customer details incorrectly entered onto system	❏ One-to-one comparison of key details by accounting staff on new business proposition form under lease evaluation process to information produced by main lease system before lease accepted	Nil	Accounts manager
		❏ Failure of system to accurately collect rentals	❏ Monthly comparison by regional manager of collection system and management information on unpaid amounts	Nil	Regional manager
	Contract risk	❏ Non-standard leasing contracts do not reflect the business which XYZ wishes to take on, or put XYZ at a disadvantage	❏ Professional qualified legal personnel, supported by external firms of solicitors review lease documentation for non-standard deals. (Some residual risk remains that a poorly drafted lease is taken on.)	£50,000 every 5 years	Head of legal documentation
	Product complexity	❏ Customers do not understand the commitment taken on	❏ "Plain English Guides" on the products provided to customers prior to signing and on very large deals customers are recommended to use solicitors.	Nil	Relationship managers
Management Information	Insufficient, inaccurate or untimely	❏ Ongoing information produced for relationship managers over rental collection and insurance of assets is not produced on a timely enough basis to make action effective	❏ Regular rental collection reports produced automatically and must be signed off by relationship manager by the 10th working day each month	Nil	Regional managers
			❏ List of outstanding insurance renewals reviewed by regional manager each month		

Embedding good operational risk and control practices

Getting people to change the way they work can be very difficult. How a bank approaches this will vary tremendously according to the banking "culture" that is involved. In the UK, the banking environment is used to working by the spirit rather than the letter of law. However, this is not the case in many other countries in Europe and the rest of the world, where people prefer to work within strongly codified boundaries or detailed policies and procedures.

To start with, it is important to gain acceptance for improved operational risk management and control practices. This may be done in a number of ways such as:

❏ *Business buy-in* In order to gain acceptance for improvements in operational practice, a number of pilot projects in selected areas can be used to demonstrate the benefits of the improvements for other business areas to see.

❏ *Sell the ideas* Many people in risk management believe that a mathematics background is required to be a good risk manager. While that is undoubtedly helpful, strong inter-personal skills are very important. These skills include the ability to persuade and sell. It can also helpful to use career bankers to sell the message, rather than specialists who may not understand many of the cultural problems.

❏ *Bring out the emotive issue* Not surprisingly, people do not always find operational risk issues that interesting. At times it is easier to focus management's attention by drawing them into emotive issues that "grab" their attention. Remember that a far higher percentage of people express a fear of flying than admit to a fear of driving, when statistically it is well known that, mile for mile, driving is far more dangerous. (The distorted way in which people perceive risk is discussed in Panels 2 and 3 of Chapter 10.) I suspect that the key reason for this type of distortion is that people believe that they will not survive a plane crash, whereas they know that drivers often have minor accidents in cars. Therefore, if one were trying to stress the

6. Operational risk event online entry form

Operational Risks Event Online Entry Form

Name of Institution	ABC Bank	
– Abbreviation		
Parent Institution	ABC Corporation	
– Abbreviation		
Parent Institution		
Organisation Type	ABC Conglomerate	
Business Activity	Trading – Securities & Commodities	

Location of Head Office	Country:	Japan
	City/Town	Tokyo
Location of Incident	Country:	U.K.
	City/Town	London
Regulatory Body	SIB, LME	

Incident Description: Unauthorised Copper trading. Forgery/falsification of documents.

Date of Occurrence				
Start Month:	January	Year:	1986	
End Month:	June	Year:	1996	
Date:	17 June 1996			
Source:	Newspaper			
Multiple Sources?	Y			

Operational Risk

Process Risk

Pre-transaction			Fraud		
Marketing Risks			Contract Risk		
Selling Risks			Product Complexity		
New Connection			Capacity Risk		
Transaction error			Managing Information		
			Erroneous Disclosure Risk		

People Risk

Integrity			Competency		
Fraud	✓		Management		
Collusion			Key Personnel		
Malice			Health & Safety		
Rogue Trading	✓				

System Risk

Data Corruption			Compatibility Risks		
Programming Errors/Fraud			System Failure		
Security Breach			Network Failure		
Capacity Risks			Strategic Risks		
Systems Suitability			(platform/supplier)		

External Environment Risk

Change Management			Strategy		
Project Management			Political		

External Environmental Risk

Outsourcing/External Supplier Risk			Tax		
Physical Security			Legal (Litigation)		
Money Laundering			Natural Disaster		
Compliance			Terrorist Threat		
Financial reporting			Strike Risk		

Impact

	Currency	GBP	
	Reported	1261M	Note:
	Total		Note:

Direct Impact

Assets Stolen – Customers
Assets Stolen – Banks
Damage to Physical Assets
Other Charge to Physical Profit & Loss Account
Loss on Transaction/Contact
Legal Costs
Irrecoverable Erroneous Funds Transfer
Irrecoverable Erroneous Asset Transfer
Lost Income
Penalties
Unbudgeted Staff Costs
Regulatory Fines
Accounting Error

Indirect Impact

	High	Medium	Low
Increased Insurance Costs			
Loss of Major Customers			
Loss of Market Share			
Loss of Deposits			
Loss of Key Staff			

Reputational Impact		✓	

Bank Analogs

Retail	
Corporate	
Operations	

Lessons/Actions

Lessons/Actions

Completed by:	Name
	Date
Input to Database by:	Name
	Date

risks of travel, one might choose to debate air travel first. In the same way, it can be useful to use some emotive examples of operational risk issues.

❑ *Make policy documents snappy* Most people feel they are very busy at work and do not believe their time is best spent reading through long policies. So keep policy documents concise, clear and practical. Ensure that staff have read the policy and understand it through some form of feedback (such as a quiz).

❑ *Look at the results of recent events* For similar reasons, it is often useful to review the results of the most recent operational risk incidents in the bank in question. Bank management and staff, like most people, tend to be interested in real life events rather than potential outcomes. Therefore, it can help to build a database of internal or external incidents that can be analysed or referred to (eg Figure 6).

❑ *Use IT* Mundane and repetitive tasks that are performed by humans – eg copying details onto a form or carrying out manual checks – are prone to error. Where possible, technology should be used to help avoid errors. While historically computers have been used to carry out basic edit checks, as technology advances it will be possible to build in controls that are less intrusive to the customer, but more effective. Already profiling technology and neural networks (systems with some in-built logic that looks for unusual transaction patterns) are being used in banks to identify fraudulent and money-laundering transactions.

❑ *Performance appraisal process* In general, people will make things happen if they know that it affects their career. Therefore, building in the right attitude to risk in the performance appraisal process is key. If staff are only judged on their sales performance with no reference to risk they will focus their attention on generating sales without considering the cost of risk. This is an area that the Bank of England has taken an interest in, particularly in terms of the risk/reward profile of bank employees' salary packages (see Chapter 9). There are no easy answers to this issue, however, as market practice often dictates salary packages. However, management needs at least to recognise it as an issue – and not only in terms of trader bonuses. For example, at The Royal Bank of Scotland we found that when we first introduced a key control self-assessment questionnaire, asking branch staff to complete it on a regular basis, there was initially a poor response rate. On investigating,

PANEL 3

CHANGING A BANK'S OPERATIONAL RISK CULTURE

The culture of an organisation is very difficult to express tangibly. There has been much talk in recent years about instilling a "control culture" in banks, but it is difficult to define exactly what is meant by this.

If defining organisational culture is difficult, changing it is even more challenging. While we cannot cover in detail the rich topic of change management, here are some starting points.

1. Remove the "blame culture"

Most organisations find it easy to criticise and difficult to praise. If it appears to the employees that the bank's only communication about operational risk is to sack or severely reprimand poor-performing personnel after a *major* operational risk incident, the example set is that it is acceptable to do things badly providing you do not get caught. This will lead to staff trying to cover up what they are doing wrong. Problems will tend to be discovered only once they have grown to be very sizeable.

To avoid this, the performance appraisal process must be designed to pick up poor management and staff at an early stage so that, where appropriate, these employees can be counselled well before an incident happens. When an incident does occur, the staff involved should be helped to improve and made to feel less concerned about admitting their mistake. In this way, small incidents can be stopped from turning in to major ones.

2. Promote personal responsibility

Many banks suffer, to an extent, from what might be termed "silo thinking". This means that staff only focus on the narrow range of tasks they are asked to do without thinking about the impact of what they do on others in the bank.

This can result in departments "throwing their rubbish over the fence into the next-door garden". For example, to meet a schedule, a department may complete their processing to a sub-standard level and pass it to the next department who are left to "clean up" the transactions – or pass the problem on to the next department in the chain. Yet a small error in a transaction in one part of the bank can end up being a major operational risk issue in another.

Two ways to engender a culture of personal responsibility are:

(1) to ensure that all parts of the organisation have full knowledge of the business and the business processes from end to end, not just their part of the process, so they understand the significance of what they are doing; and

(2) to develop department performance targets that explicitly consider the quality of the output and information that flow to other areas.

At The Royal Bank of Scotland, the introduction and eventual certification of processes under ISO 9000 has helped a number of departments improve the quality of work and reduce errors.

3. Raise the status of operations-related functions

Historically, banks have focused their brightest and best staff on developing new business and looking at credit-related issues. In some cases, operations-related functions have had to make do with the staff that other areas did not want. An effective bank operations area needs good managers who have the resources to hire and motivate bright staff.

we found that none of the staff's performance was measured on completing this questionnaire. As soon as we included the questionnaire as one of staff's key result areas, the completion rate dramatically improved.

❏ *Timely, accurate information* The easiest way for bank personnel to sidestep the issue of operational risk is to say that they do not have enough information, or the right information, to do anything about it. Attention needs to be focused on improving the flow of operational risk information to business managers and staff. As a stopgap, proxy information that is easier to obtain can help to indicate risks such as error rates, staff turnover, system capacity or security breaches.

❏ *Formal training* A 1997 survey of operational risk management practices in UK banks by the British Bankers' Association and Coopers & Lybrand found that only 16% of the banks linked their risk evaluation to training within the organisation. We have found that, to be useful, training needs to be focused on practical day-to-day implementation of the policy and the tasks surrounding it. It is not appropriate simply to make high-level statements about where the policy should be used; it must also be shown in context. Consequently, training needs to be developed in conjunction with each business. The training should be rolled out as soon as possible after the policy is implemented. In the same way that the bank would not implement a new computer system without providing training, policies need similar support. Some training now is better than a full course later. Training needs to be carried out at all levels of the business. There is no point in training staff and not their managers. On the first day back at work, management will not be able to support the policy with technical back-up and, worse still, may override the policy because they do not understand what it is trying to achieve.

How can specialist teams help?

This section considers how a central team of specialists, such as a group risk function, might help a bank improve its operational risk management, apart from strengthening its control environment.

In order to be effective a central risk function or other specialist team needs the prerequisites illustrated in Figure 7:

❏ *Competency* Any central team of experts needs to have the skills within the team to be able to help the business areas master specific aspects of operational risk. These skills would include technical expertise – such as understanding processes, systems and human resources issues – as well as softer skills such as communication. The specialist will also need to have market knowledge of the areas that the bank operates in, in order to be viewed as credible within the business areas. This can be challenging for an operational risk expert working in a very diverse banking group.

❏ *Authority* Any central risk function must have the explicit authority of the board and be seen to have this authority, either through policies or communications.

Table 8. What can central units or specialist teams offer?

1. Consistent levels of risk taking and risk management throughout the organisation, by developing or implementing corporate standards and by monitoring the business areas.
2. Better knowledge transfer. If an approach to an operational risk issue works well in one part of the bank, passing the information on can help others avoid "reinventing the wheel".
3. A second opinion to support a business unit decision.
4. An independent view for senior bank management, particularly where there are arguments between departments on risk issues.
5. Outside help while a new business unit is building up its skills in operational risk management.
6. The "straw man" argument: it is often useful to have independent specialists step forward to initiate discussions, whether or not their original ideas are adopted.
7. Resources to develop specific tools to help the business with the different aspects of operational risk management such as risk identification questionnaires, risk mapping tools, risk assessment tools or some form of risk quantification model.
8. Training on specific operational risk issues and policy.

❏ *Acceptance* The third prerequisite is that management, staff and the board accept that the unit can add value for the key reasons summarised in Table 8. Without this, the unit is unlikely to be invited by the business areas to participate in decisions at an early stage and will need to rely on policies to influence decisions. This can lead to the central unit being seen as a hindrance to business.

Summary

This chapter has covered promoting and embedding risk-aware business practice across a diverse retail banking group. Difficulties such as data collection, and the lack of any generally accepted methodologies to measure operational risk, mean that this is not an area that can be fixed overnight. Improvements must be built up over time as data and systems become available.

There may seem to be a lot of issues for a bank to focus on, but there are three which, if tackled, will help managers achieve many of the necessary improvements:

❏ Recognition by management that it is ultimately responsible for improving operational practices, and that poor management affects the quality of service and ultimately the brand, reputation, costs and income of the bank.

❏ Recognition by staff that they must take personal responsibility for their actions.

❏ Provision of management and staff with access to the information and data that they need to take action.

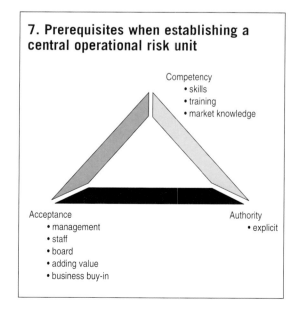

7. Prerequisites when establishing a central operational risk unit

Competency
• skills
• training
• market knowledge

Acceptance
• management
• staff
• board
• adding value
• business buy-in

Authority
• explicit

Appendix: further breakdown of the categories of risk

Type	Sub-type	Type	Sub-type
Process risk	Pre-transaction	**System risk**	Data corruption
	Marketing risks		Programming errors/fraud
	Selling risks		Security breach
	New connection		Capacity risks
	Transaction		System suitability
	Error		Compatibiltiy risks
	Fraud		System failure
	Contract risk		Strategic risks (platform/
	Product complexity		supplier)
	Capacity risk	**Business**	Change management
	Management information	**strategy risk**	Project management
	Erroneous disclosure risk		Strategy
People risk	Integrity		Political
	Fraud	**External**	Outsourcing/external
	Collusion	**environmental**	supplier risk
	Malice; unauthorised use	**risk**	Physical security
	of information		Money laundering
	Rogue trading		Compliance
	Competency		Financial reporting
	Management		Tax
	Key personnel		Legal (litigation)
	Health and safety		Natural disaster
			Terrorist threat
			Strike risk

1 *The opinions expressed in this chapter are those of the author and do not necessarily represent those of The Royal Bank of Scotland plc. The ideas and opinions expressed in this chapter do not constitute advice to any organisation or individual and should not be relied upon for any business purpose. Independent advice should be sought in all circumstances.*

DEVELOPMENTS IN ANALYSING AND QUANTIFYING OPERATIONAL RISK

8

Analysis of Mishandling Losses and Processing Errors

Mark Laycock[1]

Deutsche Bank AG

Operational risk is not unique to financial institutions – most firms manage operational risks as part of their everyday activities. However, within banks, securities firms and other participants in the financial sector there are increasing pressures to make the management of this type of risk more transparent. Some of these pressures are coming from regulators, as well as from senior management.

More active operational risk management at the corporate level is bound to lead to decisions about which risks a firm wants to avoid, transfer, reduce or assume. In some areas, for example the custody business, the management of these risks and perceived economies of scale appear to be leading to the outsourcing of certain operations. As a result, operational risk management will increasingly influence shareholder value.

In this chapter, we first offer a broad definition of operational risk, and then describe how to analyse one distinct sub-category – mishandling losses and processing errors. We show how to quantify these risks and how this information can be used to improve bank operations.

Operational risk: definition, causes and effects

DEFINITION

Financial institutions currently employ a number of different definitions of operational risk. These can usually be categorised as broad or narrow in scope. The definition that I favour is in the broad category:

> Operational risk is the potential for adverse fluctuations in the profit-and-loss statement or the cashflow of the firm due to effects that are attributable to customers, inadequately defined controls, system or control failures, and unmanageable events.

This definition is wide-ranging and yet gives an indication of what needs to be considered when measuring, monitoring or managing operational risk. Organisational issues, such as the clear allocation of responsibility and authority, would be captured under "inadequately defined controls". Information issues, such as the content and timeliness of reports, could be interpreted as an element of "inadequately defined controls", or "system or control failures". Business continuity planning and disaster recovery would be addressed by the "unmanageable events" element.

Some other definitions of operational risk are broader and less specific than the one above, and may make communication on the subject more difficult. For example, some definitions describe operational risks as being "all risks that are not market or credit risks". As a definition, this is not very satisfactory. It defines operational risk as what is left in the risk "universe" once other effects have been taken into account; as a caricature, this definition is saying that what is not a dog is automatically a cat!

One influence on the definition of operational risk is whether a firm uses risk-adjusted performance measurement techniques such as risk-adjusted return on capital (Raroc).[2] These performance measures help a firm consider the returns generated in comparison with the risks taken by various businesses, and so provide a perspective on the risk–reward relationship. If operational risk were to be excluded from this framework, then business management might be steered towards certain actions merely by the construction of the performance measures.

For example, in some circumstances, it is possible to transform market risk into credit risk by employing over-the-counter products. It is also possible to transform credit risk into operational risk, as when credit exposures are collateralised or margin calls are employed. It may also be possible to transform operational risk into credit risk, for example by purchasing an insurance contract.

The reference to fluctuations in profit and loss (P&L) in our definition of operational risk helps provide the focus of operational risk and links the measurement of operational risk to the use of Raroc performance measures. In turn, including operational risk in the Raroc calculation promotes more rational decision taking that takes into account the possibility that one kind of risk is simply being transformed into another kind of risk.

CAUSES OF OPERATIONAL RISK

Definitions of operational risk need to be segmented so that the individual causes can be identified, tools developed, management information systems enhanced and management decisions taken. As a first pass, it is useful to divide operational risk into "business risk" or operating leverage risk and "event risk".

The first segment, business risk, recognises that the P&L statement fluctuates due to changes in customer activity that are independent of any market or credit risk issues. This sort of fluctuation is generally caused by changes in the level of customer demand. Assessments of business risk might reflect, implicitly or explicitly, the firm's marketing strategy, both considered independently and in relation to competitors. Business risk is also related to whether the particular market for the product or service is growing or shrinking.

From an accounting perspective, variable costs and variable incomes are two of the driving factors in assessing business risk. Essentially, business risk is the risk that revenue will not cover costs.

The non-business risk segments of operational risk can usefully be termed as event risks. More explicitly, operational event risk represents the potential for fluctuations in the P&L account or the cashflow statement due to risks or exposures associated with:

❏ inadequately defined controls;
❏ system or control failure; and
❏ unmanageable events.

Customers are not mentioned in this definition, largely to prevent any possible confusion with our characterisation of business risk. However, customers are also a source of some kinds

of event risk and they are covered in the detailed segmentation of event risks below.

A number of dimensions have been proposed for segmenting the causes of event risk. Table 1 presents one way of looking at the broad categories and subcategories. (Similar approaches can be found elsewhere, including the JP Morgan 1997 Annual Report.)

There is plenty of room for debate over the allocation of sub-categories to categories. The decisions are likely to be influenced by details specific to individual firms, such as who takes responsibility for each of the risks.

Amongst the sub-categories are some that are extremely difficult, or impossible, to quantify, such as organisational issues. Reputational risk, which describes the risk of forgoing future income streams due to loss of reputation, is also difficult to place. There is some contention as to whether it really is a separate risk or exposure

---

Table 1. Different causes of event risk

People/employees
errors
misdeeds
employment law
employer's liability
absence/loss of key staff
organisational structure
corporate governance
wrongful trading

Customer relationships
client suitability
client capacity/ultra vires
client powers/authority to transact
money laundering

Technology
system failure
system integrity
system suitability
system age
system support
system conformance to corporate standards
model risk
data quality

Assets
business interruption
asset loss/destruction
third-party theft
environmental damage/issues
fraud

Regulator/supplier
legal risk
compliance with standards
changes in regulatory standards
supplier "failure"

Other
project risk
reputational risk

category, or simply an amplifier of the impact of an event covered by another risk category.

The causation categories of event risk listed in Table 1 are frequently further sub-divided. Sometimes this is so that they can be related to control initiatives, risk financing or risk transfer mechanisms, such as insurance from a third party or a captive insurance company. The general insurance categories used by financial firms tend to be:

❑ crime;
❑ terrorism;
❑ professional indemnity;
❑ business interruption;
❑ property damage;
❑ third-party liabilities; and
❑ employer's insurance.

It is relatively easy to see the relationship between the categories in Table 1 and this list of insurance categories. However, for some of the categories there may not be a suitable insurance category, or the risk could be allocated between several, depending upon the exact effect. It is difficult to determine whether this situation has arisen because insurance companies have not been asked to provide cover against particular causes and effects, or whether it is because it has proved very difficult to quantify some exposure categories from outside the individual firm. More recently, some insurance cover has been aimed at a specific event risk: wrongful trading.

EFFECTS OF OPERATIONAL EVENT RISK
In comparison with market risk, both the causes and the effects of event risk are difficult to model – partly due to the difficulty of obtaining data. However, we should remember that market risk quantification, particularly in the form of value-at-risk (VAR) numbers, sets a high standard. It has taken around 30 years for modern portfolio theory to find its way into the armoury of risk monitoring techniques that are used by bank-type trading operations on a daily basis (though portfolio theory has been used by fund managers for a long time).

This is not to imply that market risk was not quantified or managed by trading operations before the generation of VAR figures – merely that different techniques were used. The same can be said for the management of operational event risk. (As an aside, note that operational risk includes the risks associated with the assessment of market risk, such as the accurate capture of all positions generating market risk,

whether their features are accurately reflected in the calculations, and whether the modelling of the behaviour of these positions is accurate.)

The effects of event risk are usually easier to measure than the causes. The nature of these event risk effects can be split between low-frequency/high-impact events, and those that are high-frequency/low-impact. Those that are of relatively high-frequency/low-impact lend themselves to some form of quantitative analysis and statistical modelling, as a result of the volume of data.

The relationship between the causes and the effects of operational risk is illustrated in Figure 1. For a high-frequency/low-impact event, for example the late settlement of a security transaction, there are likely to be several possible causes (eg human error or system suitability). For low-frequency/high-impact events, such as wrongful trading, there may also be several factors involved, such as poor or ineffective controls, in addition to the propensity for an individual to commit one or more acts. Due to lack of data, it can be difficult to generate distributions of the frequency or severity of low-frequency/high-impact events that relate to the individual institution.

High-frequency/low-impact events can often be distinguished from low-frequency/high-impact events by the time lag between the operational event itself and the moment when its effect is felt by the organisation. High-frequency/low-impact events tend to make themselves felt in a relatively short period of time. A trader's handwriting error on a trade

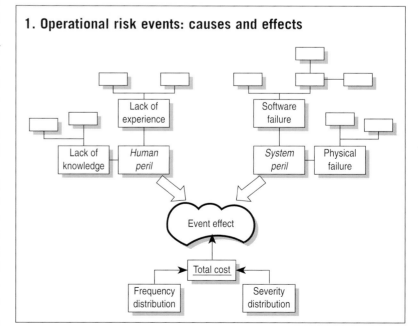

1. Operational risk events: causes and effects

ticket should generate a confirmation mismatch with the exchange or trade counterparty in a very short period of time. By contrast, a low-frequency/high-impact event, such as pricing model risk, might only generate an effect long after the model is initially reviewed and the market conditions have changed.

There are always exceptions; for example a number of settlement failures might derive from the lack of capacity of a system that is old or that does not conform to standards that have evolved in the time since the original system was implemented. Another exception would be a business interruption, such as a fire or flood. This kind of risk occurs irregularly, but the impact is usually felt very quickly!

Mishandling losses and processing errors

The rest of this chapter examines how to analyse a particular kind of high-frequency/low-impact event: mishandling losses and processing errors. For this analysis, mishandling losses are defined as the penalty or compensating payments required due to late settlement of cash or securities. Other events associated with transaction processing that give rise to losses, as opposed to increased costs – for example, penalties for late reporting of some transactions to particular organisations – are not covered here.

We first show how to put mishandling losses in perspective in relation to other operational event risks, before looking at the data and its analysis. We then look at how this analysis can be used to improve a firm's performance.

SEGMENTING THE ORGANISATION USING TRANSACTION CHAINS

In addition to segmenting operational risk by *cause*, as discussed above, it is often useful to look at how the risks relate to the *activities* or *organisational structure* of a firm, eg in terms of business line, or customer orientation.

Within many firms, certain groups are perceived to have "ownership" over particular processes, activities or customer groups. For instance, a retail banking division forms a point of interaction between the bank and the customers, and this relationship is influenced by the activities of the division and activities elsewhere in the bank that facilitate retail banking activities (eg processing retail transactions might be an activity executed by the larger operations division). Also, profit centres such as a retail banking division are likely to feel the consequences of operational events in retail banking transaction chains, either directly through the losses or indirectly through allocated costs.

One way of segmenting operational event risk within the organisation is by charting out a transaction chain (Figure 2). This chain can be broken into a number of generic elements such as pre-commitment, commitment, processing and maintenance. Transaction chains can be found in a wide variety of banking activities ranging from retail banking to corporate finance to capital markets trading. Depending upon the product or service, different elements of the transaction chain may have varying degrees of importance in relation to operational event risk and the various causation categories.

For completeness, the transaction chain should also include an expiration element. This represents activities such as the historical archiving of records, when a transaction is removed from the books and records of the firm. As some

---

2. Transaction chain

135

ANALYSIS OF

MISHANDLING

LOSSES AND

PROCESSING

ERRORS

aspects of the expiration element may be required by law or a regulator, operational event risk exists here too.

THE TRANSACTION CHAIN AND
MISHANDLING LOSSES

Mishandling losses are the effect rather than a cause of operational event risk. However, because mishandling losses are often relatively high-frequency/low-impact, and as a result there is likely to be sufficient data to support qualitative and sometimes quantitative analysis that is specific to the individual firm, their analysis allows one to quantify the risks posed by a basket of relevant causation categories.

As well as being linked to a variety of operational event risk categories, independently or in combination, mishandling losses may also be the result of actions (or inactions) at a number of the elements in the transaction chain. For example, if the counterparty static database is not maintained then settlement instructions may be erroneous and contribute directly to mishandling losses. Errors on the deal ticket, operator error in transcribing the deal ticket, unexpected system downtime and other events can all contribute directly to mishandling errors. Although there may be a range of causes of mishandling losses in the transaction chain, the effects are usually captured by the operations or processing functions.

The transaction chain also shows some of the linkages and dependencies between departments or divisions in the same firm. Often, different businesses within a firm are at different stages in their product life cycle (both in the firm and the marketplace) so that a supporting division, such as operations, will be expected to apply varying performance standards depending upon the individual transaction chain – eg spot foreign exchange, in contrast to structured credit derivatives.

The transaction chain does not capture all of the operational event risks of the organisation, but it does capture many (Figure 3).

Despite these caveats, quantifying and modelling mishandling events is useful when considering remedial action or making cost–benefit analyses – often a more difficult part of the risk management cycle than revising the controls. Figure 4 shows the stages of a framework for event risk management.

This framework can be applied to many different levels of the organisation. It can also be applied to market and credit risk, giving the firm the advantage of employing the same risk framework throughout the organisation and across risk types. In fact, in many firms such frameworks are already being applied to operational event risk, although the various steps, stages and elements may not be formally described or defined.

Looking at Figure 4, we can see that Step 4 involves making certain decisions about what to do with the identified risks: avoid, transfer, reduce or assume. The ultimate form of avoidance is to cease the activity that gives rise to the risk. As we noted at the beginning of this chapter, some forms of operational event risk transfer, for example insurance contracts, result in the transformation of the risk from operational event risk into credit risk; this kind of transformation might affect the total amount of risk incurred by the firm, or it might leave the level of risk unchanged. However, steps can be taken to reduce the event risk, for example the re-engineering of various elements of the transaction chain. Generally, capital is allocated for the risks assumed; even if a risk is reduced there will be a residual portion that is still assumed.

OPERATIONAL EVENT RISK AND
PERFORMANCE ASSESSMENT

Firms that measure Raroc to assess the performance of business units must allocate capital explicitly to cover operational event exposures

3. Segmentation of operational event risk across business processes

Non-transaction based

Environment – internal, external

Management

Transaction based

Pre-commitment commitment | Processing maintenance

Deal entry

Timeline for product/process

4. Operational event risk management cycle

Tactical operational event risk objectives and standards

Step 1 – Identify the hazard
Process/task analysis → List hazards → List causes → In-depth hazard identification

Step 2 – Assess the risk
Assess hazard exposure → Assess hazard severity → Assess event probability → Complete risk assessment

Step 3 – Analyse risk control measures
Identify control choices → Determine control effects → Prioritise risk control measures

Step 4 – Make control decisions
Select risk controls → Make risk decisions (Avoid / Transfer / Reduce / Assume)

Step 5 – Implement risk controls
Make implementation clear → Establish accountability → Provide support

Step 6 – Supervise and review
Supervise → Report → Review

mention some techniques that may assist in identifying the hazards (Step 1) that give rise to mishandling losses, but many of these hazards are already known to professionals working in the individual transaction chains. (The reason that Step 1 is discussed at this stage is that mishandling losses and processing errors arise from a number of causation categories, but the firm's data may only record that an event or effect of a certain size has occurred – in other words, we are obliged to work from effect to cause rather than the other way round.)

We then take a look at data and modelling of event frequency and severity, and examine various drivers of mishandling losses, before considering aspects such as the information contained in cancel/amend data, statistical control processes, and cost–benefit comparisons. We also take a look at techniques that allow risk managers to "drill back" from effects to causes.

QUANTIFYING OPERATIONAL RISKS REPRESENTED BY MISHANDLING LOSSES

The data for the analysis of mishandling losses are the history of penalty payments for late settlements. Payments are generally required as compensation for late settlement of cash or securities. These compensation arrangements commonly apply where settlement is categorised as "free of payment", as opposed to "delivery versus payment". The compensation is usually based upon an estimate of the overnight interest rate applied to the amount that was due to be settled for the number of days for which the settlement failed. These data will usually be held by the operations department. The analysis of the data begins with relatively simple techniques, graduating to the fitting of suitable distributions and finally the calculation of a suitable amount of capital required to support the risks. In the Raroc framework, the relevant business may decide to implement additional controls so as to reduce the risks and reduce the allocated capital.

Late payment penalties may be related to securities as well as cash movements. It is not only new transactions that initiate a movement of cash or securities. For example, an interest rate swap may not create a cash movement at inception, but it may create cash movements throughout the life of the contract. This affects the interpretation of the results of operational risk analyses, and the choice of metrics and standards.

The kinds of events that result in mishandlings that are of sufficient importance to be

and risks. For transaction chains, some of these event risks will manifest themselves as mishandling losses. Being able to quantify the impact of a basket of causes of event risk is part of the Raroc capital allocation process. We should remember, however, that while the causes of mishandling events may prove to be amenable to quantitative analysis and capital allocation, they are not the only source of event risk in a transaction chain. They may not even represent the largest risks.

Looking at Figure 4, the discussion below relates mainly to Step 2 (assess the risk) and Step 3 (analyse risk-control measures) in relation to mishandling events and processing errors. The discussion of Step 3 will look at how to make choices about enhancing controls or implementing new controls, rather than examining individual control mechanisms. We also

137

ANALYSIS OF
MISHANDLING
LOSSES AND
PROCESSING
ERRORS

investigated may be grouped together in standard error categories, eg incorrect instructions, late delivery of instructions, etc. The "granularity" of the late payment penalty data affects the kind of analysis that can be performed, and even at this early stage there may be cost–benefit considerations. For example, the cost of storing details about a particular mishandling loss will provide a cut-off for the minimum size of loss to be recorded. It is difficult to justify spending £20 to record details of a £5 mishandling loss. Although 1000 losses each with a loss value of £5 is as expensive as a single loss of £5000, the task of identifying suitable ways to control the losses may have to be approached quite differently in each instance.

ANALYTICAL TECHNIQUES
Cost–benefit considerations can have a particularly important effect during the investigation of mishandling losses. If a mishandling event is described as being due to an "incorrect description", then additional information may be required to arrive at an operational event risk category. For example, the incorrect description might have been caused by a trader's illegible handwriting, whereas a late delivery of instructions might be attributable to either unscheduled system downtime or delays resulting from the need to process larger volumes of transactions beyond the design of the system specification.

The experts in the particular transaction chain element can often provide additional texture or "colour" to the information in the database. It may be this information that forms the basis for the remedial action. Further information on a single event is expensive to collect and store, but allows for more focused remedial action. For operational risk managers, one common question is whether to amend an existing system of record keeping (often the easier and safer choice), or whether to set up a new system that may cater solely for the operational risk manager.

Risk assessments based upon the use of expert panels or intuitive "gut feeling" often distinguish between frequency and severity of the events. One frequently used tool, the risk assessment grid, can be seen in Figure 5. Managers can use this grid to vary their response to risks that are low-frequency/high-impact and those that are high-frequency/low-impact. Where a certain kind of loss has not yet been experienced by the firm, expert panels and their judgements may be the only source of information. Where the industry has experienced a loss, but a

given firm has not, then some information becomes available.

Reliability analysis and hazard analysis provide a series of quantitative techniques that are often used in engineering risk assessment. These techniques usually distinguish formally between the frequency of events and their severity. In relation to operational event risks, the drivers of the severity may be more akin to market or credit risk. For example, in the case of wrongful trading or model risk the severity may be related to market movements and to the time taken to discover the misbehaviour or error.

PROCESS ANALYSIS: FREQUENCY MODELLING
One starting point in the analysis of the frequency of mishandling events is to turn the data into a graph. A graph of the number of recorded mishandling events per day across time can reveal trends in mishandling events, such as seasonality. Although seasonality and other trends can be quantified, it may initially be easier to spot these features in a simple graph. For example, a weekly cycle might be expected: Monday mornings and Friday afternoons are generally not good times for many tasks! A seasonal cycle might also reflect holidays such as Christmas. Further, the data can also be overlaid with other information, such as the amount of overtime worked, to gauge the impact of extreme workloads. If records are kept of daily transaction volumes then it might also be possible to identify whether peaks of mishandling events are associated with significant peaks in volumes.

Figure 6 illustrates a record of mishandling events per day, and provides an impression of the average performance and how much "bad" and "good" days deviate from this. Given the

5. Risk assessment grid

138

6. Mishandling events per day over time[3]

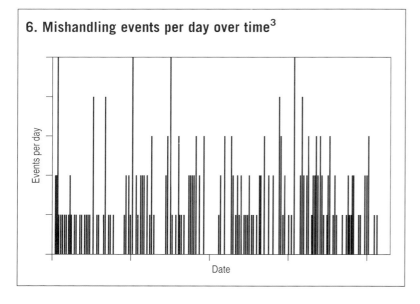

pattern of events, one might be tempted to check whether there really are days with no mishandling losses, or whether there are mishandling losses every day but that sometimes their small size means that they are not recorded, or that they are not recorded due to human error.

An alternative representation of the mishandling event frequency would be to use the ratio of events per day as a percentage of daily transaction volume or, more accurately, a percentage of movements of cash and securities. The level of performance deemed adequate or achievable is often expressed in terms of percentages, for example less than 0.2% of daily cash/security movements. Such standards are likely to vary across the range of products and will also depend upon which stage the product is at in

7. Distribution of mishandling events per day

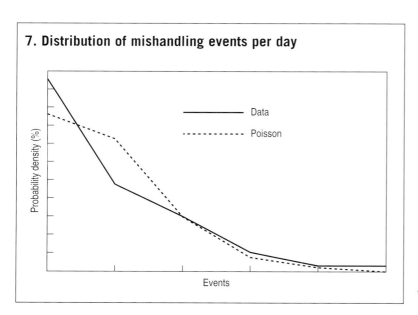

terms of its life cycle at the firm. Higher performance levels would be expected for a standard high-volume product in the mature stage of the product life cycle, eg spot foreign exchange transaction processing, than for relatively low volume customised structured products which may still be at the "innovation stage". An intuitive impression of operational performance can be gained by comparing performance at each life-cycle stage of a product to performance rates achieved in the marketplace. This sort of comparison can also be used when setting acceptable standards.

The distribution of the frequency of events can be modelled. A reasonable fit should be found with *poisson function*, which describes the arrival frequency of random events for a constant unit of time. Figure 7 shows the distribution of actual events per day in comparison with a poisson distribution. A simple review of the graph suggests that when things go wrong there is a tendency for the problems to affect more than one transaction, as the data show a higher probability of multiple events occurring than would be expected from looking at the poisson distribution and a lower probability of single events.

Other distributions that could also be used include the *exponential distribution*, which is used in reliability or hazard analysis to describe the time between events or "failures" – for example, the mean time between failures. With regard to mishandling events for a sufficiently large volume of transactions, the time between events may be less than one day; this can cause problems when using the exponential distribution from a reliability analysis perspective.

From an operational risk perspective, the graph in Figure 7 is interesting but suggests that more extensive analysis will be needed if we are to identify the *causes* of the mishandling events (ie Figure 4, Step 1: identify hazards). Some of the techniques for identifying causes are described in the following section. The analysis is complicated by the fact that a mishandling event may represent the effects of operational risk events across a number of stages of a transaction chain and due to a variety of causation categories. This can make it difficult to arrive at a specific conclusion.

Having identified the poisson distribution as a rational and reasonable description of the *frequency* of mishandling events, our focus moves to the *severity* of these events.

PROCESS ANALYSIS: SEVERITY MODELLING

As with frequency analysis, a relatively simple graphical analysis of the severity of events can be very revealing. Different inferences and amendments to controls might be drawn from a relatively large number of small losses in comparison to a small number of large losses.

These mishandling losses can be fitted to distributions such as the *Weibull distribution*, which is often used in reliability analyses and is emerging in the financial literature as a candidate for modelling continuous random variables for losses and extremes.

The exponential distribution we mentioned above is a special form of the Weibull distribution. However, the Weibull distribution does not have the same strict randomness requirement as the exponential. Further, the Weibull shape parameter, c, may take on a predictable value depending upon the nature of the problem.

The Weibull probability density function is:

$$P_x(x) = \left(\frac{c}{\alpha}\right)\left(\frac{x - \xi_0}{\alpha}\right)^{c-1} e^{-\left[\frac{(x-\xi_0)}{\alpha}\right]^c}$$

Inevitably there are some difficulties in fitting the distribution at the more severe end of the loss spectrum. This is largely caused by the lack of data. The tails of the distribution affect issues such as the allocation of economic capital, usually as part of a Raroc calculation. The problem of fitting a distribution to events is more acute where the firm has very few data points to use, or even none (for example, when trying to model the impact of wrongful trading).

If the information is available, it is often interesting to compare the distribution of mishandling losses to the distribution of transaction size. If this reveals a "good" fit, then the mishandling events would seem to be independent of the trade size. In turn, this suggests that the causes of mishandling losses are generic, as opposed to being events that tend to happen to large or small transactions.

If there is a smaller frequency of large losses than the transaction graph would suggest that this might be due to additional controls over large trades, for example checking with "six eyes" instead of "four eyes". Larger than expected losses might be attributable to the time taken to identify and remedy mishandling events; this would have implications for the reconciliation process.

The severity of mishandling losses is determined by several factors such as:

❏ size of the cash/security movement;
❏ the level of interest rates used to determine the compensation to the counterparty; and
❏ the number of days for which the compensation is required.

Keeping everything else constant, the larger the size of the cash/security movement that goes astray, the larger the penalty for late settlement and the higher the severity. This factor is likely to be the most significant determinant of the size of mishandling losses. Also, the higher the level of interest rates then the larger the penalty, and the longer the period for which the settlement "fails" then the larger the penalty.

Often firms will already possess data for each of these severity drivers. For example, the team implementing the market risk methodology will have a distribution of short interest term rates, whereas operations personnel may have collected data on transaction sizes. The main difficulty is likely to arise when constructing the relationship between these different drivers.

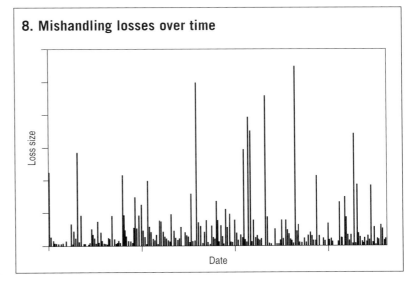

8. Mishandling losses over time

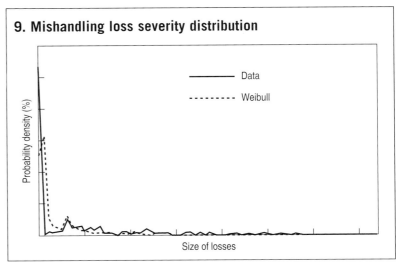

9. Mishandling loss severity distribution

This multivariate aspect of the severity distribution can also affect the interpretation of existing data on mishandling losses. For example, if the total mishandling penalties are monitored over a period as part of performance monitoring, then the total size of the penalties can be influenced by factors that are beyond the control of the settlements area – eg transaction size. A settlements area might reduce the frequency of the events, but the severity of each event might still increase because the transaction sizes have increased, or because interest rates have risen.

Once the severity data have been collected, it is possible to model the size of mishandling events on a daily basis by combining the frequency of events with the severity of the events. Fitting a single distribution enables the firm to assess the risk from the basket of causation events that can give rise to mishandling losses (ie Figure 4, Step 2) and is crucial for capital allocation.

Before we move on to the problem of capital allocation, however, note that several advantages arise from considering the frequency of events separately from their severity. For a start, this makes it possible to assess the impact of controls introduced in the past over the probability of mishandling events occurring. It also becomes possible to consider changes that are expected to happen in the future period covered by the capital allocation. For example, is the marketing emphasis towards larger but fewer transactions? Are revisions to controls, or additional controls, expected to become effective? What impact might these changes have on the distribution of mishandling losses?

MISHANDLING LOSS MODELLING AND CAPITAL ALLOCATION

While mishandling losses are effects and not causes of operational event risk, their analysis allows a firm to generate a figure for capital allocation for the portfolio of exposures, giving rise to the events that materialise into losses. Capital allocation is one of the control choices available to managers as they try to protect the firm against operational risks (Figure 4, Step 4: Make control decisions). The capital allocation figure might also eventually be included in any Raroc calculations.

The parameters used for converting the loss distribution into a capital allocation will vary from one firm to another. Under some specifications, the allocated capital is designed to represent the 99% confidence interval over 10 days, multiplied by at least three – as in the case of regulatory VAR for market risk.

Other specifications may use different confidence intervals, for example 95%, and different horizons, such as six months or a year. As a result, the distribution of "daily mishandling losses" needs to be transformed to reflect the appropriate time horizon.

Although the central limit theorem might provide a short cut, by suggesting the use of a normal distribution for moving from a distribution of daily events to a distribution of events for the desired time horizon, it is not certain that the normal distribution would be appropriate for such a heavily skewed distribution as the Weibull distribution or the distribution of illustrative events shown in Figure 10. As can be seen from the Figure, the result is dominated by days of no, or very small, losses.

Despite these concerns, obtaining data for the higher confidence intervals often stipulated in the Raroc parameters can best be derived by using a statistical distribution based on experienced events and recognising that there is model risk.

Having determined the amount of capital allocation for a settlement activity there are still a number of issues over how this information is used in the Raroc calculation itself. Firstly, the mechanisms used for estimating the capital allocation for mishandling losses should be reviewed for consistency with other capital definitions, such as market risk, before including in a Raroc calculation.

Secondly, from a firm-wide perspective there is the issue of how to aggregate capital allocations for the market, the credit, operational

10. Distribution of daily losses

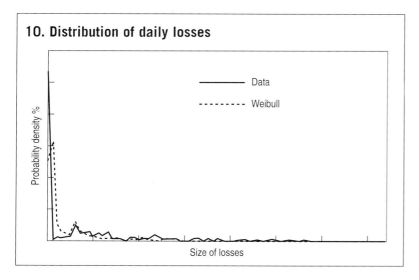

event and other risks; are these risks independent of each other and, as a result can they be aggregated by the square root of the sum of the squares? However, before reaching the firmwide level there are issues about aggregation across operational event risks at one organisational level. For example, are exposures attributable to client suitability and mis-selling independent of mishandling losses for a given product line in a particular location? This issue of the relationship between causation categories underlying mishandling losses is absorbed by the data used in determining the capital allocation. In effect, the whole basket of causation categories is embedded in the recorded mishandling losses. This leads us on to the next key issue in assessing operational risks.

CAPITAL ALLOCATION IS NOT ENOUGH

The allocation of economic capital for mishandling losses suffers from a criticism that is sometimes levied against the use of the VAR measure in the management of market risk. The measure of how much risk you are exposed to does not indicate the sources of that risk (Figure 4, Step 1: identify the hazard). This is why mishandling losses also need to be analysed in more detail as a distribution of frequency and severity. Where possible, even these figures need to be broken down further.

This more detailed analysis of frequency and severity drivers is part of Step 2 in the overall operational event risk management cycle illustrated in Figure 4 (assessing the risk). This analysis then influences Step 3 (the analysis of risk control measures), and Step 4, (making control decisions). The decisions themselves will depend not only on the causes and categories of operational events revealed by the analysis, but also upon the wider corporate infrastructure – such as the project appraisal processes already in place.

ADDITIONAL DATA

The mishandling losses reviewed in the analysis so far can be viewed as events that "escaped" through the network of controls. Analysing these events is made easier if we also review the number of cancelled/amended trades and other risk factors such as unscheduled system downtime, whether or not these led to losses. By extending the events to include cancel/amend trades, the analysis can be applied to those transactions that are delivery versus payment (where a settlement may "fail" but due to the settlement process any losses are minimal).

Some care is needed over the use of these additional data as not every cancel/amend is a potential mishandling loss. Whether these actions have the potential to turn into losses is determined by the definitions used by individual firms and by their data-collection mechanisms. For simplicity, in the discussion below it will be assumed that every cancel/amend is a potential mishandling loss.

Some control-monitoring frameworks, such as those in the category of statistical control processes, suggest grouping the data in order to reduce the amount of "noise" and to make it easier to discern patterns such as the seasonal trends we mentioned above in relation to mishandling losses.

As an illustrative example, Figure 11 aggregates the cancel/amends, as a percentage of each day's transaction volume, by calendar week. It is not easy to see trends, but it is relatively easy to see when an operational event risk may have made its presence felt more "strongly". For example, weeks three, six and 12, or weeks 18 and 19, are extremes, whereas the other weeks appear to be closer to the norm. However, although the use of percentages may make some aspects of interpretation easier, it can also mislead; for example, the good performance in week 11 could be due to low transaction volumes during that week.

The "control lines" on the graph help to determine whether the cancel/amends are within given standards – for example, the weekly average might rise above the upper control line. Control lines can be constructed using a variety of techniques. For example, exponential smoothing might be used to reflect the fact that incremental changes are constantly being made to the control environment.

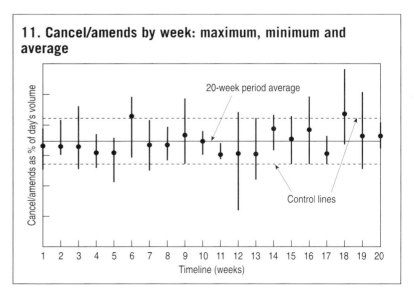

11. Cancel/amends by week: maximum, minimum and average

20-week period average

Cancel/amends as % of day's volume

Control lines

Timeline (weeks)

Figure 12 illustrates results from the same period as Figure 11, only this time the data are grouped into days of the week. As a result, each "day group" has approximately 20 data points. From the graph, it does look as though performance on Mondays is worse than on other days of the week.

USES OF THE ADDITIONAL DATA AND THE MISHANDLING LOSS MODEL

By including the number of cancel/amends in the analysis, a comparison between mishandling losses and mishandling costs can be made. For example, the ratio between cancel/amends and the number of mishandling events might be 10:1 or higher. The cost of a cancellation, for a given product, may perhaps be three times the cost of a correct transaction as the incorrect instructions have to be "backed-out" and the correct instructions inserted in addition to the original incorrect instructions.

The costs attributed to amendments depend upon how amendments are defined. But it is always true that "manhandling" a transaction on multiple occasions adds to costs: the ideal is to "do it right first time". The costs associated with processing transactions are often "fixed", in the sense that they are independent of the size of the transaction. Even errors that are captured by the control mechanisms cost the firm money, and these costs can be as painful as small losses.

Additional information can be derived from the cancel/amends. For example, the benefit of controls can be estimated by applying the frequency of cancel/amends to the severity of the mishandling losses shown in Figure 9. The frequency distribution of cancel/amends is shown in Figure 13.

The statistical distribution that best approximates this frequency of cancel/amends is the logistic distribution. By using samples from this distribution to sample from the mishandling severity distribution in Figure 9, we can produce an estimate of the capital that would be required on a daily basis to support the potential for losses, which can then be compared with the amount of daily capital required for the mishandling losses (the reduced losses). The level of comparison depends upon the definition of the cancel/amend data. Also, any estimate of the capital required that is used in a Raroc calculation will have to be made consistent with calculations and definitions in other risk areas (eg VAR for market risk, and capital for credit and related risks).

If we took a conservative and rather simplistic approach, we might assume that every cancel/amend is a potential mishandling loss. The difference between the two capital estimates would then represent the quality of the controls.[4] This is because, if there were no controls, then the mishandling loss distribution would arise directly out of the frequency distribution of cancel/amends combined with the distribution of severity of the mishandling losses. Alternatively, if the capital allocation was based upon the cancel/amend loss distribution then we would be giving no value to the controls established over the basket of operational event causation categories represented by these events.

If the controls were perfect (ie no transaction slipped through the cancel/amend controls to become a mishandling loss), then any loss severity distribution would have to be estimated as for other low-frequency operational events, as the potential still exists. The cost of these perfect controls can be compared with the estimated allocated capital derived from cancel/amend loss distribution to provide a "return estimate", which

12. Cancel/amends by weekday: maximum, minimum and average

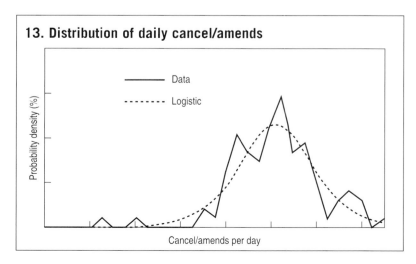

13. Distribution of daily cancel/amends

143

**ANALYSIS OF
MISHANDLING
LOSSES AND
PROCESSING
ERRORS**

can then be compared with return on equity targets used elsewhere in the firm. It might also be used in a cost–benefit analysis. The cost of the controls, as much as the losses themselves, consumes revenues and therefore capital. Ideally, the causes of the cancel/amends would be removed or "engineered out", providing a saving in terms of the cost of the controls as well as in loss reduction, and thereby reducing the capital that needs to be allocated to the business. However, reducing the frequency of mishandling events may increase exposure to the technology category of risk, such as a systems failure.

A fundamental problem when analysing transactions that are captured by an operational risk control mechanism (in this case, the cancel/amends), is that there may simply be no standardised store of information, such as a database describing the results of investigations to review. The people who operate the controls should be the first port of call in the analysis as they experience the controlled events on a daily basis. Although quantitative data may not be available, these skilled individuals can generally put their finger on the problem, if they are asked, and narrow down the scope of any data collection – for example, what happened in Figure 11, Week 12.

A mechanism for identifying the causes of particular operational risk patterns or events, and possibly for organising the storage of the results, is shown in Figure 14. The data collected using such a fault tree can be used to reinforce expert opinion in discussions on remedial action. Again, the cost of the analysis and data collection and storage will need to be weighed against the benefits likely to be obtained.

QUANTIFYING CAUSE AND EFFECT
If cancel/amend data are employed as well as loss data, the larger data set means that relationships between cause and effect can be explored quantitatively. For example, does the error rate, including those items captured by the control framework, increase as trade volumes increase, or is it only noticeable once trade volumes have increased over a particular threshold? This sort of analysis can also assist in planning for changes to trading activities. For example, as a product moves through its life cycle from the moment of innovation towards maturity, then trading volumes of the increasingly standardised product can be expected to increase. The impact this might have on the error rate can be planned for and managed.

Irrespective of this, management is likely to want to review the controls over transaction processing in order to influence the frequency and severity distribution described above. The controls over mishandling losses are intended to drive the curve describing the distribution towards the origin of the graph, reducing the area under the curve and the amount of capital required to support the business. It might be useful, for example, for the controls to differentiate between very large transactions and those of average size. This would be one way to affect the severity distribution: for example, it might allow the truncation of the distribution of daily losses seen in Figure 10, and so reduce the amount of allocated capital.

To affect the distribution of the frequency of errors, risk managers will need to drill into the data to gain an understanding of what is causing the problems. In particular, those errors that are getting through the control mechanisms can provide valuable information.

Certain techniques developed in the engineering disciplines can be used to supplement a review of existing controls and the experience of line managers. One framework, known as "fault tree analysis", begins with the effect and drills back towards the cause(s). Fault tree analysis employs a number of mechanisms, such as logic gates and dependencies, to determine where the causes arise and the one, or more, effects that they may have.

A very simple version is shown below in Figure 14. The "bushy" part of the fault tree is intended to terminate in the individual causes of errors in processing, and so a complete diagram would be much more extensive. In all likelihood multiple trees would be used, depending upon the type of processing error – for example, late delivery of instructions as opposed to incorrect instructions – and upon whether these instructions related to the counterparty or the transaction.

Like other investigative procedures, fault tree analysis is intended to enable the causes of processing errors to be identified and recorded. The analysis should enable conclusions to be drawn as to whether the fluctuations in performance are due to low frequency events, common variations, or special causes irrespective of their regularity. Fault tree analysis may also promote consideration of events that have not yet happened. Just because a cause of event risk has not yet materialised does not mean that the firm is not exposed to that risk. Some of the techniques that can be

14. Fault tree diagram of mishandling errors: causes versus symptoms

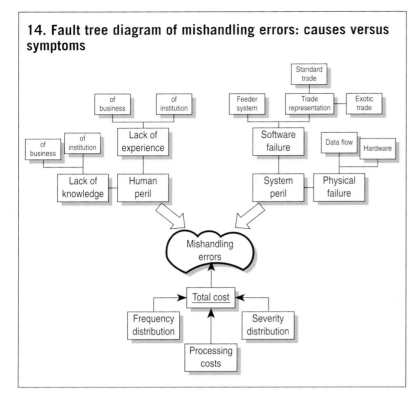

one year, or five years. The firm may also view changes in controls that generate variable costs differently from those that give rise to fixed costs – for reasons related to operational leverage risk.

The costs and benefits of changes to controls feed into the Raroc calculation by affecting the numerator (net income) and the denominator (capital for the risks). The investment in managing the operational event risks will affect the net income stream, and should result in a lower capital allocation. Risk-adjusted return on capital return targets or expectations can further complicate the cost–benefit analysis as they may influence the discounting factors for the time period over which the "savings" or foregone losses and costs are expected to accrue. Alternatively, the internal rate of returns of the "savings" can be used in the allocating of limited resources to implement the changes.

$$Raroc = \frac{\text{Risk-adjusted return}}{\text{Capital f (credit, market, business, event, other risks)}}$$

Appraising a project intended to improve controls can be made even more complicated if the limiting resources are available skills, rather than funding. Often, managers will have to consider whether action should be taken immediately, before the longer term system revisions are implemented. As a result, project appraisal can become quite complex. The quantitative result is likely to be only one of the factors influencing the management decision over whether or not to instigate change.

In the future, techniques involving the theory of "real options" may facilitate this complex analysis. This approach tries to take into account issues such as flexibility and timing in arriving at a value for a particular course of action. Real option analysis might prove particularly helpful in helping managers decide which types of changes in controls to implement – eg whether the number or type of staff needs to be changed, or whether an investment in systems would prove more beneficial – as well as helping them decide whether to implement short-term changes to controls while more fundamental changes are underway. Although this is a relatively new approach in the financial industry, real option techniques have already been applied to project and investment appraisals for the petroleum industry. Some of these aspects are raised by Dixit and Pindyck (1994) and Trigeorgis (1997).

used for further categorisation can be found amongst the methodologies of process control.

COST–BENEFIT ANALYSIS

The aim of the analyses described above is to provide management with information about the causes of variability. A different set of techniques is required when considering the cost–benefit impact of changes to controls. We have already mentioned that modelling of event frequency separately from the severity is useful. Given the drivers of severity distribution described above, it is quite possible that a business might change a process so as to produce fewer errors as a percentage of trading volume, while nevertheless posting higher mishandling *losses* in absolute terms due to increases in volumes and/or larger trade sizes.

Estimates of the cost–benefit of revisions to controls can be made using event frequency graphs such as Figure 7. Here, the aim is to drive the curve closer towards the origin. The difference between the curve describing the current loss situation and the curve describing the losses envisaged after the controls have been revised indicates the possible "benefit" to the firm. This information can be used in conjunction with the present and future costs of implementing the controls. One of the issues in such cost–benefit analysis is the period over which the benefit is expected to be felt – for example

145

ANALYSIS OF
MISHANDLING
LOSSES AND
PROCESSING
ERRORS

Conclusion

This chapter has focused on the application of quantitative techniques to a portfolio of operational risk events in the transaction chain, processing errors, as represented by mishandling losses and cancelled/amended transactions. These techniques should be viewed as supplements to the assessments of operational event risk made by the experts that work in the area – not as substitutes. The models described above do not perfectly fit the data, as the differences between the poisson distribution and actual frequency distributions in Figure 7 show. Thus they may lead to under- as well as over-assessments of capital requirements.

Processing risks may be caused by actions that occur at the pre-commitment and commitment phases as well as by errors in the processing stage itself. These are not the only risks in the transaction chain: elements of the transaction chain such as maintenance often give rise to other operational risks that are difficult to quantify; into this category fall many of the information-related risks including data quality.

In fact, in comparison with many other causes and effects of operational event risk, the analysis of processing/mishandling errors looks relatively straightforward. At least in this area there are some hard(ish) data! As we have shown, there are a number of techniques that can be applied to the analysis of processing errors. Furthermore, so long as the data relate to actual losses, it is possible to estimate the amount of capital that must be set aside – even where the losses are generated by various causes or failures through multiple stages of a transaction chain.

1 *The views and techniques described in this material do not necessarily correspond to the views and opinions of the Deutsche Bank Group or any of its subsidiaries. The author has benefited from extensive discussions with individuals inside Deutsche Bank, in particular Roland Kennett, and outside the bank, but any errors in the views expressed are his alone.*

2 *Risk-adjusted return on capital (Raroc) here is used as a generic term for risk-adjusted performance measurement, as opposed to a particular or specific performance measurement framework sponsored by a given firm or institution. For a discussion, see S. Punjabi, 1998 "Many Happy Returns", Risk, June, pp.71–6.*

3 *The data used in this article, and occasionally described as actual, are in fact illustrative. These illustrative data have been derived from models based on real data and subsequently altered to emphasise its various aspects.*

4 *A related topic arises in market risk. VAR/P&L backtesting can be performed on a "buy and hold P&L" effectively assuming that the trader does nothing to control the risks on a real-time basis, or on an amended "actual P&L" recognising the impact of the trader activity on the distribution of actual P&L in comparison to the market risks taken and possibly even the persistence of the trader.*

BIBLIOGRAPHY

Ansell, J. I., and M. J. Phillips, 1994, *Practical Methods for Reliability Data Analysis*, Oxford, Oxford Scientific Publications.

Dixit, A. K., and R. S. Pindyck, 1994, *Investment under Uncertainty*, Princeton, Princeton University Press.

Embrechts, P., C. Klüppelberg, T. Mikosch, 1997, *Modelling Extremal Events for Insurance and Finance*, Springer-Verlag.

Johnson, N. L., S. Kotz, N. Balakrishnan, 1994, *Continuous Univariate Distributions*, vol.1, Chichester, John Wiley.

Kaplan, R. S., and D. P. Norton, 1996, *The Balanced Scorecard: Translating Strategy into Action*, Harvard: Harvard Business School Press.

Oakland, J.S., 1996, *Statistical Process Control*, Butterworth–Heinemann.

Pecht, M., 1995, *Product Reliability, Maintainability and Supportability Handbook*, CRC Press.

Trigeorgis, L., 1997, *Real Options, Managerial Flexibility and Strategy in Resource Allocation*, MIT Press.

US Air Force, 1997, AFPAM 91-214, *Operational Risk Manual, Implementation and Execution*.

9

Securities Fraud and Irregularities

Case Studies and Issues for Senior Management

Norvald Instefjord, Patricia Jackson and William Perraudin

Birkbeck College; Bank of England; Birkbeck College

This chapter looks at the implications for financial firms of irregular activity in securities trading and, in particular, assesses measures that could help to reduce the likelihood of such activities. A series of prominent cases (for example, the well-publicised problems encountered by Barings, Daiwa, Drexel Burnham, Kidder Peabody and Salomon Brothers) has focused attention on the way in which such irregular behaviour may undermine the solvency of apparently solid, well-capitalised institutions and impose costs on other financial market participants.

In the words of Sir Andrew Large, former Chairman of the UK's Securities and Investments Board (SIB):

> The interesting thing here . . . is the common thread that runs through many of these cases. It is not – as might have been expected – that the regulatory rules which applied to the business were inadequate. No, it is that the organisations' own knowledge and control of their business was shown to have been seriously lacking. Control procedures were breached or were non-existent . . . one serious failure of internal controls may be an accident; but more than half a dozen suggests that there is more going on than a series of individual cases. (Large, 1996)

In this chapter we consider what action management and regulators can take to make firms less vulnerable to these risks. To shed light on these issues, we employ a mixture of case study analysis, drawing on detailed descriptions of four prominent episodes of securities fraud or irregular activity involving US, UK and Japanese companies, and more formal investigations using simple principal–agent models of securities trading operations.

The case studies, presented in Panels 1-4, comprise: the collapse of Barings; the fraudulent activity of Daiwa's New York bond dealer Toshihide Iguchi; Morgan Grenfell and the Guinness affair; and the Drexel Burnham affair.

Two criteria guided us in selecting these episodes. Firstly, we only included cases for which a substantial amount of information was publicly available. Secondly, we focused on episodes in which a firm's employees acted unbeknown to shareholders and most senior managers. These criteria mean that the episodes are representative to a varying degree in different countries. In all countries, however, regulators and senior managers in financial firms regard this kind of case as a serious and growing problem.

The main conclusion we reach is that it is not sufficient to rely on penalising those directly responsible for dealing irregularities and/or fraud. Firms must introduce strong incentives for managers to develop good control environments. The failure of managers who should have spotted irregular behaviour by their subordinates is very apparent in many notorious cases. The failures are variously attributable to ignorance of the nature of the business or to omissions in operating the risk control and accounting systems available to them.

Our formal analysis using principal–agent models of dealers and managers underlines this point. Within our models, imposing strong penalties directly on fraudsters has no impact on the prevalence of fraud. Instead, in equilibrium, it simply reduces monitoring by the dealers' supervisors. Raising penalties on dealers, for example, leads managers to reduce their monitoring so much that, overall, the prevalence of

THE COLLAPSE OF BARINGS

In 1984, the merchant bank Barings & Co acquired a team from a UK broker, Henderson Crosthwaite, and began building a subsidiary, Barings Securities Limited (BSL), specialising in trading Far Eastern securities. Barings recruited Nick Leeson in July, 1989, to work in futures and options settlement in its London office. In March, 1992, Leeson was transferred to Singapore to run the back office of Barings Futures Singapore (BFS), a Barings subsidiary involved in futures dealing on the Singapore futures exchange, Simex. He was promoted rapidly and by late 1992 he was BFS's general manager and head trader.

Much of BFS's business consisted of own-account trading aimed at exploiting small pricing differences between similar contracts on the Singapore and Japanese exchanges. It also acted as broker for clients wishing to trade on Simex. From late 1992 until early 1995, Leeson reported increasingly large profits on apparently risk free arbitrage trading in which positions on Simex were supposedly hedged by equal, offsetting positions on Japanese exchanges.

In fact, Leeson was conducting an elaborate deception. From the first, he made losses. To conceal the losses, Leeson employed a hidden Simex account numbered 88888, persuading a back office programmer to alter Barings accounting systems so that information about 88888 would not be reported back to London. The fact that Leeson was in charge of both dealing and back office operations in BFS was crucial in facilitating the deception.

In August, 1994, an internal audit of BSL concluded that the lack of segregation between front and back offices should be rectified but Barings' management did not implement the recommendation. In January, 1995, Simex became concerned that Barings might be financing its clients' trading, in particular on account 88888, against the rules of the exchange. It wrote to BSL to query this. Also in January, the BFS auditors, Coopers & Lybrand Singapore, became concerned about a receivable of £50 million, apparently due from a New York-based trader. In fact, Leeson had forged the documentation on this receivable in his efforts to cover up his activities in raising funds for margin payments on his increasingly large losses.

In early February, Barings despatched London staff to Singapore to establish what was happening. In the week beginning February 13 a settlement clerk sent from London found an apparent gap of $200 million in BFS's positions. On the evening of February 23, Leeson and his wife fled to Kuala Lumpur, from where he faxed his resignation. Strenuous efforts by the Bank of England to organise a rescue of Barings in the following three days failed largely because it was impossible to gauge the Barings' exposure accurately. On the night of Sunday 26, Barings was therefore declared insolvent and administrators were appointed. The cumulative loss on Leeson's positions at February 27, 1995, was £827 million. The cumulative loss after liquidation was £927 million. A week later, Barings was taken over by Internationale Nederlanden Group NV (ING), a large Dutch banking and insurance group. The SFA took disciplinary action against individual directors of Barings resulting in several being banned as directors or managers.

fraud remains unchanged. By contrast, raising penalties for managers who have not monitored their subordinates directly reduces the prevalence of fraud. Of course, in reality, the incentives faced by dealers and managers will be rather more complex and therefore substitution effects may not be as strong as our simple models imply.

Our analysis suggests that the ability to impose penalties at a range of different levels within the firm is valuable. Penalising managers directly responsible for monitoring *is* likely to assist in reducing fraud. Firms also need to focus on improving their overall control environments to make monitoring easier for individual managers.

Types of dealer fraud

The panels in this chapter provide accounts of four major episodes of fraud or irregular activity by insiders in securities trading operations. Broadly speaking, these case studies and other notorious examples fall into two categories. In the first category, individuals in financial firms deceived or manipulated market participants outside the firm to gain an advantage either for themselves, for their firm or for clients. For example, between 1989 and 1991, Salomon Brothers traders broke rules limiting the fraction of a US Treasury auction for which a firm could bid, at a single price, to 35%. As another example, in 1986, Morgan Grenfell's corporate finance director, Roger Seelig, was involved in the

Guinness share support scheme, which breached the UK Companies Act.

In a second broad category of cases (Barings and Daiwa), weaknesses in control systems led to the concealment of losses and to reports of spurious profits. In such cases, the misreporting can induce firms to pay large bonuses to the traders involved.

In many such cases we examined, the firms' equity-holders suffered substantial losses, in some of the cases partly because of damage to the firms' reputations.[1] For example, following revelations about Salomon's manipulation of Treasury auctions, many counterparties significantly reduced their trading with Salomon, forcing the firm to shrink its balance sheet by a third and thus substantially affecting the firm's profitability. In the Daiwa case, the firm had to absorb not only $1.1 billion in losses but fines totalling $340 million. In one of the cases (Barings) the losses directly caused the failure of the firm and in another (Drexel Burnham) the problems contributed to later failure or closure.

What steps might have prevented the fraud or irregular activity in the cases covered in the case studies? In almost all the episodes we consider, if managers had operated the monitoring systems available to them appropriately, problems would have been uncovered much more quickly. This is most obviously true in the case of Barings. Leeson's actions could have been revealed much earlier if management had acted on the recommendations of internal auditors to separate front and back office operations in Singapore, or had operated Barings' systems for reconciling payments and controlling large exposures as they should.

In other cases, the basic problem appears to have been that senior management allowed itself to become distracted or that it failed to comprehend its subordinates' actions.

Table 1 summarises the various types of case. In each type of case, the firm may be exposed to damage to its reputation and regulatory or legal sanctions. In cases of false reporting or accounting, the firm may also be exposed to heavy book losses. Even book losses may imply substantial economic costs to a firm since bonuses may already have been paid out based on exaggerated measures of the firm's earlier profitability.

The growing importance of dealer fraud

The role of fraud in bank failures is not new. An FDIC study found that fraud was the main

---

Table 1. Types of case

1. Breach of market rules
2. Aiding a breach of the law or market rules by clients
3. False reporting / accounting (disguise of losses)
4. Fraudulent transactions

---

contributing factor in 25% of 92 bank failures in the period 1960–77. The proportion rises to 83.9% if one includes improper lending to individuals or groups connected with the bank as "insider fraud". A review by the Bank of England has suggested that, in the UK in the period 1984–96, fraudulent concealment was a contributory factor in 7 out of 22 cases of problem banks (see Jackson, 1996). In many cases, however, these traditional bank frauds were perpetrated by senior mangers or the bank's owners and hence are not comparable with the specific type of irregularities on which we focus in this chapter.

An unusual feature of the securities business is that even quite junior employees may be in a position to take on substantial exposures in the firm's name. Hence, substantial frauds may be initiated at low levels in the organisation without senior managers or owners knowing. The problem is especially great in fast-moving markets in which highly geared exposures can be created with little up-front expenditure.

Huntington and Davies (1995) believe that dealing fraud is a potential problem in banks of all sizes. They believe that the most common vulnerability is misvaluation of positions but they cite other types of irregularity, for example cases in which possibly small losses are concealed leading to further substantial losses before the problem comes to light. They also mention firms' vulnerability to traders dealing at false market prices to reap personal rewards.

Several factors have contributed to an increase in the kind of large-scale securities fraud we study here. Firstly, securities trading is becoming increasingly complex, making it more difficult for senior management to monitor subordinates. Secondly, the greater globalisation of major players raises their exposure to illicit activity. With groups spanning sometimes 300 legal entities in 30 jurisdictions, management control lines can become strained. It is noticeable that three of the cases in our study involved fraud in small dealing rooms in far-flung locations (Barings and Daiwa) or offices geographically separate from the main operation (Milken's West Coast Drexel operation). Thirdly, the number of firms heavily engaged in securities trading has greatly increased. Banks, as well as traditional securities firms, are now exposed to the risk of securities fraud. Building up monitoring expertise among senior managers and regulators is a major challenge.

Huntington and Davies (1995) see the main factors that determine whether a firm is vulnerable to fraud as structural (complex structures, remote locations), cultural (results at any cost, poor commitment to control), personnel, and business risks (mismatch between growth and systems development).

Incentives

An important question for shareholders is whether contracts can be written to give the management within the firm appropriate incentives to put in place adequate systems and controls and also ensure that they are fully implemented. One problem for shareholders is that it can be very difficult to obtain accurate information on the internal controls and appetite for risk of the financial institutions in which they invest. The development of models to assess risk across a whole portfolio (value-at-risk models and eventually credit risk models) makes it easier to disclose information on the risks taken. Pressure by shareholders for greater disclosure of information may be appropriate.

The Group of Thirty in its study of global institutions, national supervision and systemic risk, suggests that global institutions should subject their worldwide operations to review by a single independent external audit firm, assessing whether the risk management process and procedures promulgated by senior management have in fact been implemented. Information from this audit would be made public.

If adopted, this approach would improve shareholders' understanding of the quality of control environments although it would not necessarily eliminate difficulties they might have in providing managers with appropriate incentives. It may not be easy for either shareholders or the top management of the firms to put in place contracts that will, in all circumstances, provide appropriate incentives for managers and traders. Daripa and Varotto (1997) show that if managers in financial firms care about non-pecuniary benefits (such as status) it may well not be possible to write appropriate contracts. One feature of several of the cases (in particular Barings) is that the traders/managers seem to have been driven as much by concerns about

status as by concerns about salary or bonus. One issue for Leeson was that disclosure to senior management of the (initially small) losses on his dealing operation could well have led to the loss of his job as a dealer and a return to the back office from which he had recently escaped.

This is not to say that the structure of the remuneration package within financial firms can be ignored, because it could considerably worsen the adverse incentive structures that may already exist. If the link between bonuses and profits is too rigid then some dealers may well be encouraged to report fictitious profits, or take excessive risks in the hope of making extra profit. This does not apply only to the danger of fraud. It is clearly very important that incentive schemes take into account the risks to the firm in any strategy (not just the profits earned). The Swiss Federal Banking Commission makes this point in its report on the losses (Sfr 625 million) sustained by UBS in 1997 on its global equity derivatives business and on trading in Japanese convertible bonds. They also highlighted the fact that, whereas traders to some extent participate in short-term, partly unrealised profits, losses that can emerge much later – in the case of long-dated exposures – remain with the bank. The structure of the remuneration package can also affect managers' willingness to exercise tight control, particularly on star traders. Nonetheless, in the highly competitive and mobile labour markets that are a feature of the financial services industry, it may well be difficult for firms to go against market trends in remuneration.

Regulation

If the market does not provide appropriate incentives for firms or managers to create adequate control environments, regulators may need to play a role in creating the right incentives. Regulators can intervene *ex ante* by requiring firms to create mechanisms for combating fraud, or *ex post* once irregularities have been uncovered. The range of actions that can be taken is as follows:

Ex ante
❏ Issuance of guidance concerning systems and controls.
❏ Inspections by regulators or review by external auditors of systems and controls.
❏ Increases in capital requirements to reflect higher risks or more intensive monitoring if the regulator has concerns about the adequacy of systems and controls.

PANEL 2

DAIWA AND TOSHIHIDE IGUCHI

Daiwa Bank had opened its New York Branch in 1956 but it only began to undertake significant global activity in the 1980s. Toshihide Iguchi was chosen to head Daiwa's bond-trading operations in 1983. According to *Financial Times* reports, Iguchi's first loss-making trade ($200,000) occurred in 1984. Iguchi responded to the loss by attempting to trade his way out of his difficulties.

Iguchi's losses over 11 years amounted to $1.1 billion by way of an estimated 30,000 unauthorised trades, an average loss of $400,000 for every working day. The case was considered extraordinary, not only because of the sheer size of the losses and the length of period over which they had been built up but because of the fact that they had been achieved in a "plain vanilla" market – the buying and selling of US Treasury bonds – and the apparent ease with which Iguchi had disguised his losses.

Iguchi had hidden his losses by selling securities held by Daiwa Bank on behalf of customers without authorisation. He concealed these sales by hiding the related trade confirmations and forging statements of securities holdings provided by the custodian of the securities and concealing the originals. This was possible for Iguchi because, until 1993, he was in charge of both front and back office. After the separation of the two departments the discrepancy between actual securities holdings and Iguchi's forged statements was not picked up. It is thought that only the admission by

Iguchi in July 1995 of what he had done alerted Daiwa's management to the true position.

When announcing the losses, Daiwa also announced that the pay of senior management would be temporarily cut for their responsibility. On October 2, 1995 the Federal Reserve Board and New York State Banking Department issued a cease and desist order against the New York branch.

In a joint statement in November 1995 by the Federal Reserve, the FDIC, NYSBD and several other state banking departments it was announced that a joint order terminating the banking operations of Daiwa Bank in the US had been made. Orders were also made requiring the termination of the Daiwa Bank Trust Company's operations. The actions were taken on the basis of information indicating that Daiwa Bank and DBTC and their officials "had engaged in unsafe and unsound banking practices and violations of law over an extended period of time" that were "most serious in nature". Daiwa agreed to terminate or sell its business in the US by February 2, 1996. In addition, the bank was faced with a 24-count indictment claiming criminal fraud.

In February 1996, Daiwa pleaded guilty in a US district court to a conspiracy to conceal the trading losses. Under the plea agreement, Daiwa agreed to plead guilty to 18 of the 24 original charges against it in exchange for which the US government agreed not to prosecute Daiwa Bank and its affiliates. It was required to pay fines of $340 million.

Ex post
❏ Penalties on the firm – fining and de-authorising are intensive and costly to the firm – investigations/supervision.
❏ Penalties on management for not supervising traders or implementing adequate control systems – fining/banning from the industry.
❏ Penalties on traders carrying out the illicit activity – fining/banning from the industry and/or imprisonment.

The difficulty with relying on *ex ante* action is that regulators cannot and should not attempt to check activities within the firms in minute detail. Irregular activities generally constitute a tiny fraction of the huge volume of *bona fide* transactions carried out by the firm and hence are difficult to spot from outside the firm. This point was evident in the Drexel case.

In the latter case, problems existed with a

small number of shell companies in a fraction of the many funds handled by the firm. Furthermore, lax control environments are seldom characterised by the absence of key control systems, which is relatively easy to observe from the outside, but by the controls being overridden or set aside. Spotting this from outside the organisation is quite difficult. Barings provides a good example. Their internal audit of the Singapore operation had identified the fact that Leeson had control over both the front and back office as a significant problem. However, line management overrode their recommendations for change. Such actions by managers are very hard to observe from outside the firm.

In fact only senior management within firms can tell whether systems and controls, at all levels, are being operated appropriately. This has led the regulators to consider ways of holding the senior management of the firms responsible for control systems. The UK Securities and Futures Authority (SFA) has introduced a new rule imposing a direct duty on senior executive officers to take all reasonable steps to ensure that employees of the firm act so as to avoid serious damage to its reputation as a registered firm.

It may well be important for the regulator to impose penalties on both those who fail to ensure tight controls in the firms and the fraudsters. If shareholders find it difficult to

write contracts that establish appropriate incentives for management, regulation provides a backstop. The regulators can also apply *ex post* penalties in a way not open to the firms themselves. A firm can sack a manager or dealer but would find it difficult to claw back a bonus already paid and could not stop the individual from being hired by another firm. In contrast, regulators can ban individuals from the industry and impose fines on both individuals and firms. Table 2 sets out the types of penalty used by the SFA over the period 1991–7. Of 129 cases involving individuals there were 66 fines and 59 individuals were declared not fit and proper (effectively preventing them from seeking certain types of employment in the industry). In 55 cases against firms, there were 45 fines and seven were expelled from the industry. Table 3 sets out the magnitude of the fines.

If shareholders find it difficult to set appropriate incentives for managers, one may ask whether firms (and therefore shareholders unless the firm is a partnership) should be fined or whether the fines should be concentrated on individuals. Overall, securities regulators have tended to be more willing to fine firms and individuals than have banking supervisors. Although most banking supervisors do have the power to fine (see Table 4) in most countries it is used rarely, if at all. Furthermore de-authorisation is usually only employed when the culture of the firm is regarded as irredeemable. The main penalty exerted is a change of management. As the changes sought by banking supervisors tend to be at the top of the firms, this does raise questions about the ability of supervisors to penalise individuals lower down in the organisation.

The role of capital

A further issue is the role that capital should have as a buffer against large securities frauds. The first line of defence against operational risk may be systems and controls within the firms but there is also a role for capital. Operational risks may be placed in three categories:
❑ the steady flow of small losses caused by mistakes such as failure to execute trades;
❑ spike losses caused by operational failures that have a small, but not extremely small, likelihood; and
❑ extremely unlikely but (if they occur) potentially devastating events such as difficulties experienced by Barings.

Capital certainly has a role as a buffer for the first two types of operational risk but it would

Table 2. SFA type of penalty: January 1991 to March 1997

Individuals

Year	No of cases	Fines	Costs awarded	Not fit and proper	Reprimand
1991	11	0	1	1	11
1992	12	4	4	6	3
1993	10	3	3	10	0
1994	34	28	25	12	5
1995	22	10	11	12	8
1996	37	18	34	17	16
1997	5	3	4	1	4
Total	129	66	82	59	47

Firms

Year	No of cases	Fines	Costs awarded	Expelled	Reprimand	Restrictions imposed
1991	19	19	7	0	1	0
1992	11	5	1	5	1	1
1993	3	1	1	0	1	1
1994	4	3	2	2	0	0
1995	6	5	7	0	1	1
1996	11	11	11	0	4	0
1997	1	1	1	0	1	0
Total	55	45	30	7	9	3

Explanation of penalties:
❑ Fines: fine imposed.
❑ Costs awarded: costs of the SFA in processing the penalty awarded against the individual or firm.
❑ Not fit and proper: an individual has breached the criteria for SFA registration and is no longer regarded as fit and proper to conduct particular activities.
❑ Expelled: when the conduct of a firm is such that it is no longer considered fit and proper to carry on authorised business, its authorisation to perform investment business is removed.
❑ Reprimand: the SFA may write a public reprimand in response to an individual's or a firm's conduct.
❑ Restrictions imposed: the SFA may limit, in part, a firm's authorisation to conduct investment business.
Source: SFA notices

Table 3. Analysis of SFA fines, 1991 to date

	(i) Control failures	(ii) Fraud or deception (theft)	(iii) Breach of reporting requirements	(iv) Exceeding dealing authority	(v) Misleading information advertisements
No. Cases	58	95	17	10	6
Max. Fine (£)	240,000	200,000	25,000	18,000	200,000
Min. Fine (£)	2,000	1,000	1,500	5,000	9,000

Notes:
(i) Fines on firms or senior management.
(ii) Usually individuals who are also often banned from the industry.
(iii) Usually firms.
(iv) Sometimes individuals, sometimes firms.
(v) Usually firms.
Source: SFA notices

PANEL 3

MORGAN GRENFELL AND THE GUINNESS AFFAIR

Morgan Grenfell is one of the UK's oldest merchant banks. It remained family dominated until rights issues in 1974 and 1978 diluted the firm's equity. In 1981, the new chief executive, Christopher Reeves, began an aggressive expansion of the firm's corporate finance operations. In 1980, Morgan Grenfell advised 15 clients in bids valued at £341 million. By 1986, this had increased to 111 take-overs worth £15.2 billion.

In 1986 a major scandal hit the firm. It concerned the tactics used by a Morgan Grenfell client, Guinness, in its successful take-over of the whisky manufacturer, Distillers. The take-over was bitterly contested by a food producer, Argyll. One of Morgan Grenfell's star corporate finance directors, Roger Seelig, was helping to advise Guinness. Guinness resorted to tactics that contravened both the non-statutory rules of the UK Takeover Panel and also, more seriously, provisions of the Companies Act.

Bids in the UK typically comprise shares of the bidding company (with a discounted cash offer generally given as an alternative). In the last month of the struggle for control of Distillers a complex network of share support was arranged for Guinness stock, to enhance the value of Guinness's offer to Distillers' shareholders.

Indemnities against loss and success fees totalling £25 million were offered by Guinness to a "fan club" of friendly investors (an offence under the Companies Act) without consulting the Guinness board or shareholders. The operation was successful and Guinness won control of Distillers in April 1986. Problems arose after the take-over, as members of the "fan club" sought to liquidate their positions. To limit the impact on the Guinness share price, Guinness, bought back a block of shares. In November 1986, the SEC alerted the Department of Trade and Industry to the share support schemes arranged by Guinness. When the scandal broke, Seelig left Morgan Grenfell immediately. In May 1987, Ernest Saunders, chief executive of Guinness, was arrested and later convicted.

---

not be efficient to require all firms to hold capital against catastrophic but very unlikely events such as the Leeson episode. As other chapters of this book explain, some firms are trying to develop models to estimate how much capital should be set aside against the first two types of operational risk and they are also using stress tests to estimate their exposure under extreme circumstances.

However, capital buffers may play a different role in reducing the likelihood of catastrophic but rare control problems. In countries with variable capital requirements, the level of capital required could be used as a lever to encourage firms to improve their systems and controls and to strengthen management to make it better placed to avoid large operational risks.

The largest financial intermediaries can (through the sheer size of their capital and earnings) withstand huge operational losses. This is highlighted by the cases of Daiwa and Barings. The loss to Daiwa from rogue trading amounted to around $1.1 billion whereas the Barings loss was £800 million, yet the former survived and the latter did not. Large players tend to have a substantial extra buffer of capital to cover operational and legal risk in part because of the way the capital requirements are calculated. This is because the current additive treatment of credit risk in the Basle Accord does not recognise diversification benefits and tends to create a larger buffer for the biggest, and therefore most systemically important, firms. If there were a move towards a more risk-based treatment of credit risk in the Basle Accord, which were to take diversification into account, this would raise a question of how buffers for operational and legal risks could be incorporated in the standard. It might be argued that extreme operational risk was unlikely to be highly correlated with other types of risk (credit and market) and therefore that any buffer should not be additive. However, there is some evidence that frauds do tend to come to light in poor market conditions. In fact, in terms of securities frauds and in particular the cases which fall into Huntington and Davies' (1995) "downward spiral" category,[2] it is the worsening of market conditions that creates the huge exposure.

Sackings, bans and fines

In this section we draw on some simple theoretical models set out in more detail in our paper "Securities Fraud", *Economic Policy* (1998). These models help us to examine how equity holders, senior management and regulators may affect the behaviour of dealers and their managers by altering the control

Table 4. Fines – banking supervisors

Country	Power to exercise	Frequency	Amount
Germany	Yes	Usually 10 to 20 cases of enforcement fines and about 4 to 10 cases of administrative fines per annum.	Current enforcement fines DM10,000 (£3,500) up to DM500,000 (£175,000). Administrative fines not exceeding DM1 million (£350,000) and should reflect benefit gained from infringement. In practice usually between DM200 (£70) and DM 25,000 (£8,750).
Norway	Yes	Authority not used so far.	No maximum. The amount would depend on the size of the institutions and the severity of the issue.
Austria	Yes	N/A	Enforcement fines up to Sch300,000 (£14,850).
Greece	Yes	N/A	N/A
Iceland	Yes	Seldom used.	N/A
Luxembourg	Yes	Not frequently used.	Lfr5,000 (£85) to Lfr5,000,000 (£85,000) and/or three–eight days' imprisonment depending on the nature of the infringement.
Liechtenstein	No. Power rests with the Government and the district court.	No cases within last few years.	Depending on the specific case up to Sfr50,000 (£21,000) or Sfr100,000 (£42,000).
Belgium	Yes	Not used so far.	Fines under administrative law are Bfr10,000 (£170) to Bfr1 million (£17,000) per calendar day and a global upper limit Bfr50 million (£850,000).
France	Yes	Rare. In most cases fines are imposed for late transmission of financial information to supervisors or failure to comply with money laundering regulations.	Fines may not exceed the minimum amount of capital required for the institutions. They have ranged between Ffr 10,000 (£1,000) and Ffr 300,000 (£30,000).
Ireland	No		
Italy	Yes	Some 80–85 cases on average over the three years 1994–6.	Breaches of prudential rules, integrity requirements etc L1 million (£360) to L50 million (£18,000). Corporate officers who breach the rules regarding disclosure to customers of terms and conditions of contracts L2 million (£720) to L25 million (£9,000).
UK	No		
Spain	Yes	Authority used frequently but usually for not meeting complex reserve requirements.	Maximum amount for very serious infringements, 1% of own funds or Pta5 million (£20,500), for serious infringements 0.5% of own funds or Pta2.5 million (£10,250). Maximum fine for a manager Pta10 million (£41,000).
Netherlands	No		
USA	OCC – yes Federal Reserve – yes	This type of action usually reserved for individuals except where a bank has filed a false or misleading report. A total of 614 fines in the last six years. Powers to fine firms for law violations, eg misreporting, 5–10 cases a year, all foreign banks. Individuals can be fined for their actions – perhaps two cases a year.	The amount depends on the seriousness of the case but most fines for individuals are $10,000 (£6,200) to $25,000 (£15,500). Maximum $1 million or 1% of assets per day for a firm. Largest fine BCCI $200 million (£124 million). Fines for individuals usually $10,000 to $100,000 (£6,200 to £62,000).
Japan	Ministry of Finance – yes Bank of Japan – no	Only one case of a bank being fined. Other penalties are used as well such as restrictions on business activities.	Maximum of ¥500,000 (£2,600), likely to be revised upwards.
Denmark	Yes	Used only once for failure to submit annual accounts.	There is no limit on fines.

environment or *ex post* penalty structure that they face.

The first model we will consider provides a framework for studying the behaviour of reasonably junior dealers and their managers in securities trading operations. For this model, we assume that each individual decides whether or not to expend effort in monitoring subordinates. If the individual decides not to monitor, he then chooses whether or not to commit a fraud. We suppose that each agent experiences:

❑ a fixed utility gain from committing fraud undetected;

❑ a cost of being caught either committing fraud or not monitoring when a subordinate is caught committing fraud;

❑ a utility gain if he detects fraud by a subordinate; and

❑ a cost of monitoring.

An important parameter of the model is the number of subordinates for which an individual is held responsible. We suppose in this version of the model that individuals are only held responsible for monitoring the one or more subordinates immediately below them.

Our analysis of this model indicated that, to reduce the incidence of fraud and increase monitoring effectiveness by individual managers, firms need to reward staff for detecting fraud. In fact, in none of our four case studies did those who discovered the problems obviously benefit. However, one should probably interpret this result in the broader sense that firms should reward managers who identify control failures even when no fraud has actually arisen. Recently, in deciding on remuneration, a major firm awarded an exceptionally large bonus to an individual who had spotted potential problem areas in control. Managers and – in particular – internal auditors may well be discouraged from highlighting control weaknesses if line management overrides their recommendations. This seems to be a wide ranging problem and has been evident in fraud cases such as Barings and in cases involving mismanagement such as the derivatives losses experienced by UBS.[3] One solution might be for firms to introduce a dedicated risk control/risk assessment line that reported to board level. This would make it impossible for line management to override recommendations before they had been put before the board.

In addition, in order to increase the amount of monitoring and reduce the amount of fraud, firms need to reduce the costs of monitoring to individual managers. This makes it essential that firms improve the overall control environment. Structural changes may be necessary to accomplish this. Matrix management, without clear lines of responsibility, can make it more difficult for individual managers to exercise their control functions. Indeed, they may not even recognise their responsibility for the control environment. It is noticeable that, following the rash of recent fraud cases, many firms have responded to shareholder and regulatory pressure by improving their control systems and also by changing the structure of the firm to facilitate monitoring (for example, by pulling back dealing from small, overseas, operations to larger centralised dealing rooms).

How many levels to penalise?

Another important question for senior management and regulators is which managers should be penalised if monitoring turns out to have been deficient? We analysed these issues within the framework of our model by increasing the number of subordinates for whom a manager is held responsible.

The key finding from the model is that greater responsibility for detecting fraud at different levels in the hierarchy has a beneficial effect – for a given amount of monitoring, there is a lower incidence of fraud. It may well be important for firms to make clear, within their internal procedures, that when failures in control occur, the working of the whole hierarchy would be reviewed to see if, at all levels, managers were taking their responsibilities seriously and ensuring a robust control environment. When allocating bonuses, systems and controls issues (how well individuals are implementing systems and enforcing rules) as well as cultural issues (for example whether there is a culture of cutting corners) should be fully taken into account. A number of firms have incorporated such elements in the design of their bonus packages.

Bonus schemes and monitoring

One area of concern is that internal bonus structures may have discouraged managers from exercising control. If the bonus payments of senior managers depend on profit generated lower down, they may well have an incentive not to upset star traders by monitoring or questioning their activities too closely.

To analyse this potential problem, we formulated a model in which a trader, who observes the true profits of trading activities, can cheat

DREXEL BURNHAM AND MICHAEL MILKEN

Until the 1970s, Drexels was a well-established, if lack-lustre, member of the second tier of American investment banks. In 1974, it recruited as head of corporate finance Frederick Joseph, who subsequently rose to be chief executive officer of the firm. Michael Milken was a rising star within the firm who had already made a name by trading low-grade industrial bonds. Milken persuaded Drexels to create a high-yield bond department (HYBD) independent of Drexel's trading in more conventional investment grade bonds. The HYBD was so successful that the firm was forced to acquiesce when, in 1978, Milken announced he was moving the department to Los Angeles. The move had the effect of removing the HYBD from the day-to-day control of Drexel's New York headquarters.

During the 1970s, most of the HYBD's business consisted of trading "fallen angels", investment-grade bonds that had been downgraded when their issuers encountered financial difficulties. In the late 1970s and early 1980s, however, Milken and his HYBD encouraged issuers to create new offerings of high-yield debt, guaranteeing that Drexels would make a market and hence maintain liquidity. By the mid-1980s, a new breed of corporate raiders eager to raise debt capital combined with Milken's well-developed networks for placing junk bonds to create a large new market for such debt.

Some of Milken's networks involved irregular activity. For example, a fund manager might be paid inflated prices for bonds and in return benefit from tax losses for his personal trading account. Other alleged activities included trading on inside information regarding imminent take-overs. Milken's networks were entwined with those of the notorious arbitrageur, Ivan Boesky.

In September, Boesky surrendered to the authorities and agreed to co-operate in uncovering the activities of Milken and others. A slip by Boesky's bookkeeper in March 1986 had led to Milken receiving a cheque of $5.3 million for "consultancy services" from Boesky. This gave the authorities an invaluable paper trail that they were able to follow up. Under investigation, and with the equity and junk bond markets crashing, Drexels' net income fell 79% in 1987.

In December 1988, Drexels pleaded guilty to six of the 100 felony counts against it and agreed to pay fines of $650 million. It also agreed that Michael Milken and his brother Lowell would leave the firm and not be paid their 1989 bonus of $200 million. The firm had been forced to concede because of the authorities' threat to use the Rico statutes against it. In 1990, Milken pleaded guilty to six related counts and agreed to pay a fine of $600 million, of which $500 million was restitution to those injured by the fraud. In 1992, he agreed to pay a further $300 million to resolve civil suits.

when reporting the profits to the firm; the trader's manager can decide whether or not to take action to verify the reported profits (see Figure 1). We further assume, and this is key, that both the trader and the manager receive bonus payments that are a function of the profits generated by the trader. We use this model to look at the effect of different remuneration structures on the misreporting of profits.

A complete breakdown of internal control can occur in this environment if managers care more about short-term loss of earnings than the long-term profitability of the business and therefore choose not to monitor star traders closely. The trade-off is influenced by a number of factors other than remuneration. Promotion prospects are a prime example. But, the sheer size of bonus payments may make a short-term focus attractive, particularly given the mobility of staff in the industry. The average time that staff in dealing areas spend with one firm in the City is currently thought to be as little as three years. In some of the cases we examined, the profits earned by managers because of rogue trading lower down the hierarchy were very substantial indeed.

The model indicated that problems associated with short-termism in internal control can be mitigated through the optimal use of penalties for managers who do not discharge their control responsibilities and rewards for those who do. It is important that managers who carry out control responsibilities well are rewarded for it, and that managers who do not are penalised, regardless of whether problems have actually occurred because of the lax control environment.

Regulators can reinforce the incentives for managers by penalising severe breaches in control that come to light when there are problems. This, however, is not as effective as the adoption by the firms of reward systems that fully recognise adequacy of management.

Conclusion

"It is very hard to know what is going on in a financial services company." This prescient remark was made in 1990 by Warren Buffett, the investor who the following year was to rescue Salomon Brothers after senior employees were caught breaching rules in US government bond auctions. As a relatively new member of the Salomon board, Buffett was probably referring to the difficulties faced by independent directors monitoring developments in a complex financial institution. The problem is broader, however.

In this paper, we study the problems faced by senior management and regulators, attempting to limit fraud by firm insiders. The following conclusions deserve stress.

❑ Firms must focus on improving their overall control environment. This facilitates the efforts of managers to monitor their subordinates and prevents the firm from slipping into a culture where corners are cut.

❑ Firms should assess control strengths at all levels in the organisation. Where control breaches have occurred the firms should not rely on simply penalising the immediate supervisor of the level where the breach occurred but should also consider whether more senior managers have been enforcing an adequate control environment. Regulators, too, may need to be able to penalise management at different levels for severe control breaches.

❑ Firms should reward managers who discover actual or potential control lapses and avoid (to the extent that this is possible) too close an alignment between the pay of managers and profits reported by the dealers they manage.

❑ Remuneration for managers should reflect the adequacy of the control environments that they oversee.

1. A formal model of misreporting by a dealer

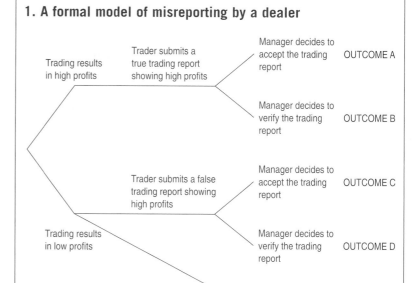

The figure above summarises the formal dealer misreporting model described in Instefjord, Jackson and Perraudin (1998). The model's basic assumptions are:

❑ only the trader can observe the true trading profits directly;

❑ the manager can observe the true profits if he exerts (costly) effort verifying the trader's report.

We suppose that profits can take two values, high or low. The trader decides whether to report high or low, and the manager decides whether or not to check the report. The sequence of moves is shown in the figure. The outcomes listed from A to E are as follows:

OUTCOME A: If profits are high, the trader has no incentive to disguise this. If the manager accepts the report without checking, both dealer and manager receive high bonuses.

OUTCOME B: Again, profits are high and the trader correctly reports them but now the manager decides to verify the trader's report. Again, both receive high bonuses.

OUTCOME C: Profits are low but the trader decides to report them as high. The manager decides not to verify. Both trader and manager are then exposed to the risk of an external audit. If the audit fails to uncover the false report, both receive high bonuses. If the false report is discovered both suffer penalties.

OUTCOME D: Profits are low but the trader reports them to be high. The manager in this case verifies that the report is untrue. The trader receives no bonus and is subject to penalties. The manager receives a low bonus since profits are low.

OUTCOME E: In this case, the true profits are low and both manager and dealer receive low bonus payments.

1 *The reputational costs of corporate fraud have been examined in two interesting papers cited in our bibliography. In "The Reputational Penalty Firms Bear From Committing Criminal Fraud", Karpov and Lott (1993) look at corporate fraud and in particular the costs for the firm caused by reputational damage against the cost of criminal fines. They use US data on 132 cases of alleged and actual corporate fraud from 1978 to 1987. To investigate the reputational costs, they calculate the change in the market value of the common stock over the date of the announcement of the fraud. For all 132 events, the median change in market value is a loss of $5½ million. The largest losses occur when the initial announcement concerns allegations or investigations of fraud within a firm. The median loss for these cases is nearly $9½ million. They investigate whether these losses reflect expected legal penalties and conclude that most of the loss incurred is because of lost reputation.*

Knight and Pretty (1998) in "The Impact Of Catastrophes On Shareholder Value" look at the effect of catastrophes for non-financial firms on shareholder value. They believe there are two elements to the impact. The first is the immediate estimate of the associated loss. The second hinges on the markets' assessment of management's ability to deal with the aftermath and a general re-evaluation by the market of management strengths/weaknesses.

2 *In their 1995 paper, "Management Fraud in Banks", the authors categorise various types of fraud including:*
❑ *Downward spiral. One unauthorised or fraudulent transaction leads to a complex web of transactions which eventually give rise to a significant loss. A dealer may incur a small loss or create a false profit and then take positions to hide this which, when the market moves against the positions taken, could generate a larger loss and so the process goes on.*

❑ *Off-market rings. Other frauds may include the use of false market prices, for example using offmarket rings or related party deals. Concentration of business through particular brokers may indicate kickbacks. Discretionary dealing accounts in the hands of experienced dealers may provide an opportunity for hiding losses or manipulating profits.*

❑ *Roll-up contracts. In markets where immediate settlement is not required (eg some FX and derivative contracts), a key factor might be that counterparties allow deals to be rolled up without settlement.*

❑ *Misvaluation. The most common vulnerability in the dealing area is misvaluation of positions.*

3 *In the latter episode, the Swiss Federal Banking Commission concluded that the losses were in part due to misconduct by individuals. The risk exposures entered into with complex products were not fully recognised by the business units concerned and were inadequately monitored. Internal reports within UBS pointed to deficiencies in the management process that were insufficiently heeded.*

BIBLIOGRAPHY

Board of Banking Supervision, 1995, *Report of the Board of Banking Supervision into the Circumstances of the Collapse of Barings,* HMSO, London.

Daripa, A. and S. Varotto, 1997, *Agency Incentives, Reputational Distortions and the Effectiveness of Value at Risk and Precommitment in Regulating Market Risk,* Working Party, Bank of England, London.

Eccles, R.C. and H.C. White, 1988, "Price and Authority in the Inter-profit Center Transactions", *American Journal of Sociology,* 94 (supplement), S17–S51.

Fay, S., 1996, *The Collapse of Barings,* Richard Cohen Books, London.

Franks, J. and S. Schaeffer, 1993, *The Costs and Effectiveness of the UK Financial Regulatory System,* Subject Report II, City Research Project, London Business School.

Hobson, D., 1990, *The Pride of Lucifer, Morgan Grenfell (1938–1988): The Unauthorised Biography of a Merchant Bank,* Hamish Hamilton, London.

Instefjord N., Jackson, P. and W. Perraudin, 1998, "Securities Fraud", *Economic Policy,* 27.

Huntington, I., and D. Davies, 1995, *Management Fraud in Banks,* Central Banking 94/95.

Jackson, P., 1996, "Deposit Protection and Bank Failures in the UK", *Financial Stability Review.*

Karpov, J.M. and J.R. Lott, 1993, "The Reputational Penalty Firms Fear When Committing Criminal Fraud", *Journal of Law and Economics* 36, pp.757-803.

Kochan, N. and H. Pym, 1987, *The Guinness Affair,* Christopher Helm, London.

Knight, R. and D. Pretty, 1998, *The Impact of Catastrophes on Shareholder Value,* The Oxford Executive Research Briefings.

Large, A., 1996, Regulation and Management (Speech delivered by the Chairman of the SIB at the FT European Life Assurance Conference, London).

Leeson, N., 1996, *Rogue Trader,* Little, Brown & Co, London.

Lewis, M., 1989, *Liar's Poker,* Coronet Books, London

Lynch, G.G., 1994, *Report of Inquiry into False Trading Profits at Kidder, Peabody & Co, Incorporated.*

Meyer, M., 1993, *Nightmare on Wall Street: Salomon Brothers and the Corruption of the Marketplace,* Simon & Schuster, New York.

Walker, J.L., 1995, "Daiwa Losses Spell a Scandal Too Far", *International Financial Law Review,* pp. 12–14.

Zey, M., 1993, *Banking on Fraud: Drexel, Junk Bonds and Buyouts,* Aldine de Gruyter, New York

10

Psychological Theory and Financial Institutions

Individual and Organisational Influences on Decision Making and Behaviour

Emma Soane, Mark Fenton-O'Creevy, Nigel Nicholson and Paul Willman
Centre for Organisational Research, London Business School

How did one man bring about the collapse of Barings Bank? Why did it take over a decade for managers at Daiwa Bank to realise that Toshihide Iguchi was hiding losses equivalent to about $450,000 per day? What are the pressures and motivations that drive traders to build up portfolios of highly speculative investments instead of low risk ones?

Barings and Daiwa are two organisations that have recently lost millions of dollars, as the case histories in Chapter 9 describe. Such losses are often attributed to the actions of one employee who was considered a "star". It is not clear how much these employees gain from their behaviour in financial terms. However, Nick Leeson, Toshihide Iguchi and other such traders all experience huge psychological gains from being regarded as highly influential people.

Many factors are involved in each case, and it seems that the lengths to which these individuals were prepared to go in the pursuit of status, and the lack of management controls over them, are unusual. However, it also seems reasonable to think that replicas of these behaviours on a minor scale might be quite commonplace. Not all of these may be conscious attempts to deceive others; they might instead involve self-deception by individuals about the factors that actually control their actions. Some of these factors – deeply embedded in the psychology of trading – elude existing controls, as we shall show.

Various surveys indicate that "rogue traders" are a major concern in financial institutions. For example, research by the Centre for the Study of Financial Innovation asked participants (banking practitioners) to rank the key "banking banana skins" or risks in the industry (Table 1). The survey was carried out in February 1997 and the results represent the views of 170 respondents (Centre for the Study of Financial Innovation, 1997).

Are these fears overstated, or rather misdirected? Are businesses vulnerable to everyday human psychology – to complex but common interactions between individual propensities and organisational factors, such as management systems and pay structures? Risk in financial institutions is usually calculated using ratios of risk to return, distributions of probabilities of a range of events, variance and covariance of returns, risks of individual stocks versus risks in whole markets and so on. Can we apply a similar set of procedures to people?

We shall argue that we can use psychometric tests to measure quantitatively a number of psychological factors, but also that we need to think about the way people make decisions using a rather different, more qualitative approach that examines how people process information and evaluate actions and their consequences.

The aim of applying psychology in the workplace is to increase understanding of motivation, perception and performance with the ultimate purpose of bringing about improvements (Dipboye, Smith and Howell, 1994). This chapter provides an introduction to the field and shows how psychological approaches can be used to analyse, explain and predict behaviour, drawing examples from current research being carried out by the authors in investment banks. This research employs interviews, a computer-based

Table 1. Banking banana skins

1996	1997	Banking banana skin
1	1	Poor management
–	2	EMU-related turbulence
4	3	Rogue trader
5	4	Excessive competition
2	5	Bad lending
6	6	Derivatives
10	7	Fraud
3	8	Emerging markets
–	9	New products
9	10	Technology "snafu"[1]
8	11	Back office failure
7	12	Settlement systems
11	13	Macro economy
12	14	Under-regulation
–	15	Labour victory in UK election
–	16	Over-regulation

[1]technology-related problems

measure which presents participants with a series of decision-making tasks in the form of a game to predict and bet on the outcomes and a questionnaire to examine a number of issues which influence trader performance, such as individual learning experiences, management of losses and gains and organisational culture.

The individual

RATIONAL DECISION MAKING

Rational decision making is usually considered to be essential in financial institutions. People are encouraged to consider facts and weigh up alternatives before coming to a conclusion. However, high-profile cases in recent times have drawn attention to the fact that excessive risk taking, irrational thought and poor decision processes occur at a number of organisational levels.

When attempting to understand these decisions it is critical to understand the context within which they were made. There is a consistent human tendency to attribute more importance to the character of the decision-maker than to the situation within which he or she is acting (Ross, 1977). Organisational analysis suggests that a greater awareness of the diverse factors influencing decision making can suggest systemic measures to improve performance and reduce unwanted risk.

To make a rational decision, six steps should be followed:
❏ define the problem;
❏ identify the criteria by which the problem needs to be considered;

❏ weigh the criteria;
❏ generate alternatives;
❏ rate each alternative on each criterion;
❏ compute the optimal decision.

Most people rarely take the time and effort to go through all of these stages, if necessary repeating steps as they obtain new information or as situations change. Instead, they base their decisions on their inclinations, momentary influences, interpersonal dynamics, belief systems, concerns about unintended outcomes, and cultural norms and values.

PERSONALITY

We usually give plausible reasons for our actions, saying that we did them in our own characteristic way. When we consider peoples' actions we may question their reasoning but agree that they acted from personal biases or with their own personal style. In effect, we see others allowing their decisions to be governed by personal needs, emotional responses and particular styles of thought to a greater extent than ourselves. These dispositions lie at the core of personal identity or personality – a largely inborn, genetically determined profile of tendencies, which we recognise as having a hidden yet powerful effect on the choices that we make, how we implement them and what emerges from them.

Personality has been defined as a "set of non-physical and non-intellectual psychological qualities which make a person distinct from other people" (Adler, 1995). Whether the study of personality is relevant to organisational behaviour is debatable because it has not been clearly established how it impacts on many job-related outcomes. Many factors overlay personality and amplify or attenuate it. A sales-oriented job could enhance extrovert tendencies, or an organisation's culture could encourage people to behave in a way counter to their natural tendencies. This makes it difficult to separate personality from the work environment. A consideration of personality does, however, have special value in that once personal strengths are identified, they can be enhanced by encouragement and resourcing; conversely, weaknesses or vulnerabilities need to be guarded against, buffered or compensated for by support, training, working partnerships and managerial control.

Personality is relatively unchanging once adulthood is reached and is now commonly considered to comprise five dimensions (or trait clusters): neuroticism (emotional stability),

Table 2. Personality traits

Trait scales	Characteristics of the high scorer	Characteristics of the low scorer
Neuroticism Assesses adjustment versus emotional instablity. Identifies individuals prone to psychological distress, unrealistic ideas, excessive cravings or urges and maladaptive coping responses.	Worrying, nervous, emotional, insecure, inadequate, hypochondriac.	Calm, relaxed, unemotional, hardy, secure, self-satisfied.
Extroversion Assesses quantity and intensity of interpersonal interaction; activity level; need for stimulation and capacity for joy.	Sociable, active, talkative, person-oriented, optimistic, fun loving, affectionate.	Reserved, sober, unexuberant, aloof, task-oriented, retiring, quiet.
Openness Assesses proactive seeking and appreciation of experience for its own sake; toleration for and exploration of the unfamiliar.	Curious, broad interests, creative, original, imaginative, and untraditional.	Conventional, down-to-earth, narrow interests, inartistic, unanalytical.
Agreeableness Assesses the quality of one's interpersonal orientation along a continuum from compassion to antagonism in thoughts, feelings and actions.	Soft hearted, good natured, trusting, helpful, forgiving, gullible, straightforward.	Cynical, rude, suspicious, uncooperative, vengeful, ruthless, irritable, manipulative.
Conscientiousness Assesses the individual's degree of organisation, persistence and motivation in goal-directed behaviour. Contrasts dependable, fastidious people with those who are lackadaisical and sloppy.	Organised, reliable, hard working, self-disciplined, punctual, scrupulous, neat, ambitious, persevering.	Aimless, unreliable, lazy, careless, lax, negligent, weak-willed, hedonistic.

extroversion, openness, agreeableness (nurturance) and conscientiousness. These qualities can be measured using specially designed personality tests, which can only be purchased by professionally trained and approved practitioners in psychological assessment.[1]

Table 2 defines each personality trait (Costa and McCrae, 1985). These traits interact and form relatively consistent approaches to situations. This general model of personality does not classify particular traits as "good" or "bad", but it does suggest that certain aspects of these traits make some people more suitable for a particular type of environment than others.

The environment in financial institutions is highly demanding. It requires workers to make numerous decisions with incomplete information under the threat of loss of money and loss of status. It is highly competitive and there are long working hours. Some aspects of the traits mentioned above may well be more beneficial than others in the financial industry. For example, a low score in neuroticism enables individuals to deal with ambiguous and incomplete information; an average score

in extroversion helps in teamwork and when dealing with others. It is necessary to be open to new approaches to working and new information. As far as agreeableness is concerned, people need to be tough-minded enough to negotiate in the interests of their firm, or present a new or challenging idea to the team, yet sufficiently nurturing to develop and maintain trusting, supportive client and colleague relationships. Conscientiousness has clear value when order and control are needed, coupled with determination to see decisions through to completion.

It is possible that personality traits form the basis of a number of behaviours observed in so-called "rogue traders". For example, an average score in neuroticism might enable someone to be sufficiently anxious to want affirmation of status from others, yet not so anxious as to be unable to deceive; he might be a low scorer on the agreeableness dimension, inspired by mistrust, competitiveness and self-advancement. In conscientiousness, he may have high ambition and self-discipline but low commitment to rules, order and approved paths to achievement.

There are, however, many psychological and organisational factors that enhance these traits, or allow "rogue" tendencies to be carried out in practice.

MOTIVES AND ABILITIES

If personality is viewed as the core of a person, motives and abilities form the next layer between internal sub-consciousness and external, observable characteristics and behaviours. Two factors, self-efficacy and motivation, are critical to effective functioning in the uncertain financial services environment where confidence and drive are key attributes.

Self-efficacy is the extent to which a person feels capable and effective in accomplishing a particular task. Many jobs in financial institutions comprise numerous different elements and self-efficacy can vary across tasks. Where performance does vary, feedback from managers giving constructive advice about how to carry out the particular problematic tasks assists development of self-efficacy.

Self-efficacy is a key link between motivation and performance. Motivation can be conceptualised in a number of ways. It is useful to consider its effects on behaviour in terms of the extent to which individuals are attuned to internal and external stimuli. This difference relates both to underlying personality factors and to how goals are structured in the work environment. Internally motivated people are usually found in high-discretion environments and are accustomed to operating with little external control. They are typically driven to achieve for personal gratification. External motivation is more related to the outcomes of goal achievement, with satisfaction coming from rewards and positive feedback administered by managerial control systems, or the informal approval of other people, including reputation within one's team or the positive regard of subordinates (Deci and Ryan, 1985). Different job environments thus tend to suit internally and externally motivated people, for example research and sales, respectively.

COGNITIVE BIASES

A set of cognitive systems also underlies decision making that is used to process information and make decisions. Often these processes are subconscious and decisions are made without conscious intervention. This is generally a highly successful strategy that allows us to avoid danger or to protect our feelings of worth and identity. When complex decisions are being made, however, the inappropriate application of heuristics (personal rules of thumb) can result in sub-optimal outcomes.

Cognitive biases are inherent in much of our decision making. For example, we are affected by whether a problem is framed in terms of a loss or a gain, an opportunity or a cost. In our research, we have found that susceptibility to these biases is prevalent among people in financial institutions, despite training to the contrary.

Consideration of cognitive biases can be particularly important in financial markets where there is much ambiguity and uncertainty. Efforts to avoid biases can be made. This can be done, firstly, by acknowledging their existence and influence rather than assuming that immunity can be simply guaranteed by experience and training. Secondly, biases can be avoided by using decision processes that force individuals to question choices and assumptions. Where groups, or teams, are involved in decision making there needs to be opportunity for individuals to share the basis for their judgements and have them challenged before a decision is made.

Panel 1 shows four main categories of decision-making biases that influence information gathering, information processing, taking decisions and reactions to outcomes of decisions. Within each there is a number of biases. Examples of each type of bias are given in italics. It can be seen clearly that there are many ways that decision making can be biased. Bazerman (1997) discusses cognitive biases in greater depth.

LOSS AND GAIN

A frequently occurring, but often disregarded, cognitive bias that requires repeated managerial intervention is differential reaction to loss and gain. In our research we are finding this bias to be particularly pervasive. It is not simply a difference in reaction to the way a problem is framed, as illustrated in Panel 2. There are other associated issues, such as position in relation to a target, status associated with making money or emotional aversion to loss.

One of the bases for trading is the "flat book" approach, where traders are encouraged to trade as if they had no prior losses and gains. This is, in practice, very hard to achieve; losses and gains tend to have considerable influence on subsequent decisions. There can be short- and long-term influences. In the short term, traders usually experience positive and negative

COGNITIVE BIASES AND DECISION MAKING

Cognitive bias	Effects on decision process
❏ Influences on information gathering	
Retrievability and availability bias	Selective attention is given to what stands out, or springs easily to mind
Base-rate insensitivity	Focus is on objective not relative frequency
Failure to apply sampling theory to small numbers	True likelihoods are miscalculated
Conjunction fallacy	Unconnected data are is falsely assumed to be linked
Framing and order effects	Different weights are assigned to first versus last in a sequence
Subjective frequency estimates	Infrequent events are overestimated, frequent events underestimated
Confirmation bias	Search is biased towards confirming rather than disproving hypotheses
❏ Influences on information processing	
Loss aversion not risk aversion	Lottery behaviour occurs – gambling on long odds
Miscalculated probabilities	Only hits are scrutinised, not misses, or vice versa
Gambler's fallacy	Connections are mistakenly perceived between unconnected events
Over-confidence and self-esteem	Optimism is greater than objective chances merit
Ego-involvement	Too little or too much emotional attachment is given to events or outcomes
Stress	Load, uncertainty and conflict affect ability to think and act clearly
Framing of targets	Behaviour changes according to whether a target is conceived of as "avoid worst case" or "achieve goal"
Representativeness bias	Isolated events or information are assumed to be representative
❏ Influences on decision taking	
Asymmetries of loss and gain	Losses are chased more than gains
Endowment effects	What you have to sell is overvalued relative to what you buy
Social norms	The risk or decision profiles of the local culture are followed
"Groupthink"	Intragroup momentum governs a decision and dissent is censored
Herding	Instead of making individual rational choices, we imitate what others do
Incentives	Risk–reward outcomes are distorted by personal payoff system
Impression management	It is more important to look good than do good
Competitive pressures	It becomes more important to win than to achieve
❏ Influences on reactions to decision outcomes	
Hindsight bias	History is rewritten; "I knew this would happen"
Regression to the mean	Random variations are perceived as systemically caused
Rationalisation of outcomes	Failures are re-evaluated as benefits
Illusions of control	It is believed uncontrollable outcomes can be controlled
Escalating commitment	Good money is thrown after bad; motivated by sunk costs
Failure reactions	Learning is for future avoidance rather than analytical or constructive insight
Attribution errors	Errors are over-attributed to will and personality, and too little to situation and chance

RISK PERCEPTION: THE FRAMING EFFECT

The existence of the particular type of cognitive bias called the "framing effect" was illustrated in an experiment performed by Tversky and Kahneman (1981). They presented participants with one of the following:

a) Imagine that the US is preparing for the outbreak of an unusual Asian disease, which is expected to kill 600 people. Two alternative programs to combat the disease have been proposed. Assume that the exact scientific estimates of the consequences of the programs are as follows:

❑ If program A is adopted, 200 people will be saved.
❑ If program B is adopted, there is 1/3 probability that 600 people will be saved and 2/3 probability that no people will be saved.

OR

b) Imagine that the US is preparing for the outbreak of an unusual Asian disease, which is expected to kill 600 people. Two alternative programs to combat the disease have been proposed. Assume that the exact scientific estimates of the consequences of the programs are as follows:

❑ If program C is adopted, 400 people will die.
❑ If program D is adopted, there is 1/3 probability that nobody will die and 2/3 probability that 600 people will die.

The outcomes of the first and second alternatives of (a) and (b) are identical. The key difference between them is the presentation of the consequences of the programme. In (a) the focus is positive, on lives saved, and in (b) the focus is negative, on lives lost. When these problems were given to a group of people it was found that:

(a) Programme A was chosen by 72% and programme B was chosen by 28% (N = 152)
(b) Programme C was chosen by 22% and programme D was chosen by 78% (N = 155)

Clearly, the presentation of the problem in terms of lives saved or lives lost has a big effect on choice. The authors also found that if the same person is given (a) then (b), their preferences will change according to the positive or negative framing. These findings have wide-ranging implications for decision making and show how simple semantic changes can result in different choices.

---

outcomes of decisions at least several times a day – in some cases more frequently. Reactions to loss and gain by traders, peers and managers have important influences on future treatment of similar opportunities and the way losses and gains are viewed. Gains are treated in a psychologically different way from losses. They create good feelings, but usually only in the short term; gains are more easily forgotten than losses. In contrast, losses are the focus of much more attention and reflection, and are also more likely than gains to result in management intervention. The negative emotions associated with loss usually last longer and act as powerful reinforcers of particular decision-making strategies, such as creating aversion to situations where certain types of decision are required – "I need to recover from losses and be more emotionally stable before I start trading again".

In financial markets traders can be affected by previous outcomes. There is a reference point around which subsequent decisions are made; above this psychological base point events can be regarded as the domain of gain and below

this point they are in the domain of loss. There can be four possible reactions. First, as profits accumulate, traders can become risk averse because they seek to conserve their gains and protect any related bonus – "when I've made my target, I just don't trade". Second, traders can feel they have a buffer of money in the bank and therefore they can take a little more risk, loss having the non-linear effect of being felt less by traders who have already made profits – "I think there is a certain comfort factor when I have made money; I am more willing to lose it". Third, if losses escalate, traders can take larger positions, or more risky ones, in the hope they will regain losses – "it's easy to double up and double up". This was the strategy of Nick Leeson at Barings. Fourth, traders can accept their losses and cut their losing positions, insofar as this is possible – "when I've reached my stop loss point, I just cut the position". Cutting losses and letting profits run is the ideal strategy for trading, however this runs against the grain of human nature and most traders find it very difficult to achieve in practice despite encouragement by managers.

ARE RISKS COMPARED OBJECTIVELY?

Risk perception is a person's view of the risk inherent in a situation. One of the key papers in this field is Slovic, Fischhoff and Lichtenstein (1980). This discusses the perception of risks in our environment such as radioactive waste or genetic engineering, and how risks are managed. This summary focuses on the aspect of the authors' work that examines lay perceptions of risk.

The authors found that, if asked to estimate the approximate number of deaths per year from a variety of causes, heuristics come into play that lead people to overestimate the number of deaths from causes such as accidents or homicide and underestimate deaths from causes such as stomach cancer or asthma. These errors in estimation are in part linked to newspaper coverage of some events, for example high-profile accidents. These make accident-related death more salient than other non-reported deaths from illnesses such as stomach cancer. They might also be related to people's tendency to be overconfident in their estimates of uncertain factors, to beliefs that "it won't happen to me" and to general preferences for certainty over uncertainty. There are also hazard-related issues that affect risk perception and help to explain why we drive cars and accept risk of death but protest loudly about the use of nuclear energy.

A list of activities (eg smoking), substances (eg pesticides) and technologies (eg handguns) were rated according to the present risk of death from each to help elucidate the concept of risk perception. It was found that there are a number of key dimensions on which risks can be rated, which is why some risks are accepted and others are judged unacceptable. The three main factors are:

❑ The dread associated with the hazard, eg are the effects uncontrollable or controllable, fatal or not, involuntary or voluntary, easily reduced or not?

❑ The knowledge associated with the hazard, eg is the risk known to people or not, are the effects known to scientists or not, is the risk observable or not?

❑ The number of people exposed to the hazard.

These three dimensions can explain most of the variance the authors found in the participants' rating of hazards. Hence, a hazard that is considered particularly dangerous is one that is essentially uncontrollable, unknown to science and can affect a large number of people.

The acceptance of motor vehicles can be explained by the perception that they are not risky on all of these dimensions – the hazard might affect a large number of people, it might be uncontrollable to some, but the nature and extent of the risks are, for the most part, well known.

In addition to the different ways risks are perceived on these three dimensions, there are individual differences that relate to people's values, beliefs and experiences. Clearly, the scope for differences in risk perception needs to be remembered in any organisation that needs to manage risk.

It needs to be acknowledged by both traders and their managers that the reference point held internally by a trader is not necessarily the reference point held by the manager. For example, some traders believe that their targets are not high enough, so they might set themselves a personal target to achieve, which might be considerably higher than the organisational target.

Thus, when the trader is doing well and above target from the manager's point of view, the trader might still feel that he is in a position of loss because he has yet to attain his personal target.

This can be true of any situation where there is loss and gain. An awareness of employees' perceptions of their positions and targets can be an important approach to understanding their reactions to loss and gain.

GROUP FACTORS

In addition to the influences on individual decision making that have already been discussed there are a number of group-related decision-making factors that can operate within or across teams and result in a group making a decision that no individual really supports. These require management over the long term – for instance selection and training of group members – but they have important short-term implications for managers.

An example of this is "groupthink" (Janis, 1972), where the view that a consensus opinion is optimal prevails. It is therefore possible for more powerful members of the group to shape the behaviour of those who are less powerful and persuade them to go along with a decision that they privately have reservations about. It is also possible that decision makers in stressful and challenging situations cope by demanding conformity from subordinates, isolating or threatening those who go against the dominant position. Some high-profile examples of group-think have been the Bay of Pigs fiasco and the *Challenger* disaster.

A second effect is group polarisation (Myers and Lamm, 1976). When groups make decisions, choices reached can be more extreme, for example much more risky, than any individual would usually prefer. This can be because, when the decision maker compares himself with others immediately around him, he tends to put himself in a position closer to the others rather than retaining the integrity of his initial position. This is most likely to happen when a group has just formed, or is faced with an unusual or crisis situation.

Group decision-making processes can affect individuals in several ways, depending on the nature of the groups. The primary group in an organisation is the team. Where teams are homogeneous, similar decision-making strategies might be preferred by all team members. The advantages of this type of team are cohesion and mutual support. Disadvantages can be a lack of creativity and innovation. Alternatively, teams might be very heterogeneous with different decision-making strategies being favoured by different team members. This might enhance team performance, but a disadvantage may be that group polarisation, which occurs most commonly in heterogeneous groups, could lead the entire group towards excessively conservative or risky postures. Different groups may, in this way, generate quite different sets of norms to which they adhere. This can be positive in situations where introduction of new ideas or perspectives to a group would enhance group performance. It can be negative if individuals have widely different perspectives and work more for self-interest than team benefit. Clarification of these kinds of issues can be achieved through focused discussion with team members. However, even an awareness of these factors and their potential influence can assist in understanding why people have made particular decisions.

MEASUREMENT OF INDIVIDUAL AND ORGANISATIONAL FACTORS USING PSYCHOMETRIC TESTS

The factors that have been described so far are, for the most part, seemingly intangible constructs. However, these constructs can be measured with an acceptable amount of accuracy if appropriate tests are used. As mentioned in the introduction, testing is not just the reduction to numbers of people and their characteristics. Tests can produce useful findings about what employees think and feel about their work, the organisational systems, or other key influences on performance, and such findings might then be used to predict behaviour. This requires the application of appropriate measures and analytical procedures by competent professionals.

Psychometric tests are useful because they can provide standardised, unbiased quantitative, or sometimes qualitative, data about topics of interest or concern to managers. At a basic level, a summary of this kind of information can give managers an insight into what is going on in the organisation and this can be used to shape views about how employees might behave in, or react to, certain situations. More complex analysis can give more detailed information about the nature and strength of the relationships between factors, for example: which is more of an influence on performance – individual motivation or feedback from managers? This type of question can only be answered by thorough and appropriate testing and analysis.

There are four main categories of test:

❑ *Ability tests* can be general or specific and might cover areas such as verbal, numerical, diagrammatic, mechanical or spatial abilities. Ability tests can also be combined with particular work sample tests and so can be a useful part of the recruitment process.

❑ *Personality inventories* can be used for development, counselling and team building.

❑ *Attitude questionnaires* measure specific orientations and opinions, such as job commitment, perceptions of compensation systems and assessments of management style. This information can be of use in helping to understand and predict decision-making behaviour.

❑ *Interest inventories* are designed for career guidance, evaluating non-work as well as work values, associated, for example, with hobbies and general life experiences. They can help to define the occupational directions in which individuals wish to develop.

There are some general issues concerning design of tests and how testing is carried out. Tests such as those described above need to be designed by qualified people, such as an occupational psychologist or a human resources manager with the appropriate training. There are two key design features. First, a test should

PANEL 4

ATTITUDES TO RISK: AN EXAMPLE OF A QUESTIONNAIRE

In our research, we are interested in considering people's propensity to take risks; that is, are people consistently prone to seek or avoid risks? To answer this question, we ask participants in the research to complete the following item:

We are interested in everyday risk-taking. Please could you tell us if any of the following have ever applied to you *now* or in your adult *past*?

Please use the scales as follows:

1 = never, 2 = rarely, 3 = quite often, 4 = often, 5 = very often

	Now	In the Past
a) recreational risks (*eg rock-climbing, scuba diving*)	1 2 3 4 5	1 2 3 4 5
b) health risks (*eg smoking, poor diet, high alcohol consumption*)	1 2 3 4 5	1 2 3 4 5
c) career risks (*eg quitting a job without another to go to*)	1 2 3 4 5	1 2 3 4 5
d) financial risks (*eg gambling, risky investments*)	1 2 3 4 5	1 2 3 4 5

	Now	In the Past
e) safety risks (*eg fast driving, city cycling without a helmet*)	1 2 3 4 5	1 2 3 4 5
f) social risks (*eg standing for election, publicly challenging a rule or decision*)	1 2 3 4 5	1 2 3 4 5

The pattern of answers to this item allows us to assess whether people take or avoid risks in general, whether they take or avoid risks in specific areas of their lives and whether their risk taking is different now compared with the past.

Statistical analysis can be used to study the data of large numbers of people and compare their answers on this item with answers to other questions. For instance, we have found that people do consistently tend to take or avoid risks across different areas of their lives, risk taking does change over time and certain types of risk taking are significantly related to specific personality traits, eg career risk taking is significantly related to openness, but not to extroversion.

be valid; it should measure what it purports to measure. For example, if a test is needed to measure commitment to a job, it should not look at just the number of hours worked or the amount of output. These factors might relate to job commitment, but they are not the essence of commitment. Other, more internal, factors thus need to be measured, such as individuals' involvement with their work and whether they are satisfied by their achievements at work. The second key factor is reliability. If a test were to be carried out on another day, even weeks apart, or if another person administered it, an individual's results should be almost the same (unless the test was designed to measure changes over time). Pre-designed tests supplied from test publishers will usually fulfil these criteria. Tests created in-house require thorough development and checks by qualified staff to ensure that these criteria are met.

There are a number of practical issues to be dealt with before testing can begin in an organisation:

❑ Staff need to be trained in administration, scoring, interpreting results and feeding these back to individuals. Appropriate feedback of results is important so people gain something from the testing session and learn for the future.

❑ The appropriate test needs to be selected.
❑ Confidentiality is crucial. Access to test results should only be open to those who really need to know them.

Test management should include regular monitoring, reviews and training updates if required. There is potential for the misuse of tests. This needs to be considered and prevented where possible as it is potentially damaging to individuals and to the company's reputation, threatening relationships between managers and current or potential employees. A clear policy and reflection on these issues should mean that these problems can be avoided and a strategic approach to introducing and using tests within the organisation should be developed.

The organisation
ORGANISATIONAL CULTURE
The culture of an organisation is what distinguishes it from similar organisations in the same industry. Culture is relatively stable over time and is represented in the practices and norms within a firm (Handy, 1993). There are a number of dimensions on which cultures of firms in the financial industry differ, particularly now that there are fewer firms that have been built up

through the consolidation of a larger number of more diverse or specialist firms. Examples of aspects of culture include:

❑ the basic objectives of the firm, for example whether it specialises in commercial banking or merchant banking;

❑ the national culture of the organisation;

❑ whether the firm is a partnership or owned by shareholders; and

❑ whether it has a risk-seeking or risk-averse tradition.

There are also divisions, or subcultures, within the main organisational culture. These subdivisions can be important and useful where different sections of the organisation have different functions but subcultures can be a major threat. An example of a sub-culture which completely undermined a larger and more established culture was Baring Futures Singapore, which enabled a set of systems to be developed that were counter to those of the main organisation (Barings Bank) and ultimately led to the bank's collapse.

A strong organisational culture can be beneficial because it gives employees a clear message about what is valued and what is to be avoided, helping people to develop and maintain direction in their work. Strong cultures convey a sense of identity to individual members, enhance stability of social systems and encourage commitment to identifiable organisational goals. In organisations with a strong culture, assessing someone's "cultural fit" will be an important part of the recruitment process. Socialisation into the culture is often a large part of the training process; one trader said "I think you get moulded by the culture". This can take place through formal methods, such as management systems that reward specific behaviours and punish others. Informal methods can, however, be more pervasive and more influential. These might include the telling of stories, the language people use to reflect underlying values, the physical organisation of desks and the location of senior and junior staff in relation to each another.

Strong cultures can also have negative effects. They can create such homogeneity that creativity and innovation are stifled, reducing an organisation's ability to adapt to changing environments. One trader who was interviewed felt that the culture in his organisation "does remove some of the entrepreneurial element of trading", which resulted in non-optimisation of opportunities. Study of an organisation's culture, or specific aspects of the culture, reveals critical insights into and explanation of the strengths of the company. These strengths will help it to succeed in competitive environments, to identify potential weak points that could be exploited, guide the overall aims and direction of an organisation and the behaviour of individuals within the organisation.

SELECTION AND RECRUITMENT
The introduction of a new employee into a job and organisation is a complex process involving interactions between what people believe about themselves, their abilities and preferences, perceived job characteristics, and responses to management systems and organisational culture. Many of these factors are not explicit and it is up to the individual to make inferences about what is valued and what is unacceptable. Managers therefore need to be vigilant about what new employees infer from their early experiences to ensure that their learning is balanced and realistic.

The recruitment process itself needs to be designed to ensure appropriate applicants are not rejected and that applicants are not selected and trained at great cost and then found to be unsuitable. This requires a thorough evaluation of what the job comprises in terms of the tasks an individual is required to carry out and the skills needed to perform well at the job. Techniques for distinguishing applicants who possess these particular skills from those who lack them then need to be developed.

In general, many managers adopt an interview approach to selection. Interviews provide an opportunity to meet candidates, discuss their experience and so on. This approach, however, can raise a number of problematic issues if interviews are not heavily structured. Problems arise if:

❑ the interview has no standard format, so the interviewee might appear different if interviewed again with questions framed in even a slightly different way;

❑ the interview is not based on an analysis of what skills and aptitudes the job requires; it is not then likely to be effective in selecting the right person to carry out the job; and if

❑ the interview is a social encounter; this encourages the use of stereotypes and preferences in interpersonal judgements, for example the interviewer's rating of the interviewee's attractiveness (Herriot, 1989).

A number of other techniques can be used alongside an interview in the recruitment

PANEL 5

TRADER RISK PERCEPTIONS

Traders juggle many types of risk to reach decisions and take positions. They require a clear set of external risk management controls that indicate when risk limits are reached. Yet external limits are not the complete answer. Let's consider two traders who both require careful management to encourage an appropriate amount of risk taking.

The first is an equities trader who, like all his colleagues, has a target for the end of the year. However, this target is not challenging enough, so he has set a personal target that is 50% above the organisational target. His hobbies are high-risk sports.

The second trader is also in equities, but considers himself risk averse compared with his colleagues. He has to be pushed to take risks and often uses external factors, such as the small size of the companies he deals with, as reasons to commit less capital, as befits his preference. He believes that "bear traders like me are maturer than bull traders, but I admit that I do sometimes miss opportunities."

The approaches of these two traders are clearly different and require different management strategies. In the first case, the critical factor is the trader's internalised view of risk and his reference point. His personal target is considerably higher than the one set for him. It might therefore appear to a manager that he has reached a target, yet he might still be observed taking more risk than is optimal. This is predictable once it is known that the trader is still in his "domain of loss" and will be driven to take action to move himself to a "domain of gain" and reach his personal target.

In the second case, the trader might feel he has achieved enough and stop taking risks at some point ostensibly below the set target. His manager needs to persuade him that he has not yet achieved enough and encourage him to reach the target.

The point of these examples is to emphasise that, even where targets are set, definitions of loss and gain remain highly subjective. Managers must understand their traders' internal perspectives if they are to predict behaviour.

---

process. Following completion of a job analysis, simulated versions of "live" tasks can be developed to be used as part of the recruitment process. The use of such job-related tasks as a method of assessment allows managers an opportunity to observe performance on tasks in ways that are directly applicable to what new recruits are expected to do.

ISSUES REQUIRING LONG-TERM MANAGEMENT

The learning process

When someone joins an organisation, the initial period of learning is critical. Significant events during this period often shape all subsequent development. There are two types of learning: "cumulative" and "critical incident". Cumulative learning takes place on a day-to-day basis and is the slow build-up of knowledge and ability to translate knowledge into practice. Comments by traders include: "the year is a continuous progression of trading experiences", "learning is an extended process, it is not a matter of a single event". This type of learning should continue throughout a career, however, often a small number of significant events have a disproportionately large impact on learning and subsequent behaviour – critical incidents.

Critical incidents are usually those that are personally important, for example, big trading gains or losses. The result can be long-term changes in decision-making strategy. The way managers respond to critical incidents like this and longer term learning also have an effect on future behaviour. If employees are supported, encouraged to reconsider their strategy and develop new ideas about different approaches, negative effects can be reduced and the experience can be reconstructed as positive learning.

Appraisal and compensation

The appraisal and compensation systems in financial institutions are key management systems and important shapers of behaviour. Remuneration is often in the form of an annual bonus added to a lower base salary. This has clear advantages for the organisation in that it allows profits and losses over the year to be calculated before bonuses are paid, but the method has a number of negative side effects. These effects can be both immediate, such as employees quitting after being paid their bonus, or subtler, such as the often unacknowledged changes to risk perception that occur over the year as a result of anticipated performance evaluation.

DECISION MAKING AND DISASTERS: PIPER ALPHA AND THE CHALLENGER SPACE SHUTTLE

Piper Alpha

Piper Alpha, one of a network of four offshore oil plat-forms in the North Sea, was destroyed by a series of explosions and a fire on 6 July, 1988. Of 226 men, 165 died, including two rescue workers. The financial loss was more than $3 billion. This disaster was the result of a string of poor decisions and inattention to safety procedures, and offers managers some lessons about risk management. The key events were:

❑ a leak that caused vapour release;

❑ small explosions that led to a petroleum line being severed, resulting in a fire;

❑ gas piped in from another platform caught fire;

❑ the design of the platform allowed the fire to spread quickly, destroying the control and radio rooms;

❑ electronic power generation, public address, gen-eral alarm, emergency shutdown, and fire detection and prevention systems failed soon after the initial explosions;

❑ the platform superintendent was not able to make effective decisions and died during the accident;

❑ evacuation was not ordered; if it had been, it would not have been possible due to the design of the platform and extent of the fire – evacuation routes were blocked and lifeboats were only accessible from one point;

❑ fireboats were present, but waited for orders to begin fighting the fire; when action was taken indepen-dently of orders, fire-fighting monitors were ineffective;

❑ despite the visible signs of explosion and fire, the other platforms linked to Piper Alpha continued pro-duction and continued to feed fuel to it for some time. Two of the platforms stopped when they saw the sever-ity of the situation, but one platform continued for an hour, optimistic of the fire fighting capability. (Paté-Cornell, 1993)

In summary, the appalling extent of the disaster was caused by:

❑ design faults of the platform, which restricted access to life boats;

❑ poorly maintained equipment;

❑ oil platforms that were physically closely linked, but with little overall management;

❑ bad decisions and errors during the crisis;

❑ a lack of trained, capable management and promo-tion of several people above their normal position when

---

Perceptions of a current situation in terms of whether it lies in the domain of loss or gain, because of internalised targets can result in different strategies as discussed earlier. This applies to longer time scales, such as the compensation year, as well as short-term decision outcomes. Towards the end of the trading year, for exam-ple, traders who have reached their target and are assured of a good bonus may quietly slacken off their risk profile to protect what they have already achieved. Once the bonus has been received, the trader starting the new trading year may, in contrast, wish to build up slowly with-out making big losses in the first month or two, and thereby avoid a few potentially risky oppor-tunities to reduce exposure to possible loss. This can result in sub-optimal performance for up to six months of the trading year.

In addition to cyclical annual effects, percep-tions of the appraisal system and how it affects compensation also affect behaviour and motiva-tion. A common perception of traders is that their profits and losses are much more important than their appraisal, despite the reassurances of managers – "I believe I'm compensated much more on profit and loss than I am told". Motiva-tion is then shifted towards making larger prof-its, possibly by taking more risk – "if you put a huge bet on and make money, you will look good". The upside of risk taking in this case exceeds the possible downside – loss of money that is not the trader's own. This is the essence of what is known as the "principal agent pro-blem", discussed more formally in Chapter 9.

A second important influence on motivation is perceived inequity in distribution of bonuses – "the system is so arbitrary it affects my motivation". This feeling can be exacerbated in organisations that celebrate "star" employees. In these cases, the "stars" might be paid considerably more than their colleagues would consider justifiable, and might also be given greater freedom and latitude than colleagues, as was the case in the high-profile events outlined at the start of this chapter. Greater transparency of the compensation system both within management and between managers and

they did not have sufficient experience and had not had the opportunity to show how they would behave in crisis situations or the training to deal with such situations;

❑ industry pressure to maintain a high level of production, even at the expense of safety.

This was a physical disaster, but managers in the financial industry will have no difficulty spotting the relevance to their organisations. In particular, the disaster revealed the importance of structural design, the management of organisations, selection and training of employees, rewards for adhering to safe practices and the development of a safety culture.

The *Challenger* space-shuttle disaster

A second and similar case is the *Challenger* disaster. The space shuttle *Challenger* exploded 73 seconds after lift-off on 28 January 1986. Seven people were killed, the replacement shuttle cost more than $2 billion and the credibility of NASA was shattered. The explosion was the result of the failure of an O-ring seal, which allowed hot gases to burn through and ignite the fuel tank.

Was this an unforeseeable technical failure? No. Responsibility for several aspects of the shuttle programme rested with the Marshall Space Flight Centre. There were a number of procedures that Marshall needed to follow before it could permit a launch. In particular, Marshall needed certification of the readiness of each component, including the O-ring seal.

Investigation of the disaster revealed that managers at Marshall had pressured the producers of the O-ring seal to agree to say that the seals were safe and would function in the conditions of the launch (Heimann, 1993). Some of the senior experts at the producer company did not believe that either point was certain, yet the risk was considered acceptable by Marshall and launch procedures went ahead.

The decision to launch the space shuttle was similar to most decisions to execute an action. There were four possible choices and consequences:

❑ the shuttle is safe and the mission goes ahead;

❑ the shuttle is not safe and the mission is abandoned;

❑ the shuttle is not safe and the mission goes ahead (type I error);

❑ the shuttle is safe and the mission is abandoned (type II error).

This was an example of the third scenario. The cost of abandoning a potentially successful mission was placed above the risk of an unsafe shuttle, loss of life and considerable expense. The context was a need for cost efficiency and recent reductions in personnel in a number of organisations related to the launch of a shuttle.

The *Challenger* disaster led to a number of changes in the way decisions are made at NASA, intended to reduce the likelihood of missing risks, and of choosing to accept known risks.

employees is necessary to enhance motivation and performance and to reduce the negative effects of the annual cycle of bonus distribution.

Summary

❑ Rational decision making is often thought of as the basis for most business-related decisions. However, many decisions are made as a result of other processes on which there are many influences. The analyses in this chapter have sought to show that, even when working within the most disciplined and structured financial institutions, people make non-rational and biased decisions.

❑ There are a number of relatively stable factors that influence decision making: individual personality, psychological make-up and organisational culture. Knowledge of these factors provides an overarching view of the possibilities and limitations of an organisation and the individuals within it. This can assist understanding and prediction of behaviour. A systematic approach to these factors can help managers to maximise individual and organisational potential within a realistic framework.

❑ Day-to-day management of individuals' successes and failures and teamwork is crucial for overall good performance. Insights into what is guiding decision making and behaviour are essential for good management. This is particularly important in an industry where good performers are promoted to management but might not possess, or have been trained in, the skills required to manage people and teams effectively.

❑ Psychometric tests are powerful tools for measuring a variety of psychological factors in a standardised and equitable fashion if correct procedures are followed. The results of testing can be useful to both individuals and organisations seeking to maximise person–role fit and performance potential.

❑ There are various aspects of organisational procedures and practices that can have long-lasting directional influences, both positive and negative, on performance. These include:

selection processes, induction-learning experiences and how employees and managers process them, and the operation of appraisal and compensation systems.

1 *For further information about personality testing, contact the British Psychological Society.*

BIBLIOGRAPHY

Adler, S., 1995, Personality. Entry in N. Nicholson (ed.) *Encyclopedic Dictionary of Organizational Behavior,* Oxford: Blackwell, pp. 419–25.

Bazerman, M.H., 1997, *Judgment in Managerial Decision Making,* Fourth Edition, New York, Wiley.

Centre for the Study of Financial Innovation, 1997, *Banking Banana Skins,* London, Centre for the Study of Financial Innovation.

Costa, P.T. Jnr and R.R. McCrae, 1985, *The NEO Personality Inventory Manual,* Odessa, Florida, Psycholoical Assessment Resources.

Deci, E. and R. Ryan, 1985, *Intrinsic Motivation and Self-determination in Human Behaviour,* New York, Plenum Press.

Dipboye, R. L., C. S. Smith, and W. C. Howell, 1994, *Understanding Industrial and Organisational Psychology. An Integrated Approach,* Fort Worth, Harcourt Brace College Publishers.

Handy, C., 1993, *Understanding Organizations.* Fourth edition, London, Penguin.

Heimann, C. F. L., 1993, "Understanding the Challenger Disaster: Organizational Structure and The Design of Reliable Systems", *American Political Science Review,* 87(2), pp. 421–35.

Herriot, P., 1989, The Selection Interview. In P. Herriot (ed.) *Assessment and Selection in Organizations,* Chichester: Wiley, pp. 433–8.

Janis, I. L., 1972, *Victims of Groupthink,* Boston, Houghton Mifflin.

Myers, D. G. and H. Lamm, 1976, "The Group Polarisation Phenomenon", *Psychological Bulletin,* 83, pp. 602–27.

Nicholson, N., 1995 (ed.), *Encyclopedic Dictionary of Organizational Behavior,* Oxford: Blackwell.

Paté-Cornell, M. E., 1993, "Learning from the Piper Alpha Accident: A Postmortem Analysis of Technical and Organizational Factors", *Risk Analysis,* 13(2), pp. 215–32.

Ross, L., 1977, The Intuitive Psychologist and His Shortcomings: Distortions in the Attribution Process. In: L. Berkowitz (ed.) *Advances in Experimental Social Psychology* 10, New York, Academic Press.

Slovic, P., B. Fischhoff, and S. Lichtenstein, 1980, Facts and Fears: Understanding Perceived Risk. In: R. C. Schwing and W. A. Albers (eds) *Societal Risk Assessment: How Safe is Safe Enough?* New York, Plenum Press.

Tversky, A. and D. Kahneman, 1981, "The Framing of Decisions and the Psychology of Choice", *Science,* 211, pp. 453–8.

11

Measuring the Risk of Using the Wrong Model

A New Approach

Yiannos A. Pierides and Stavros A. Zenios

University of Cyprus; University of Cyprus and the Wharton School, University of Pennsylvania

Operational risk has been studied extensively in manufacturing industry, where techniques such as total quality management have been used to manage such risk. Somewhat surprisingly though, the financial services industry has not traditionally devoted much effort and resources to the explicit measurement and management of operational risk. Recently, it has started to pay more attention to such issues. The driving force has been a number of well-publicised financial disasters such as the losses at Metallgesellschaft (oil futures) and elsewhere.

The aim of this chapter is to discuss a new way to analyse and measure a particular aspect of operational risk – model risk. However, as other chapters in this book stress, any discussion of operational risk must be based on a framework for managing financial operations. Accordingly, the first main section describes two different approaches to managing financial operations, namely functional management and integrated product management, and argues that the latter is superior. The next main section identifies the four sources of operational risk that continue to arise under integrated product management: model risk, management information systems risk, legal risk and employee fraud risk. The penultimate section focuses on model risk and employs as an example a new approach to one aspect of model risk – ignorance of the correct functional form for the interest rate stochastic process.

Managing financial operations – functional versus integrated approaches

Consider a financial intermediary that offers a single product (liability) to investors to fund its assets. It faces the following tasks: first, designing the product; second, pricing it; and third, as time passes, making decisions on changes in its asset mix. Under *functional management*, each of the three tasks is considered independently of the other two and is undertaken by a separate department within the intermediary.

As pointed out by Holmer and Zenios (1995), this separation of functions can create significant asset/liability management problems. Consider, for example, an insurance company that instructs its mortgage portfolio manager to try to track the Salomon Brothers mortgage index. The portfolio manager may do extremely well, as measured by the tracking error of the portfolio vis à vis the index. Nevertheless, this performance is not ideal for an insurance company that has liabilities with a pattern of returns that have little correlation with those of mortgage securities. Holmer and Zenios (1995) advocate the use of *integrated product management* (IPM) to avoid such asset/liability management problems. Integrated product management integrates the segmented functional approach into a single process. The essence of this approach is to offer investors products (liabilities of the intermediary) whose cashflow pattern will closely mimic that of the assets of the intermediary. Financial simulations can be used to generate horizon returns under various interest-rate scenarios for the different products that can be used to fund the assets. From these products, the intermediary should choose the one whose horizon returns are closer to the horizon returns of the assets. It is becoming widely accepted that integrated product management is a superior technology of financial intermediation, and many intermediaries are in the process of adopting it.

An intermediary that adopts a functional management approach will unavoidably assume more risks than an intermediary adopting an integrated product management approach. One could argue that some of these additional risks should be classified as operational risks, and indeed many issues raised by the functional management approach are discussed in other chapters of this book. In this chapter, however, we will focus on the sources of operational risk that *continue* to arise under integrated product management.

Sources of operational risk under integrated product management

Integrated product management enables a financial intermediary to manage financial risks such as market risk and credit risk; however, the process of managing these financial risks gives rise to operational risks that, in turn, need to be managed. The following four sources of operational risk can be identified:

❏ model risk;
❏ management information systems risk;
❏ legal risk; and
❏ employee fraud risk.

Model risk is the risk of using a model that is unrealistic. Any model represents a simplified way of describing the complexities of the real world. As such, no model is completely accurate. Nevertheless, different models can have different degrees of accuracy and the use of a model that is not sufficiently accurate can result in significant problems. As mentioned above, a basic characteristic of integrated product management is the use of financial simulations to generate horizon returns under various interest rate scenarios of different products that can be used to fund assets. These simulations are based on a model of the evolution of the interest rate. The use of an inaccurate model will result in the generation of inaccurate horizon returns for different products that can be used to fund assets and for the assets themselves. As a result, the intermediary will choose from the different products the one whose inaccurate horizon returns are closer to the inaccurate horizon returns of the assets. Upon the future realisation of the actual returns of the chosen product and of the assets, it will be discovered that they differ significantly and this can have a negative effect on the net income and net worth of the intermediary.

Management information systems (MIS) risk is the risk of a malfunction will in the computer systems that support integrated product

management. To operationalise integrated product management one needs to use computer-intensive Monte Carlo simulations and to solve large-scale optimisation problems. High performance computers, networks of workstations and parallel architectures can provide the required computational power. Any malfunction in these systems can result in sub-optimal decisions and this can have a negative effect on the net income and net worth of the intermediary. This is especially true in the case of the use of a multi-period stochastic programming model that requires frequent changes in the composition of the assets and liabilities of the intermediary. If there is a system malfunction, the required changes may be delayed and may have to be implemented at less favourable trading prices at a later point in time.

Legal risk is the risk that the intermediary may be sued by one or more counterparties for damages that they have suffered from doing business with the intermediary. These lawsuits may result in fines being paid and indirect damage to the intermediary in the form of lost business as clients could refuse to do business with a counterparty that has violated the law.

Employee fraud risk is the risk that an employee of the intermediary may engage in inappropriate actions that violate the intermediary's internal regulations. For example, a trader may take positions far exceeding the approved limits, which could lead to significant trading losses if this trader's views are wrong, as illustrated by the case histories in Chapter 9 of the present volume.

Model risk

The deficiencies of financial modelling have been usefully analysed by Derman (1996). He points out that financial modelling is concerned with describing phenomena (such as asset prices) that are influenced by the actions of economic agents who change their views often and unpredictably. As such, financial models are analogies that are useful in explaining and categorising phenomena but lack the degree of compelling truth and depth that characterises models in other disciplines, such as physics. It follows that more than one model can be used to describe the same phenomenon.

A practitioner faced with more than one model describing the same phenomenon may have difficulty choosing among them. We will now investigate the risks involved in this choice. The analysis is presented within the context of a particular example of integrated product management.

The example we use is described in Consiglio and Zenios (1997). The intermediary is assumed to be a federal agency that owns mortgage assets that it wants to fund by selling callable bonds to investors. The rationale for the choice of callable bonds should be obvious: as interest rates drop and the mortgage assets prepay, the agencies can call the callable bonds, thereby achieving a good asset/liability match. Nevertheless, the agency needs to specify the characteristics of the callable bond that it will issue; the choice will depend on the specific characteristics of the mortgage assets it wants to fund, and it is here that integrated product management becomes useful.

A callable bond is defined by the following four parameters:

❏ lockout period (L);
❏ redemption price at first call date (R);
❏ time to maturity (M); and
❏ schedule of redemption price (K).

Assume that the correct model for describing the evolution of the interest rate is the Black, Derman, Toy (1990) model. Consider a discrete probability space, denoted by a set of scenarios $\Omega = \{1,2,3,\ldots,S\}$. A target distribution of holding period returns of the mortgage assets is assumed given and denoted by $\tilde{r}^s, s = 1,2,3,\ldots,S$. This assumption implies that we also have a correct model of the returns on the mortgage assets for a given change in the interest rate. The chosen callable bond should replicate the given holding period returns of the mortgage assets. The distribution of the holding period returns of the callable bond is a function of the design parameters:

$$r^s = f(L, R, M, K)$$

There is no closed-form expression for f; instead, it is obtained from a simulation procedure that relates the cashflows of the callable bond with parameters L, R, M, K to the interest rate scenarios in Ω. By changing the parameters, we can change the distribution of the holding period returns of the callable bond until we design the optimal bond that closely replicates the mortgage assets. Note that this simulation procedure assumes that we know the model that correctly gives the returns on the callable bond for different changes in the interest rate.

To summarise, we have made three important assumptions about the correct models that describe the way the interest rate changes and the way these changes affect returns on mortgage assets and callable bonds:

❏ assumption 1: the correct model for describing the evolution of the interest rate is known;
❏ assumption 2: the correct model for describing the returns on the mortgage assets for a given change in the interest rate is known;
❏ assumption 3: the correct model for describing the returns on the callable bond for given changes in the design parameters or the interest rate is known.

In this paper we focus on the validity of the first assumption, it is assumed that the other two are valid.

VALIDITY OF ASSUMPTION 1

There is disagreement among practitioners and academic researchers on the appropriate stochastic process for the short-term interest rate. Different researchers have proposed varying stochastic processes. The most widely used ones are those of Cox, Ingersoll and Ross (1985) henceforth CIR, Hull and White (1990) henceforth HW, and Black, Derman and Toy (1990) henceforth BDT. The interest rate stochastic processes that these authors proposed are shown in Table 1. This also shows the Vasicek (1977) process that, even though not widely used, was the first to be proposed.

We begin the description of these processes with the Vasicek model, which assumes that the interest rate follows an Ornstein–Uhlenbeck process: a, b and σ are the parameters of the process and W(t) is a standard Brownian motion. This is a Gaussian process that leads to relatively simple closed-form solutions for the price of Treasury bonds and for the price of plain vanilla options on such bonds. It has two main drawbacks. Firstly, it implies that the interest rate may become negative and secondly, it implies that the volatility of the interest rate is independent of the level of the interest rate.

Cox, Ingersoll and Ross (1985) proposed a stochastic process for the interest rate that does

Table 1. Interest rate stochastic processes

Model	Stochastic process
Vasicek	$dr(t) = (a + br(t))dt + \sigma dW(t)$
CIR	$dr(t) = \kappa(\theta - r(t))dt + \sigma(r(t))^{0.5}dW(t)$
HW	$dr(t) = (\theta(t) + a(t)(b - r(t)))dt + \sigma(t)\,dW(t)$
BDT	$d\log r(t) = (\theta(t) + a(t)(b - \log r(t)))dt + \sigma(t)\,dW(t)$

not suffer from the drawbacks of the Vasicek process. As in the case of the Vasicek process, κ, θ and σ are the parameters of the process and W(t) is a standard Brownian motion. This became known as the square root process because it implies that the volatility of the interest rate is not independent of the interest rate; instead, it is proportional to the square root of the interest rate. The interest rate cannot become negative. Cox, Ingersoll and Ross showed that this process leads to closed-form solutions for the price of Treasury bonds and for the price of plain vanilla options on such bonds.

Hull and White (1990) point out that a major drawback of both the Vasicek model and the CIR model is that they are not consistent with any initial term structure of interest rates and interest-rate volatilities observed in the market. In other words, these models do not imply a perfect fit to the initial term structure of interest rates and interest-rate volatilities observed in the market.

Hull and White (1990) proposed an extension to the Vasicek process that provides a perfect fit to the initial term structure of interest rates and interest rate volatilities in the market. The process became known as the extended Vasicek or Hull and White (HW) process. Here a(t), θ(t), b and σ(t) are the parameters of the process and W(t) is a standard Brownian motion. Note that, unlike the Vasicek and CIR processes, three of the four parameters are time dependent and this enables one to estimate these parameters in a way that provides a perfect fit to the initial term structure of interest rates and interest-rate volatilities observed in the market. Unfortunately, the HW process suffers from the same drawback as the Vasicek process, namely that the interest rate can become negative. Hull and White (1990) showed that this process leads to closed-form solutions for the price of Treasury bonds and for the price of plain vanilla options on such bonds.

Another process that provides a perfect fit to the initial term structure of interest rates and interest-rate volatilities that are observed in the market is the BDT process. This process, unlike HW, implies that the interest rate cannot become negative. Its major drawback is that it does not lead to closed-form solutions for the price of Treasury bonds and for the price of plain vanilla options on such bonds. The implication is that these prices have to be calculated numerically, thereby increasing computational costs.

It is not surprising that different researchers have proposed different functional forms for the short-term interest rate stochastic process. The reason is simple: on theoretical grounds, it is not clear what the functional form should be because the interest rate is not a traded asset. In the case of equity derivatives, the underlying instrument is a traded asset and theoretical arguments can be made for describing the evolution of its price using a geometric Brownian motion.

A surprising perception among some practitioners and academic researchers is that the disagreement about the correct functional form of the short term interest rate stochastic process is *not* so important for the task of valuing complex financial instruments such as mortgage assets and callable bonds. It is argued that, if one estimates the parameters of the short-term interest rate stochastic process in a way that ensures that the process is consistent with the current term structure, the type of functional form used does not significantly affect the price obtained for complex financial instruments. This estimation condition is usually referred to as the *consistency* condition.

Pierides (1996) argues that the above view is not necessarily correct even if the consistency condition is met. That paper considers the pricing of a particular complex financial instrument – a European lookback put option on a zero coupon Treasury bond – using the CIR and HW stochastic processes. It demonstrates that the price obtained for the lookback option is very different if one uses the CIR process rather that the HW process.

Pierides (1996) does not propose any approach that will solve the pricing problems. It simply states that future econometric research will hopefully be convincing enough to ensure that everybody, or almost everybody, will agree on the correct functional form of the interest rate stochastic process. At present, econometric research does not provide convincing evidence in favour of a particular functional form. For example, Ait-Sahalia (1996) tests each of the above functional specifications and rejects all of them. The test is based on a comparison of the probability density of the interest rate data implied by the particular parametric model and the same probability density estimated non-parametrically. Each of the above parametric models is rejected because it is not capable of producing an implied probability density that is sufficiently close to the actual probability density observed in the market. Hence, disagreement on the correct functional form of the interest rate stochastic process persists thereby rendering the task of valuing financial products difficult.

If assumption 1 is not valid, the simulation procedure on which integrated product management is based will lead to the generation of the wrong interest rate scenarios. This type of model risk can have a significant impact on a financial institution as described below.

QUANTIFICATION OF MODEL RISK IF ASSUMPTION 1 IS NOT VALID

We will quantify model risk by referring to the earlier example of the optimal design of a callable bond. The simulation procedure that relates the cashflows of the callable bond and the mortgage assets to the interest rate scenarios in Ω presumes that the correct interest rate stochastic process is one of those above. In this context, model risk is the risk that the correct process is one of the others considered above. To explain how this risk can be quantified, suppose a financial institution raises \$100 by issuing callable bonds at par and invests \$E of equity to purchase \$(100 + E) of mortgage assets. The value of the equity of the financial institution (V) at the end of the holding period is given by:

$$V = 100(\tilde{r}^s - r^s) + E(1 + \tilde{r}^s)$$

Where $\tilde{r}^s$ = return on mortgage assets and r^s = return on callable bond. The return on equity (ROE) is given by:

$$ROE^s = (1 + \tilde{r}^s) + 100\,((\tilde{r}^s - f\,(L,\,R,\,M,\,K))/E)$$

The design parameters should be selected so as to maximise the ROE. However, note that the ROE is scenario dependent and the optimal choice of design parameters will differ from scenario to scenario. Nevertheless, we can choose the optimal design by considering the utility function of the decision maker.

Let U denote the utility function of the decision maker. Then, the financial institution will prefer the bond that maximises the expected utility:

$$(1/S) \sum_{s \in \Omega} U(ROE^s)$$

With each bond we associate the certainty equivalent ROE (CEROE) as follows:

$$U(CEROE) = (1/S) \sum_{s \in \Omega} U(ROE^s)$$

We can rank bonds by their CEROE by inverting the previous function for each bond. We can choose the bond with the highest CEROE as the optimal one.

Let us now consider again the simulation procedure for the interest rate that forms the basis for the calculation of the CEROE. As mentioned above there are three possible models of the evolution of the interest rate: the BDT, CIR and HW models. Assume that the objective probability that each of these models is correct is 1/3. Nevertheless, the financial institution assumes that the correct model is the BDT model and uses this model for integrated product management. Assume that three bonds, referred to as A, B and C could potentially be used to fund the target mortgage assets. The CEROE associated with each bond ($CEROE_i$ for bond I) is as follows:

$$CEROE_A = 1.5$$
$$CEROE_B = 1.4$$
$$CEROE_C = 1.3$$

Based on the above, the financial institution chooses bond A as the optimal design given that it has the highest CEROE.

If the correct model were either the CIR or the HW, the CEROE associated with each bond would be different as detailed in Table 2.

Suppose the correct model is CIR. Then, the loss to the financial institution arising from the use of the wrong model (the BDT one) is given by:

$$Loss = CEROE_{B,CIR} - CEROE_{A,CIR} = 1.6 - 1.4 = 0.2$$

If the financial institution knows that the correct model is CIR, it would choose bond B, which has the highest CEROE under the CIR model, defined as $CEROE_{B,CIR}$. However, the financial institution erroneously uses the BDT model and chooses bond A, which has the highest CEROE under the BDT model. Given that the correct model was CIR, the CEROE earned by the financial institution ends up being the

Table 2. Certainty equivalent ROEs for three bonds under CIR and HW

	CIR	HW
$CEROE_A$	1.4	1.5
$CEROE_B$	1.6	1.7
$CEROE_C$	1.5	1.8

CEROE of bond A under the CIR model defined as $CEROE_{A,CIR}$. By subtracting $CEROE_{A,CIR}$ (the actual CEROE earned) from $CEROE_{B,CIR}$ (the CEROE that could have been earned if the correct model were used), we arrive at the loss to the financial institution (in terms of CEROE) arising from the use of the wrong model.

Suppose, now, that the correct model is HW. From the same principles, the loss arising from the use of the wrong model is given by:

$$Loss = CEROE_{C,HW} - CEROE_{A,HW} = 1.8 - 1.5 = 0.3$$

It follows that the expected loss is a weighted average of the two previously calculated losses with weights equal to the probability of incurring each of them, namely 1/3. Hence

$$Expected\ loss = (1/3)(0.2) + (1/3)(0.3) = 0.167$$

This expected loss may be considered too high: note that as a percentage of the CEROE that will be earned if the model actually used ends up being the correct one (1.5) it amounts to 11%. One way to reduce the expected loss is to use an averaging procedure to choose the optimal bond as detailed below.

AVERAGING PROCEDURE TO REDUCE
EXPECTED LOSS

The idea behind the averaging procedure is for the financial institution to acknowledge that it does not know which is the correct model; instead, it knows that there is a 1/3 probability that each of three models is the correct one. Using these probabilities as weights, we can calculate the CEROE associated with each bond under this averaging procedure (defined as $CEROE_{i,AVER}$ for i = A, B, C):

$$CEROE_{A,AVER} = 1.466$$
$$CEROE_{B,AVER} = 1.566$$
$$CEROE_{C,AVER} = 1.533$$

Based on the above, the financial institution will choose bond B, which has the highest CEROE.

Suppose, now, that the correct model is BDT. The loss to the financial institution arising from the use of the averaging procedure is given by:

$$Loss = CEROE_{A,BDT} - CEROE_{B,BDT} = 1.5 - 1.4 = 0.1$$

If the financial institution had known that the correct model is the BDT, it would choose bond A, which has the highest CEROE under the BDT

model defined as $CEROE_{A,BDT}$. However, the financial institution erroneously uses the averaging procedure and chooses bond B, which has the highest CEROE under this procedure. Given that the correct model was BDT, the CEROE earned by the financial institution ends up being the CEROE of bond B under the BDT model defined as $CEROE_{B,BDT}$. By subtracting $CEROE_{B,BDT}$ (the actual CEROE earned) from $CEROE_{A,BDT}$ (the CEROE that could have been earned if the correct model were used), we arrive at the loss to the financial institution (in terms of CEROE) arising from the use of the wrong model.

Now, suppose the correct model is CIR. From the above principles, the loss to the financial institution arising from the use of the wrong model is given by:

$$Loss = CEROE_{B,CIR} - CEROE_{B,CIR} = 1.6 - 1.6 = 0.0$$

Finally, suppose the correct model is HW. The loss to the financial institution arising from the use of the wrong model is given by:

$$Loss = CEROE_{C,HW} - CEROE_{B,HW} = 1.8 - 1.7 = 0.1$$

The expected loss is a weighted average of the three previously calculated losses with weights equal to the probability of incurring each of them ie 1/3. Hence:

$$Expected\ loss = (1/3)(0.1) + (1/3)(0.0) + (1/3)(0.1) = 0.067$$

The expected loss has been reduced from 0.167 to 0.067 through the use of the averaging procedure. This is a significant percentage reduction.

Conclusion

This chapter has described the different types of operational risk that can arise in financial intermediation. It has analysed in detail a particular type, namely model risk. Model risk can arise whenever the wrong model of the evolution of the values of financial variables is used in integrated product management. This risk can have a significant impact on the returns earned by a financial intermediary as demonstrated in the case of the optimal design of a callable bond to fund mortgage assets. A procedure for reducing this risk has been suggested. This procedure requires the intermediary to recognise its ignorance of the correct functional form for the interest rate stochastic process.

This chapter has focused on only one aspect of model risk, namely ignorance of the correct functional form for the interest rate stochastic process. It has been pointed out that other aspects of model risk include ignorance of the correct model for describing the returns on financial products (in the case of the example, the mortgage assets and the callable bond) for a given change in the interest rate. These aspects of operational risk will be the subject of future research.

BIBLIOGRAPHY

Ait-Sahalia, Y., 1996, "Testing Continuous Time Models of the Spot Interest Rate", *Review of Financial Studies,* vol. 9(2), pp. 385–426.

Black, F., E. Derman and W. Toy, 1990 "A One-Factor Model of Interest Rates and its Application to Treasury Bond Options" *Financial Analysts Journal,* (January/ February), pp. 33–9.

Consiglio A. and S. Zenios, 1997, "A Model for Designing Callable Bonds and its Solution using Tabu Search", *Journal of Economic Dynamics and Control,* vol. 21, pp. 1445–70.

Cox, J. C., J. Ingersoll and S. Ross, 1985, "A Theory of the Term Structure of Interest Rates", Econometrica, vol. 53, pp. 385–407.

Derman, E., 1996, "Valuing Models and Modeling Value", *Journal of Portfolio Management,* (Spring), pp. 106–14.

Holmer, M. and S. Zenios, 1995, "The Productivity of Financial Intermediation and the Technology of Financial Product Management", *Operations Research,* vol. 43(6), pp. 970–82.

Hull, J. and A. White, 1990, "Pricing Interest-Rate-Derivatives", *Review of Financial Studies,* vol. 3(4), pp. 573–92.

Pierides Y., 1996, "Legal Disputes about Complex Interest Rate Derivatives: Part of the Problem is the Current State of Complex Interest Rate Derivative Valuation Theory", *Journal of Portfolio Management,* (Summer), pp. 114–18.

Vasicek, O., 1977, "An Equilibrium Characterization of the Term Structure", *Journal of Financial Economics,* vol. 5, pp. 177–88.

On the Quantification of Operational Risk

A Short Polemic

Michael K. Ong
ABN AMRO

Nothing strikes more fear in the financial industry than the risk of a headline-grabbing, catastrophic loss stemming from a risk management failure. These breakdowns can include breaches of operational guidelines or policies, settlement snafus, back-office mistakes, errors of judgement, rogue trader actions, audit oversights, risk control lapses, technological problems like the "millennium bug", and other failures associated with the daily running of different business lines. The queasiness such failures engender in financial industry executives is probably similar to that which the dinosaurs felt 65 million years ago when they noticed a sudden bright light in the sky. There, streaking across the heavens, was a brilliant blob with a tail of fire; what we know as a comet was to them an unknown, fearful force.

Fear of the unknown in the financial industry over the past five years has spawned a cottage industry around issues cleverly disguised and lumped together under the heading "operational risk", which is widely defined as everything (and I mean everything) outside of market risk and credit risk. With the advent of value-at-risk (VAR) modelling for market risk and the more recent techniques for modelling credit risk, there is now intense pressure to quantify operational risk – what I like to think of as the blazing trail of the dinosaur comet. The need to quantify is driven primarily by the same fear of the unknown experienced by the dinosaur. While the urge to quantify translates into job security for risk quantification specialists – myself included – I question the rationality of such faith in numbers.

There has been much talk about operational risk and its quantification. Many conferences have been convened on the subject, but nothing substantive has actually emerged. That is because operational risk is one big confused blob. In our haste to quantify, we have failed to identify its many components. The truth is that some are quantifiable, but most are not. By trying to develop such risk-adjusted performance measures as a risk-adjusted return on capital (Raroc) process for enterprise-wide risk management, we have blurred the distinction between operational risk capital and the mechanism for risk control. The two are complementary: the former is a buffer against extinction; the latter, prevention. Operational risk capital shields the institution from unanticipated financial losses due to mishaps, while daily risk control mechanisms prevent an institution from disaster in the course of doing business. Does it make sense, therefore, to quantify prevention when it really should be part of the risk management process?

Amassing voluminous amounts of internal data, which may not even be possible, is not necessarily the answer. Returning to the dinosaur comet model, we realise that if the dinosaurs had understood physics they could have determined its trajectory of doom. Would this have saved them? What arrogance do we possess that makes us think a single measure of operational risk is sufficient to save us from disaster?

The crux of the problem is our irrational desire to measure what we fear most, even if it is immeasurable. Measuring or quantifying operational risk is meaningful only in the context of capital attribution and risk-adjusted performance measurement. Prevention, as a proactive function of risk control, should not be confused with the more strategic function of measuring performance and, therefore, of performing capital attribution across the enterprise. The only buffer against operational risk is not

STATISTICAL MODEL

The philosophy underlying this kind of statistical modelling is to gather both internal and external failure and mishap data on the institution and its peers. The steps are:

❏ Collect data on the past losses due to mishaps.

❏ Take a stratified sample of collected data based on business units subject to operational losses.

❏ Attach probability of loss distribution and ascertain the number of standard deviations necessary to cover a confidence interval.

❏ The number of standard deviations multiplied by the standard deviation from the mean determines the operating risk capital necessary to cover operational losses.

Some of the chapters in this book provide detailed examples of this approach, especially Chapter 8 and Chapter 5.

some quantified measure but educated people who are careful, technologically aware, informed and compliant with internal policies.

Operational risk is more of a management issue and less a quantification issue. Because it entails a series of processes necessary for the institution to conduct its daily business, operational risk should be managed in partnership among the different business, corporate governance, internal and external audit, and risk management units. As financial institutions are very dissimilar to, say, manufacturing facilities, the operating processes within the financial institution are not identical to the assembling processes of an automobile manufacturer. Quality control of these assembling factories can be successfully quantified using a branch of operations research called reliability theory, wherein statistics are properly used to sample the likelihood of failures and defects.

In financial institutions, however, the daily process is the "assembling" of human capital and its interaction with a network of systems. The products at the end of the assembly line are not countable objects such as light bulbs or automobiles, but services. The implementation of corporate risk policies, the establishment of good communication channels among the human capital, and the building of a sound IT infrastructure are, therefore, more logical measures of operational risk than some mathematically contrived set of numbers. Because quantifying the breakdown of underlying processes is really much more difficult than computing the possible trajectories of the dinosaur comet, prevention is still the key.

Unlike our dinosaur ancestors who, had they been able to project the comet's trajectory, would have realised they were doomed, we have a choice. We can begin education programmes to create a risk-aware corporate culture. We need not wait for a back-office systems failure before the next audit cycle. We can take the role of the internal and external audit process seriously. And we can sample the frequency of errors in our payments and securities services areas and come up with policies to minimise errors. We must stop blindly seeking data, which for the most part do not exist, and stop trying to measure failures and mishaps. These are integral to doing business and competing. The key should be prevention, not just measurement.

There is some still-to-be-proven wisdom in allocating economic capital to operational risk as part of a strategic risk-adjusted performance measurement framework. To distinguish this from the broadly defined operational risk, we shall call it *operating risk capital*. In an attempt to quantify operating risk capital, there are three major schools of thought, summarised in the three panels.

Other than prevention, I'm not sure which of the three approaches I prefer. For now, I am reluctant to propose a solution akin to sending a spaceship to shoot down the incoming dinosaur comet and, in so doing, breaking it into smaller pieces that cause other catastrophes. Financial losses arise not from lack of measurement but from complacency and management inattention. In good times (when the dinosaur comet is far from sight) it is easy to ignore signs of potential danger. In lean times, management attention is focused on survival. So, when is the right time to initiate preventive measures and good controls?

In today's merger-mad world, is the irrational pressure to quantify operational risk the result of bank executives wishing to protect their own reputation and merger rewards, or an

RISK CATALOGUING

The risk rating catalogue is a report card of an institution's business operations and their foibles (see the table). Such catalogues can be used to determine the frequency and severity of mishaps. Each risk is given a score and then operating risk capital is calculated for each business unit. The score determines allocation of operating risk capital. Some of the chapters in this book provide detailed examples of this approach, especially perhaps the illustrative examples that conclude Chapter 1.

Table. Operational risk catalogue

Risk types	Business unit		
	Derivatives	Leasing	Credit card
Processing			
Technology			
Recording			
Disaster Recovery			
Control			
Valuation			
People:			
Number			
Knowledge			
Compliance Risks			
Legal risks			
Tax risks			
Fraud			
Audit report			
Business complexity			
Infrastructure quality			
Other			
Overall operational risk assessment			

Risk assessment: Use "low", "medium" and "high" or assign a numerical value.

enlightened reading of the skies and a desire to heed the comet's warning? We need not look far for evidence. The lifelessness of the moon and the countless craters on earth all are testaments to previous encounters. In finance, the ghosts of past great companies and the shadows of those that barely survived are still with us.

If, 65 million years ago, dinosaurs knew not just how to measure the chance and magnitude of the impact of the comet of doom, but also knew how to prevent the impact from actually occurring, perhaps some of them would be sitting in posh boardrooms, chomping on fat cigars and planning their next acquisition. From them, there is indeed a lesson a dinosaur banker can learn. Next time someone preaches about quantifying operational risk in very broad terms, I'm going to look toward the heavens and implore the cosmos to hurl the largest dinosaur comet down the preacher's way.

1 *This is a revised version of an article that was first published in the October/December 1998 edition of* Infinity World.

"FOLLOW THE PACK" BENCHMARKING

Also known as the "market comparables" method, the benchmarking method borrows ideas from the capital asset pricing model (CAPM) approach in finance. Beta, a measure of a company's risk relative to the market, is the key component of this methodology.

The main idea behind the CAPM benchmarking approach is that CAPM employs market data (via the beta measure), together with revenues and expenses, to split the total capital of a company into portfolio (ie financial) risk and business (ie operating) risk components.

The equity beta thus represents two components of riskiness in an institution, namely:

❑ *financial risk* due to the amount of leverage in an institution's capital structure; and

❑ *asset risk*, or the riskiness of an institution's business activities.

The financial risk or "leverage effect" can then be removed from the equation, using an appropriate tax rate and the debt to market value of equity for the institution. This leaves us with the portion that represents business or operating risk.

To put the methodology into practice, risk managers would need to:

❑ Identify publicly-traded companies with businesses that correspond in some sense to the institution's activities, so that these companies can be used as market benchmarks.

❑ Collect data on each market benchmark's assets, equity, debt and beta risk.

❑ Strip away or "unlever" the financial risk of each benchmark firm.

❑ Using the *unlevered* beta and the CAPM model, calculate the institution's *unlevered* required return.

❑ Finally, adjust the data for these market benchmarks to reflect the institution's own beta and target hurdle rate, and then determine the imputed leverage ratio (ie capital divided by assets).

Critics of this approach to measuring operating risk capital point to the general inadequacies of benchmarking. Following the pack may not be a safe practice, and may not always lead to capital ratios that are appropriate to the unique features of an institution. After all, every firm that stands out from its competitors *necessarily* possesses unique features.

INDEX